Plagues of the heart

Manchester University Press

Plagues of the heart

Crisis and covenanting in a seventeenth-century Scottish town

Michelle D. Brock

MANCHESTER UNIVERSITY PRESS

Copyright © Michelle D. Brock 2024

The right of Michelle D. Brock to be identified as the author of this work has been asserted in accordance with the Copyright, Designs and Patents Act 1988.

Published by Manchester University Press
Oxford Road, Manchester, M13 9PL

www.manchesteruniversitypress.co.uk

British Library Cataloguing-in-Publication Data
A catalogue record for this book is available from the British Library

ISBN 978 1 5261 6090 4 hardback

First published 2024

The publisher has no responsibility for the persistence or accuracy of URLs for any external or third-party internet websites referred to in this book, and does not guarantee that any content on such websites is, or will remain, accurate or appropriate.

Typeset by Newgen Publishing UK

Contents

Author's note	*page* vi
Acknowledgements	vii
Introduction	1
1 Clergy and covenants	18
2 Plague	44
3 Saints and sinners	69
4 Occupation	94
5 Restoration and rebellion	123
6 The old protestor	147
Epilogue: afterlives	174
Select bibliography	189
Index	201

Author's note

Original spellings throughout have been very slightly modernised for the benefit of non-specialist readers. When necessary for clarity, contractions and abbreviations have been expanded, and the Scots letters thorn and yogh have been transcribed as 'th' and 'y', respectively. I have generally used the spelling of surnames as they appear the records, unless the person was particularly prominent, in which case I have used the standard spelling in the scholarship of the period (i.e. minister William Adair rather than 'Adaire', provost John Moor rather than 'Muir', or minister George White rather than 'Whyte').

Expanded abbreviations related to source materials are provided at their first mention in each chapter, as well as in the bibliography. Dates are given in the 'new style', with the year beginning 1 January.

Regarding currency, one pound Scots was the equivalent of one-twelfth of a pound sterling and comprised twenty shillings (each of which equalled twelve pence). One dollar was worth four merks, with one merk valued at about thirteen shillings, six pence in Scots money. All amounts are given in Scots currency unless otherwise noted.

Acknowledgements

This book centres on two themes that have also been at the heart of its creation: crisis and community. My interest in the people of Ayr and their experiences of the 'crisis of the seventeenth century' began in early summer 2016, on the precipice of the two countries central to my life and work – Britain and the United States – entering bewildering new chapters of angst and instability. In 2018, when I published an exploratory article on the plague in Ayr, I had no idea that I would soon write the fuller story of the town while living through a modern pandemic. The topics that appear on the pages that follow – political polarisation, disease, war, refugees, and religious extremism, to name a few – have felt far closer to home in recent years than I could have imagined.

In 2012, Robert Orsi wrote in his introduction to the *Cambridge Companion to Religious Studies* that 'religions are lived, and it is in their living, in the full and tragic necessity of people's circumstances, that we encounter them, study and write about them, and compare them, in the full and tragic necessity of our circumstances'. I often thought about his words while writing this book, wading through seventeenth-century documents that provided, despite their own complexities, some respite from the political chaos and global tragedies going on around me. It has, in short, been a strange but fitting time to write about people in the distant past living through a series of overlapping crises.

I have been profoundly lucky in this work because of the second theme of this book: community. At every step of the way, I have been surrounded and supported by the best people. The history department at Washington and Lee University is a wonderful place to call my academic home, and I am grateful for the collegiality and friendship of those with whom I share the space of Newcomb Hall. In particular, Molly Michelmore and Sarah Horowitz, my 'work wives' for the past decade, deserve a special shout out: thank you for all the texts, second pairs of eyes, podcast and product recommendations, and, at times, gallows humour. Any summer research behind this book has been generously supported by the W&L Lenfest fund, and further support for publication was provided by the Class of

1956 Provost's Faculty Development Endowment at Washington and Lee University. I do not take for granted my access to resources that not everyone has, and I am genuinely humbled to have landed so well.

The Scottish history community continues to be made up of the most brilliant and encouraging people. The list of those whose generosity in conversation, sharing of sources, and friendship made writing this book a genuinely enjoyable journey could fill pages: Roger Mason, Julian Goodare, Alasdair Raffe, Chris Langley, Valerie Wallace, Karly Kehoe, Brian Levack, Steve Murdoch, David McOmish, Jamie Reid Baxter, Craig Gallagher, Louise Yeoman, Alan MacDonald, Robert Urquhart, and so many others. Elizabeth Ewan deserves a special mention for accompanying me on my first trip to Ayr – despite an eventful train ride, it was the perfect first visit. Michael Graham and Elizabeth Armstrong offered me a home away from home – and many evenings of great food, libations, and conversation – in their beautiful Stockbridge flat. James Brown and Ashlyn Cudney graciously located and photographed a few important archival sources for me when I was unable to make it to Scotland. I was also lucky enough to spend time among the wonderful people at the Institute for Scottish Historical Research at the University of St Andrews and the Institute for Advanced Studies in the Humanities at the University of Edinburgh during key stages of this project. Funding was also provided by the American Philosophical Society. And of course, none of this work could have happened without the talented archivists and librarians at the National Library of Scotland, National Records of Scotland, and Ayrshire Archives.

Outside of the Scottish history world, my fellow devil-historians and friends Richard Raiswell and David Winter have been constant sounding boards for my ideas and questions, demonic or otherwise. Martin Farr, Jake Ivey, Jess Hower, Justin Quinn Olmstead, Brandon Marsh, John Mitcham, Laura Seddelmeyer, Sue Thompson, Jon Shipe, Leslie Rogne Schumacher, Arunima Datta, and Jamie Gianoutsos have become dear friends well beyond our shared attendance at British history conferences. Julie Hardwick's generous mentorship and guidance helped me think about the relevance of this book to audiences beyond Scottish historians. My 'writing wrens', Anne Proctor and Lisa Diller, have been the best writing/academic-support buddies imaginable. Meredith Carroll and Siobhán Poole at Manchester University Press have been fantastic to work with, patient and supportive as this book slowly but surely found its way into the world.

Last but certainly not least, thank you to my family. To Dad, Kristina, and David, for reminding me that there is so much that matters beyond my work. To Ron and Marilyn, for being the most wonderful in-laws I could ask for. To my four-legged family members (yes, even the cat), for bringing me joy when I have needed it most. And above all to Jared, my first, favourite, and forever reader, for everything. This book is dedicated to you.

Introduction

Plague, war, witchcraft, invasion, rebellion: for the generation of Scottish protestants who witnessed the tumultuous period between the British civil wars and the Revolution of 1688, there was little doubt that God was angry and that the gains of the Reformation were at stake. In these years, alongside dramatic moments of crisis, spiritual and civic leaders grappled with challenges like sabbath-breaking and sexual impropriety – long-running concerns of a hyper-disciplinary church preoccupied with sin for reasons both pragmatic and providential. As one preacher put it, whatever his parishioners did in life, they must 'be zealous', for there were abundant 'snares without, and corruptions within' seeking to lead them astray from the godly path and bring ruin on their communities.[1] These challenges were set against a backdrop of an increasingly interconnected world, as ministers and merchants alike built upon older patterns of travel and exchange to forge their place in burgeoning global networks. Indeed, these Scottish experiences were not dissimilar to those of their Reformed counterparts south of the border and across the Atlantic, men and women who spent much of the seventeenth century driven and at times riven by apocalyptic anxiety, theological debates, and political division.[2] This was, in short, a time of both peril and possibility.

This book is about the formation, practice, and performance of protestant identity amid these interlocking crises. My guiding contention is that early modern piety was not confined to confessional rituals like sermon-going, covenant-subscription, discipline, and prayer. Instead, it was fashioned through individual and collective responses to crises like pestilence and conquest, as well as more predictable problems such as sin and encounters with strangers. I argue that during the turmoil of the seventeenth century and under the stewardship of a generation of radical clergy, many in Scotland developed a distinct and durable 'culture of covenanting'. This culture was created not simply by swearing two national covenants (which the majority of Scots did), but through reimagining the post-Reformation programme of discipline and worship around hardline interpretations of those covenants. This culture of covenanting demonstrates that Reformed protestant piety, despite outdated assumptions about individualism, was fundamentally a communal project negotiated over decades of lived experience and born of moments of crisis.

To centre people and place in our understanding of the long Reformation, this book uses the port city and royal burgh of Ayr as a case study of seventeenth-century protestant self-fashioning in an urban community.[3] It is structured around the long and eventful career of minister William Adair. His tenure began shortly after the communal swearing of the National Covenant in 1638, a document composed by clerical leaders in rebellion against Charles I's imposition of the 'popish' Book of Common Prayer on the Scottish church the previous year, and ended in 1682 with his refusal to follow the orders of government directives he deemed ungodly. In these four and a half decades, the community experienced not only pandemic and warfare, but also military occupation by the Cromwellian army, an intense period of witch-hunting, an influx of refugees from Ireland, the restoration of the monarchy, and growing scrutiny from the British government. Through their responses to these interlocking challenges, Adair and his congregation forged a powerful religious ethos that shaped not only daily life in Ayr, but Scotland's place in the wider world.

An introduction to Ayr

In some respects, to study the history of Ayr is to glimpse the history of Scotland, particularly those places on the sea, in miniature. In 1197, King William I built a new royal castle near the mouth of the River Ayr, a statement of power, first in wood and then in stone, to intimidate the rebellious lords of the region. It stood on auspicious ground. Two centuries later, the royal structure shared lands with the church of St John the Baptist and, two centuries later still, with Oliver Cromwell's citadel, a sprawling fort that destroyed any remains of the castle and consumed the town's sole place of worship. By the early thirteenth century, William I had made Ayr a royal burgh, conferring on the community a range of political and economic privileges granted by the crown.[4]

Ayr's medieval era offers much fodder for myth as well as history. There are several 'Wallace caves' along the banks of the river, where the man of future *Braveheart* fame supposedly took refuge during the Wars of Independence. On one side of the water is a partial heel mark imprinted in the rock, reportedly left by Wallace as he was fleeing the English forces. A more sensational legend from the period recounts a time when the local gentry were summoned to the aforementioned castle, where they were ambushed, captured, and hung by the English. In retaliation, Wallace and his supporters set fire to the barns where the English soldiers were billeted and watched the buildings go up in flames amid the cries of the burning occupants. While this account is probably apocryphal, we do know that in 1315, Robert I held parliament in St John the Baptist in an assertion of Scottish strength, though the Wars of Independence would rage for at least another decade.[5]

Protestantism came to Ayr, as it did to the rest of the country, in fits and starts. The Catholic church, while undoubtedly central to the community as both a spiritual guide and a provider of essential services, was challenged by a growing 'tradition of dissent' in the region, spearheaded by Lollardy at the end of the fifteenth century and Lutheranism in the early sixteenth century.[6] Ayr witnessed at least one important first in the story of the Scottish Reformation. In 1533, Walter Stewart, son of the 1st Lord Ochiltree, faced charges before the Archbishop of Glasgow for 'casting doun ane image in the kirk of Ayr'.[7] The exact act may have entailed the beheading of a statue of the Virgin Mary belonging to the burgh's Franciscan monastery, but regardless, it constitutes the earliest recorded episode of iconoclasm in Scotland. Further waves of iconoclastic enthusiasm were encouraged by the local preaching of George Wishart in 1545, whose dramatic execution in St Andrews the following year made him a powerful martyr for the protestant cause. John Knox too is reputed to have visited the burgh, preaching in the parish kirk and in private houses, in the spring of 1556. As Margaret Sanderson has vividly demonstrated, the town was an important meeting place for those 'behind the increasing momentum' of what became a full-fledged religious revolution in 1559–60.[8] The protestant credentials and rebellious proclivities of the burgh were, in short, established well before the seventeenth century. The culture of covenanting grew in fertile soil.

Ayr was one of fifty-three royal burghs that formed the core of early modern Scotland's urban society. It was not the largest or most powerful burgh – on the stent (tax) rolls, Ayr declined from the ninth to twelfth largest ratepayer between 1574 and 1670 – but throughout the era, the town was an important player in the affairs of kirk, economy, and state, largely owing to its zealous religious commitments and active port.[9] Its population was one of varied means and influence; wealthy merchants lived beside those who laboured in less lucrative trades, and the winding and cobbled streets of the town would have been dotted with 'a medley of castellated mansions and mean heather-thatched cottages'.[10] The early modern period in Ayr is framed, chronologically, by the construction of two iconic bridges over its eponymous river, one dating from the fifteenth century and the other from the eighteenth. The River Ayr runs into the North Channel, the stretch of sea that brought goods and strangers from Ireland and continental Europe to the burgh during the sixteenth century and, by the second half of the seventeenth century, carried local sailors to faraway lands in the Caribbean and New England.[11] The imagined rivalry between the two structures over the river inspired Robert Burn's humorous 1786 poem, 'The Brigs of Ayr'. Indeed, the town is a common stopping point for Burns enthusiasts on their way to his home in nearby Alloway. A lesser-known fact is that on the second day of his life, 26 January 1759, the 'Bard of Ayrshire' was baptised by minister William Dalrymple in the Auld Kirk of Ayr, where Adair had preached for three decades.[12] Beyond the christening of the region's most famous resident, the walls of this old stone church, built in 1654, have many tales to tell. Some of them are at the heart of this book.

For our purposes, the most formative event in this seaside community took place on 8 April 1638, when the people of Ayr, 'men women and all bouth younge and old', publicly swore to uphold the National Covenant, which had been composed earlier that year in Edinburgh and circulated to Scotland's parishes.[13] At this point, the town's population would have been around 2,500 residents, making it a midsize burgh that could still be managed by a single parish church, in contrast to larger cities like Edinburgh which by the early 1640s had six.[14] The communal swearing of this covenant, the text of which was at once conservative in its specifics and radical in its implications, invited the Scottish people to participate in a moral, ecclesiastical, and political revolution.[15] Its subscription signalled the beginning of what would be a tumultuous year – indeed, a tumultuous generation – for the town. Another critical covenant, this time in concert with English parliamentarians, was sworn in 1643, further committing the townspeople in body and spirit to pursuit of the 'true faith', whatever the costs. By the early 1650s, the community was occupied by the Cromwellian army and its parishioners ousted from the church that had been the burgh's centre of worship for centuries. In 1660, the restoration of Charles II ushered in over two decades of varied attempts to suppress presbyterianism in the region, which intensified local divisions and provoked a general crisis of authority. In sum, this was a society, like so many others during the seventeenth century, grappling with pandemic, war, patriarchal power, religious anxieties, immigration, debates over sovereignty, and political polarisation.[16] It reminds us that perhaps the past is not such a foreign country after all.

The communal swearing of the National Covenant coincided with another decisive event in Ayr: the appointment of minister Adair, on the precipice of his long career as pastor of the parish kirk. Adair was a staunch and, in his youth, radical, covenanter, with an unshakeable commitment to Scotland's presbyterian ecclesiastical structure. Apparently a force of nature, his influence in shaping the communal identity of Ayr is hard to overstate, even if he has been little remembered in the scholarship of the period.[17] His legacy remains embodied in stone near the entrance to the Auld Kirk of Ayr, in a striking monument of the old cleric kneeling in prayer, erected the year of his death in 1684. This book tells the story of Adair and his congregation and the ways in which the relationship between the person in the pulpit and the people in the pews, especially in times of crisis, was at the heart of the covenanting project and the lived experience of protestantism.[18]

Histories of the covenanters

The historiography of the covenants and covenanters is a curious, fascinating beast. Prior to the mid-twentieth century, much of this work was essentially presbyterian hagiography, interspersed with invaluable but biased histories and bibliographies.[19] By the 1970s, historians such as David Stevenson and Ian Cowan began to approach the covenanters with a much-needed critical lens, and since then, serious scholarship on the topic has flourished, most of it centred on the ecclesiastical politics of this pivotal group.[20] Our knowledge of politics and faith in early modern Scotland has been greatly expanded by a new wave of works examining the meanings and influence of the National Covenant and Solemn League and Covenant beyond the nation's ecclesiastical politics. Laura Stewart's *Rethinking the Scottish Revolution: Covenanted Scotland, 1637–1651* has been particularly pathbreaking in demonstrating that, while the covenants were fundamentally aimed at political and social control, this did not preclude ordinary people from interpreting and using them according to their own needs and understandings.[21] Additional studies have further augmented our understanding of the covenanters beyond the specific contexts of 1638 and 1643, asking how ministers and parishioners alike understood the covenants well into later decades when the covenanting movement had lost much of its former power.[22]

The covenanters have also loomed quite large in histories of Scotland's southwest, a part of the country that remains littered with memorials to presbyterians who died during the 'Killing Time' of the 1680s.[23] Historians have frequently cited the area as the 'radical' centre of the covenanting movement, and while the term can be a misleading one, in this case it is generally apt. As Sharon Adams has demonstrated, this was a region which, for a range of complex factors including active networks of kinship and proximity to Ireland, was an incubator for presbyterian zeal and resistance.[24] Indeed, in the southwest originated a concerted push by a minority of hardline ministers for further innovations to purify the church, which to more conservative covenanters seemed like the beginning of a slippery slope towards puritanism or, worse, the separatism plaguing their southern neighbour. Adair was among the ministers who railed against the continued use of the Pater Noster (the Lord's Prayer), Gloria Patri (a short hymn of praise), and the much-hated practice of kneeling in the pulpit.[25] The congregation of Ayr was an 'enthusiastic early endorser of the Covenant', requiring that all of its members swear to uphold the document a year earlier than many other more reluctant parishes.[26] A decade after its subscription, many of the men present at the armed conventicle at Mauchline Muir – a purportedly impromptu prayer meeting which soon turned into combat against government forces – were from Ayr, including Adair.[27] Moreover, between 1638 and 1651, the presiding ecclesiastical bodies in the southwest led the country in the deposition of ministers whose covenanter credentials did not quite cut it.[28] In short, the commitment of the town, and of the region more generally, to a hardline interpretation and defence of the covenants is well-established and well-known.

And yet, for all that we do know, about both the region and the covenanting movement more generally, we still lack a full understanding of how broader allegiance to the covenants influenced, to borrow Margo Todd's phrase, the 'culture of protestantism' in specific Scottish parishes.[29] Todd's work, which has been tremendously influential in early modern Scottish studies, explores religious practice in post-Reformation Scotland through analysis of the records of the kirk sessions, the local ecclesiastical courts charged with enforcing moral discipline in every parish. The chronological reach of Todd's study ends on the eve of the National Covenant – arguably the defining religious event of the seventeenth century in Scotland – but many of the kirk sessions, of course, endure to the present day. The question, then, is to what extent the covenants – these documents seen as watersheds in the political and ecclesiastical history of Scotland – informed or reshaped religious life in local communities. We know quite a lot about what the covenants meant to a wide range of people, but considerably less about what they *did*. There was indeed a culture of protestantism in seventeenth-century Scotland, but what about a culture of covenanting? In pursuit of the answer to these questions, this book explores the innerworkings of one exemplary covenanted community in order to better understand the embodied experience of faith during one of Scotland's most tumultuous periods. By focusing on the tenure of Ayr's longest-serving minister, we can discern subtle and overt mechanisms of religious change, the dynamic and varied meanings of the covenants and covenanting, and most important, how the people of Ayr understood themselves and their relationships to each other and to their God. As will become clear, for all the lofty rhetoric and high-minded ideals of men like Adair, the practical realities of covenanting 'radicalism' were often more nuanced and more flexible than is generally assumed.

This exploration of the culture of covenanting in Ayr is fundamentally an inquiry into urban piety and religious politics. Indeed, the community's urban structure at once necessitates such a study and makes it possible. Ayr's status as a royal burgh generated copious records of not only the kirk session but also the town council, the burgh courts, and the various minute books of prominent trades, and made it a modest but noteworthy player in the convention of royal burghs and in the Scottish Parliament.[30] Moreover, the town's urban environment meant that it became, as with many of Scotland's burghs, a frequent waystation for troops in the mid-seventeenth century: Scottish forces in the 1640s, a citadel for the English army in the following decade, and the quartering site for the king's men keeping tabs on the rebellious region after the Restoration. The regular presence of soldiers in Ayr generated a wide range of disciplinary and fiscal challenges for the town council and kirk session and put the culture of covenanting to its most serious tests.[31] The comparatively dense populations of middling burghs like Ayr also made them breeding grounds for the various waves of plague, centres of recruitment into the military, ideological hotbeds for resistance and nonconformity, and testing grounds for fiscal, civic, and religious change. In short, the 'crisis of the seventeenth century' in Scotland was an especially, though not exclusively, urban experience.[32] Yet previous studies of urban religion in Scotland have tended to focus on the Reformation era.[33] As Alan R. MacDonald noted in 2019, while some illuminating work has been done on the religious politics of Scotland's towns during the covenanting era, the period between 1660 and 1690 has been 'the most remarkably unexplored'.[34] As a study of one urban community during a long period of revolutionary change in the British Isles, this book begins to fill this lacuna.

Ultimately, the goal of this study is two-fold. First, it demonstrates that following the administration of the National Covenant and the Solemn League and Covenant, covenanting became a lens through which the people of Ayr made sense of their sins and obligations as Reformed protestants. In these years, the congregation of Ayr was, thanks to the zealous efforts of its religious leadership (and the stewardship of Adair in particular), refashioned as a covenanted community, an identity that would remain in tack for more than a generation. In most ways, this was not a major departure from the previous culture and practice of protestantism at the local level; to the contrary, the making of a covenanted community depended on following the well-worn grooves of discipline and worship that had been carved, slowly but surely, after the Reformation. Godliness and covenanting became synonymous, but in the eyes of Adair and his ilk, the former could not be truly achieved without the latter. This did not mean, of course, that the town was without disagreement and disobedience during this period. The covenanting project, much like the more general disciplinary culture of Calvinism, was never about eradicating sin – an impossibility for a fallen population – but rather about interpreting those sins as the reason the covenants were necessary in the first place. In Ayr, therefore, covenanting served not only as a political practice or even an absolute mandate, but as a social lodestar for the ways in which the community ought to believe and behave.

Second, this book offers an uncommonly complete picture of early modern piety, leadership, and identity in Scotland across multiple moments of crisis. Structured chronologically to capture the story of a community over time, it reveals much about the lived experiences of 'super-protestants' throughout the Anglophone world – the men and women who were distinct not so much in their theology, but in the intensity of their spiritual praxis.[35] While the covenanters of Ayr may not have been puritans in the strictest sense, most were certainly the 'hotter sort' of protestants, joined in spirit (and sometimes in collective action) with their brethren on both sides of the Atlantic in an all-encompassing pursuit of a godlier society.[36] Moreover, Ayr, because of its location on the sea, was rarely without international visitors – Frenchmen shipwrecked in the early 1640s and again in the late 1660s, English soldiers quartered in the town during the Cromwellian occupation, and a regular influx of relatives and refugees from Ireland. The people of Ayr, too, were tremendously mobile, commonly crossing the Irish Sea and travelling south of the Tweed but also venturing, by mid-century, to Barbados and the American colonies. These interactions inspired a range of 'sinful' behaviours, exposed residents to faiths other than their own, and at times threatened the cohesiveness of the congregation. In short, this book shows how the comparatively small world of Ayr, far from being an isolated place in a peripheral country, was 'densely intertwined with larger ones' in ways that had a striking impact on the religious life and ethos of the town.[37]

Terminology, method, and sources

This book centres on the idea of a community of 'covenanters', a contested historical and historiographical term that bears further explanation. The most obvious definition of the term is someone who pledged their allegiance to the covenants and the defence of the 'true religion', which was synonymous for many Scots with presbyterianism, a protestant polity based on a system of administrative courts – local (session), regional (presbytery), and national (General Assembly) – and marked by its opposition to royal interference in ecclesiastical affairs.[38] Yet the meaning and practice of covenanter identity on the national stage proved far less clear than this neat framing might suggest. The National Covenant itself was fundamentally and purposefully ambiguous, a fact made manifest in the political controversies a decade after its composition.[39] Debates over what it meant to uphold the covenants persisted well into the post-Restoration era, when members of this fractured movement had to decide to what extent, if at all, they would cooperate with a monarch whose ecclesiastical goals were usually in direct opposition to their own.[40]

While such definitional discussions are useful, I am less interested in pinning down a precise definition for 'covenanter', because there was not one. The experiences and identities of those who attempted to live their lives according to perceived mandates of the covenants were fluid, nuanced, and varied. Still, I use the term throughout this book to refer to the majority of the people of Ayr, lay and clerical alike, as well as to diverse members of the movement throughout Scotland. Here, the term is not meant as an inflexible or even dominant marker of identity, but rather as a way to designate those whose faith, political allegiances, and understanding of individual and corporate responsibility had been deeply informed by the swearing of the covenants and their ongoing application in the community. For them, covenanting was less an absolute mandate and more a formative practice that was exercised in a myriad of ways that overlapped with and redefined older beliefs and rituals. 'Covenanter' could contain multitudes – presbyterian, nonconformist, radical, conservative, and more – and I hope the pages that follow add complexity and richness to a term that was, for much of the seventeenth century and even in places like Ayr, a moving target.[41]

Readers of a book focused on one community will invariably wonder about the limits of such a work's conclusions. This is a valid concern, and this book is not intended to be comprehensive or representative of all of Scotland. In some ways, Ayr was exceptional, or at the very least extreme. The community, as has already been noted, stood at the heart of the 'radical' southwest, and the same passionate, hardline minister tended to the congregation for over a generation.[42] Yet much of what happened here in terms of daily discipline, allegiance to the covenants, enthusiastic witch-hunting, and resistance to the Restoration settlement can also be found beyond the southwest, especially throughout the Lothians and Fife. Moreover, the myriad challenges wrought by war, the Cromwellian occupation, and the quartering of troops were shared by other burghs throughout the country; in this way, Ayr reflects the urban experience of crisis. Thus if we want to understand the impact of the covenants on Scottish communities, Ayr might not be typical – though I would argue there was not a typical covenanter, either – but it can be taken as representative of the more zealous, urban parts of the covenanting heartlands. Regardless of how much we can and cannot extrapolate from the story of Ayr, the benefit of focusing on a single place is that it provides a much more complete picture of a covenanted community over a sustained period of time, revealing not just how the covenants were administered and received, but what they did. This, then, is a study of the production and practice of a specific protestant identity and the ways in which local dynamics – in a national context, in a globalising moment – determined the lived experience of faith.

This project was, as so many histories are, borne of chance. My interest in Ayr was piqued completely by accident, when I was looking for information on sermon-going in various kirk session records from the seventeenth century. The sessions, presided over by the minister and a cadre of elders and deacons drawn from leading members of the laity in a given community, were rather ubiquitous bodies by the late sixteenth century. Because they recruited people from all levels of society to participate in the enforcement of reform – from the occasional witness to the influential merchant turned elder – sessions imbued the community with a vested interest in broader aims of the Scottish kirk.[43] It was in these rich and copious records, which are unbroken in Ayr during the seventeenth century, that I came across the town's remarkable response to the plague of 1647 (discussed at length in Chapter 2) and the figure of minister William Adair.[44] These records have constituted my principal source for understanding the experiences and beliefs of this covenanted community. The minutes of the presbytery of Ayr, which oversaw twenty-five parishes in the southwest during much of the seventeenth century, have offered a regional perspective for events in Ayr and helped to illuminate the far wider importance and influence of Adair and other community members.

The ecclesiastical court records, remarkable as they are, do not tell the whole story. Ayr's town council minutes – a vastly underutilised source representing the burgh's 'repository of elite power' – have provided further opportunity to explore the tangled intersections between civil and ecclesiastical priorities, especially following the Restoration.[45] There was substantive overlap in personnel on the session and council throughout our period, which encouraged, as in other burghs, both regular collaboration and occasional conflict.[46] I have also consulted records of the Ayr burgh court, minute books of the town's major crafts, and the records of the General Assembly, Privy Council, Convention of Royal Burghs, and Scottish Parliament to situate religious dynamics in the town within their local, national, and international contexts. The other major sources that inform this study are the sermons and letters of William Adair. While his sermons never appeared in print, a sample of his preaching and lecture notes are preserved in the Ayrshire archives, often as undated fragments written on the backsides of pages from his university notebook and occasionally as more complete sermons and lectures dating from the late 1640s and early 1650s. A few of his letters to fellow ministers have survived, and I have used Adair's own words, written for both private and public use, to understand the mental world of the elusive man at the centre of this book. The writings of contemporaries like Robert Ballie and later presbyterian polemicists such as Robert Wodrow help to round out the picture of Adair and the influence he had on his kirk and well beyond.

Even in a focused study such as this, things are invariably missed, downplayed, or left out. This is a book about religious life – the influence of the covenants, the daily practices of piety, the beliefs and experiences of the townspeople, and the divisions spurred by ecclesiastical policies – and at times, the national politics of various players in Ayr take a backseat to local stories. While the involvement of Adair and others in conflicts surrounding things like the Engagement or the Test Act are discussed throughout this book, I consider them primarily in terms of the relationships and identities of the community. The economy, too, is addressed exclusively in terms of its impact on religious dynamics, although its main driver, the sea, is ever-present behind the movement of peoples, ideas, and goods in the burgh.

While William Adair is at the centre of this book, I have tried to incorporate the beliefs and experiences of the men and women we might call 'ordinary covenanters' – how they navigated the complexities and turmoil of the mid to late seventeenth century, what they made of the covenants and religious endeavours of their kirk, and what it was like for them to spend a generation under the spiritual guidance and discipline of the same hardline minister. I have listened closely for their voices in the kirk session and town council minutes, mediated as they were by the hands of the clerks. As much as possible, I have also considered the ways in which women found agency and hardship alike in an ecclesiastical structure and covenanting movement that was, in many respects, a patriarchal project.[47] While the picture of religious life in any community in any historical period will remain, ultimately, incomplete, I hope this book does justice to the men and women who shaped, and were shaped by, Scotland's covenanting revolution.

Notes

1 National Library of Scotland (hereafter NLS), MS 5770, notebook of seventeenth-century sermons, p. 119.
2 On the shared 'puritan' experience in a transatlantic context, see David D. Hall, *The Puritans: A Transatlantic History* (Princeton: Princeton University Press, 2019).
3 On the concept of Scotland's 'long Reformation', see the introduction to John McCallum (ed.), *Scotland's Long Reformation: New Perspectives on Scottish Religion, c. 1500–c. 1660* (Leiden: Brill, 2016).
4 George S. Pryde, 'Charter of Foundation', in Annie I. Dunlop (ed.), *The Royal Burgh of Ayr: Seven Hundred Fifty Years of History* (Edinburgh: Oliver and Boyd, 1953), pp. 1–18.

5 John Strawhorn, *The History of Ayr: Royal Burgh and County Town* (Edinburgh: John Donald Publishers, 1989), pp. 28–9.
6 Margaret H.B. Sanderson, *Ayrshire and the Reformation: People and Change, 1490–1600* (East Linton: Tuckwell, 1997), p. 45.
7 As quoted in Sanderson, *Ayrshire and the Reformation*, p. 49.
8 Sanderson, *Ayrshire and the Reformation*, p. 81.
9 George S. Pryde, 'The Development of the Burgh', in Dunlop, *The Royal Burgh of Ayr*, pp. 19–53, at p. 44.
10 William J. Dillon, 'The Streets in Early Times', in Dunlop, *Royal Burgh of Ayr*, pp. 68–77, at p. 76.
11 Hugh McGhee, 'The Harbour', in Dunlop, *Royal Burgh of Ayr*, p. 199. On the general history of trade in early modern Ayr, see Tom Barclay and Eric J. Graham, *The Early Transatlantic Trade of Ayr 1640–1730* (Ayr: Ayrshire Archaeological and Natural History Society, 2005).
12 Alan Bold, *A Burns Companion* (Basingstoke: Palgrave Macmillan, 1991), p. 63.
13 Edinburgh, National Records of Scotland (hereafter NRS), CH2/751/2, Ayr kirk session minutes, fo. 293r.
14 Strawhorn, *The History of Ayr*, p. 77; Laura A.M. Stewart, *Urban Politics and British Civil Wars: Edinburgh, 1617–1653* (Leiden: Brill, 2006), p. 61.
15 Laura A.M. Stewart, *Rethinking the Scottish Revolution: Covenanted Scotland, 1637–1651* (Oxford: Oxford University Press, 2016). For the text of the National Covenant, as well as the Solemn League and Covenant, see Samuel R. Gardiner (ed.), *The Constitutional Documents of the Puritan Revolution, 1625–1660*, 2nd edn (Oxford: Oxford University Press, 1899).
16 On the general 'crisis of the Seventeenth-Century', see Geoffrey Parker, *Global Crisis: War, Climate Change and Catastrophe in the Seventeenth Century* (New Haven: Yale University Press, 2013). For a more focused look at the crises in seventeenth-century England, see Clare Jackson, *Devil-Land: England Under Siege, 1588–1688* (London: Penguin, 2021).
17 Adair's life is detailed, though with a few minor errors, in Hew Scott (ed.), *Fasti Ecclesiae Scoticanae*, vol. III: Synod of Glasgow and Ayr, new edn (Edinburgh: Oliver and Boyd, 1920), pp. 8–9. On Adair's tenure at Ayr, see Archibald Mackenzie, *William Adair and His Kirk: The Auld Kirk of Ayr, 1639–1684* (Ayr: Ayr Advertiser, 1933). Adair's background and contributions have also been discussed by Neil McIntyre, 'Saints and Subverters: The Later Covenanters in Scotland, c. 1648–1682' (PhD thesis, University of Strathclyde, 2016), pp. 27–8. On the Adair family, see John R. Young, 'Scotland and Ulster Connections in the Seventeenth Century: Sir Robert Adair of Kinhilt and the Scottish Parliament under the Covenanters', *Journal of Scotch-Irish Studies*, 3 (2013), 16–76.
18 On the social, religious, and political roles of the clergy in early modern Scotland, see Chris R. Langley, Catherine E. McMillan, and Russell Newton (eds), *The Clergy in Early Modern Scotland* (Woodbridge: Boydell & Brewer, 2021).
19 Some of these essential if biased works include James Kirkton, *The Secret and True History of the Church of Scotland from the Restoration to the year*

1678 (Edinburgh: James Bannatyne and Co., 1817); Robert Wodrow, *The History of the Sufferings of the Church of Scotland, from the Restauration to the Revolution*, 4 vols (Edinburgh: James Watson, 1722); Thomas M'Crie, *The Works of Thomas M'Crie*, 4 vols (Edinburgh: William Blackwood and Sons, 1857).

20 David Stevenson, *The Scottish Revolution, 1637–44* (Newton Abbot: Davis and Charles, 1973); David Stevenson, *Revolution and Counter-Revolution in Scotland, 1644–1651* (London: Royal Historical Society, 1977); Ian B. Cowan, *The Scottish Covenanters 1660–1688* (London: Victor Gollancz, 1976); Walter Makey, *The Church of the Covenant 1637–1651: Revolution and Social Change in Scotland* (Edinburgh: John Donald, 1979). The work of Allan Macinnes has been essential, especially in framing diverse covenanting ideology within a wider British framework; see, in particular, Allan Macinnes, *Charles I and the Making of the Covenanting Movement* (Edinburgh: John Donald, 1991) and *The British Revolution, 1629–1660* (Basingstoke: Palgrave, 2005). On the debates about and within the covenanting movement after the Restoration, see Alasdair Raffe, *The Culture of Controversy: Religious Arguments in Scotland, 1660–1714* (Woodbridge: Boydell, 2012).

21 Stewart, *Rethinking the Scottish Revolution*, esp. pp. 103–21. The influence of the covenants and ensuing ecclesiastical debates on the local mechanics of church governance has also been fruitfully explored by Chris Langley in his study of the relationship between warfare and religious practice during the British civil wars. See Chris Langley, *Worship, Civil War and Community, 1638–1660* (London: Routledge, 2015).

22 See, for example, McIntyre, 'Saints and Subverters'; Jamie Murdoch McDougall, 'Covenants and Covenanters in Scotland, 1638–1679' (PhD thesis, University of Glasgow, 2017); Kirsteen M. Mackenzie, *The Solemn League and Covenant and the Cromwellian Union 1643–1663* (London: Routledge, 2017); Chris Langley (ed.), *The National Covenant in Scotland, 1638–1689* (Woodbridge: Boydell, 2020); Sharon Adams and Julian Goodare (eds), *Scotland in the Age of Two Revolutions* (Woodbridge: Boydell, 2014).

23 These monuments have been meticulously explored by Mark Jardine at https://drmarkjardine.wordpress.com (accessed 2 January 2024).

24 For an investigation into the 'radical' reputation of the southwest, see Sharon Adams, 'A Regional Road to Revolution: Religion, Politics and Society in South-West Scotland, 1600–50' (PhD thesis, University of Edinburgh, 2002) and Sharon Adams, 'The Making of the Radical South-West: Charles I and His Scottish Kingdom, 1625–1649', in John R. Young (ed.), *Celtic Dimensions of the British Civil Wars* (Edinburgh: John Donald Publishers, 1997), pp. 53–74. See also Makey, *The Church of the Covenant*, esp. pp. 165–78. For a useful discussion of the challenges of designating covenanters 'radical' versus 'conservative', see McDougall, 'Covenants and Covenanters', pp. 24–5.

25 David Stevenson, 'The Radical Party in the Kirk', *The Journal of Ecclesiastical History*, 25:2 (1974), 135–65, at 156. After a conversation with David Dickson, however, Adair demonstrated his willingness to compromise, agreeing

to submit to the 'three nocent ceremonies' for the greater good and unity of the kirk. See Robert Baillie, *The Letters and Journals of Robert Baillie*, ed. David Laing, 3 vols (Edinburgh: Bannatyne Club, 1841–2), ii, pp. 69–71.
26 Stewart, *Rethinking the Scottish Revolution*, p. 109.
27 Baillie, *Letters*, iii, p. 53.
28 David Stevenson, 'Deposition of Ministers in the Church of Scotland under the Covenanters, 1639–1651', *Church History*, 44:3 (1975), 321–35.
29 Margo Todd, *The Culture of Protestantism in Early Modern Scotland* (New Haven: Yale University Press, 2002). Happily, a number of recent works have begun to fill this void, most notably Alison Muir, 'The Covenanters in Fife, c 1610–1689: Religious Dissent in the Local Community' (PhD thesis, University of St Andrews, 2002) and Claire McNulty, 'The Experience of Discipline in Parish Communities in Edinburgh, Scotland, 1638–1651' (PhD thesis, Queen's University Belfast, 2021).
30 On the role the burghs in parliament, see Alan R. MacDonald, *The Burghs and Parliament in Scotland, c. 1550–1651* (Aldershot: Ashgate, 2007), pp. 5–6. For a detailed study of the convention, see John Toller, ' "Now of little significancy"? The Convention of the Royal Burghs of Scotland, 1651–1688' (unpublished PhD thesis, University of Dundee, 2010).
31 On the military and attendant fiscal burdens on Scottish burghs, see Laura A.M. Stewart, 'Military Power and the Scottish Burghs, 1625–1651', *Journal of Early Modern History*, 15:1 (2011), 59–82.
32 On debates surrounding whether these conflicts constituted a 'crisis of the seventeenth century', see Geoffrey Parker, 'Crisis and Catastrophe: The Global Crisis of the Seventeenth Century Reconsidered', *American Historical Review*, 113:4 (2008), 1053–79.
33 See, for example, Sanderson, *Ayrshire and the Reformation*; Robert Falconer, *Crime and Community in Reformation Scotland: Negotiating Power in a Burgh Society* (London: Routledge, 2012); John McCallum, *Reforming the Scottish Parish: The Reformation in Fife, 1560–1640* (Aldershot: Ashgate, 2010).
34 Alan R. MacDonald, 'Urban Archives: Endless Possibilities', *Journal of Irish and Scottish Studies*, 9:2 (2019), 29–49, at 35. On urban religious politics during the civil war period, see, for example, Stewart, *Urban Politics*; Gordon DesBrisay, ' "The Civill Wars Did Overrun All": Aberdeen, 1630–1690', in Patricia Dennison, David Ditchburn, and Michael Lynch (eds), *Aberdeen before 1800: A New History* (East Linton: Tuckwell 2002), pp. 238–66; David Stevenson, 'The Burghs and the Scottish Revolution', in Michael Lynch (ed.), *The Early Modern Town in Scotland* (London: Routledge, 1987), pp. 167–91. For a welcome addition to the literature on urban Scotland during the Restoration era, see Allan Kennedy, 'The Urban Community in Restoration Scotland: Government, Society and Economy in Inverness, 1660–C.1688', in *Northern Scotland*, 5:1 (2014), 26–49.
35 The phrases 'super-protestant' and 'hotter sort' are Patrick Collinson's, in 'Elizabethan and Jacobean Puritanism as Forms of Popular Religious Culture', in Christopher Durston and Jacqueline Eales (eds), *The Culture of English*

Puritanism (London: Red Globe Press, 1996), pp. 32–57, at p. 46 and *The Elizabethan Puritan Movement* (Berkeley: The University of California Press, 1967), p. 27, respectively. John Coffey makes explicit the similarities between Scottish presbyterianism and puritanism in *Politics, Religion and the British Revolutions: The Mind of Samuel Rutherford* (Cambridge: Cambridge University Press, 1997), pp. 17–18. On the question of the terminology of puritanism as it might be applied to Scots, see Margo Todd, 'The Problem of Scotland's Puritans', in John Coffey and Paul C.H. Lim (eds), *The Cambridge Companion to Puritanism* (Cambridge: Cambridge University Press, 2008), pp. 174–88.

36 On Scottish Reformed protestants in dialogue with their counterparts in England and New England, see, most comprehensively, Hall, *The Puritans*. For insights into the influence of Scottish presbyterianism – including in its covenanted form – on burgeoning American religiosity, see Leigh Eric Schmidt, *Holy Fairs: Scotland and the Making of American Revivalism* (Princeton: Princeton University Press, 1989), esp. chapter one.

37 Thomas V. Cohen, 'The Macrohistory of Microhistory', *Journal of Medieval and Early Modern Studies*, 47:1 (2017), 54. For studies of Scotland that demonstrate the complex relationship between the local, national, and international processes of religious and political change, particularly during the Reformation, see, for example, Michael Lynch, *Edinburgh and the Reformation* (Edinburgh: Edinburgh University Press, 1981); McCallum, *Reforming the Scottish Parish*; and Catherine E. McMillan, 'Keeping the Kirk: The Practice and Experience of Faith in North East Scotland, 1560–1610' (PhD thesis, University of Edinburgh, 2016).

38 On the challenges of defining 'covenanter' in purely religious terms, as well as an overview of these definitions, see R. Scott Spurlock, 'Problems with Religion as Identity: The Case of Mid-Stuart Ireland and Scotland', *Journal of Irish and Scottish Studies*, 6 (2013), 1–29, esp. 27–9.

39 The point about the ambiguity of the National Covenant has been eloquently made in McIntyre, 'Saints and Subverters', 5 and McDougall, 'Covenants and Covenanters', pp. 41–4. For an overview of the divisions within the covenanting movement and within the way historians have discussed covenanting ideology, see Allan I. Macinnes, 'Covenanting Ideology in Seventeenth-Century Scotland', in Jane H. Ohlmeyer (ed.), *Political Thought in Seventeenth-Century Ireland: Kingdom or Colony* (Cambridge: Cambridge University Press, 2000), pp. 191–220.

40 On the meanings of covenanting in the post-Restoration period, see McIntyre, 'Saints and Subverters' and Alasdair Raffe, 'Who Were the Later Covenanters?', in Chris R. Langley (ed.), *The National Covenant in Scotland, 1638–1689* (Woodbridge: Boydell, 2020), pp. 197–214.

41 For a useful discussion of terminology, see McDougall, 'Covenants and Covenanters', 23–4. Here I primarily use 'hardline' to denote those who interpreted the covenants as a binding, pro-presbyterian mandate that placed godliness above obedience to a monarch.

42 This was an unusually long tenure. An examination of all the clergy of the Synod of Lothian and Tweeddale between 1630 and 1690 shows that the average tenure of a minister who took up his pose in this period was just over nine years. This data is from www.maps.mappingthescottishreformation.org (accessed 2 January 2024).

43 Historians generally estimate that by the beginning of the seventeenth century, 80 per cent of the thousand or so parishes in Scotland had regular, working kirk sessions. See Todd, *Culture of Protestantism*, p. 8. On the history and purpose of the sessions, see also Jenny Wormald, *Court, Kirk and Community: Scotland, 1470–1625* (Toronto: University of Toronto Press, 1981); Michael. F. Graham, *The Uses of Reform: Godly Discipline and Popular Behavior in Scotland and Beyond, 1560–1610* (Leiden: Brill, 1996); Lesley M. Smith, 'Sackcloth for the Sinner or Punishment for the Crime: Church and Secular Courts in Cromwellian Scotland', in John Dwyer, Roger Mason, and Alexander Murdoch (eds), *New Perspectives on the Politics and Culture of Early Modern Scotland* (Edinburgh: John Donald Publishers, 1982), pp. 116–32. The Ayr session met at least weekly and was composed of the minister and assistant minister (when the town had one) and a large cohort of between 20 and 40 elders and deacons. According to the *First Book of Discipline* (1560), elders were to deal primarily with maintenance of moral order while the deacons dealt with financial issues like church property and charity, but in practice there was often little distinction between the two roles. On the theoretical distinctions between these two roles, see John McCallum, *Reforming the Scottish Parish*, pp. 158–60.

44 For the kirk session minutes, see CH2/751/2–7. Separate account books, which usually kept registration of the payments made into and taken from the poor's purse as well as the recipients of poor relief, were kept from 1664 onward. See CH2/751/19–24.

45 This phrase is used by Laura Stewart to describe Edinburgh's town council, but it applies to Ayr as well. See Stewart, *Urban Politics*, p. 6.

46 Historians have identified such a significant overlap in personnel between town councils and sessions in Edinburgh and Aberdeen during the Reformation period, though unlike in Ayr, this over overlap did not persist in the capital through to the seventeenth century. See Falconer, *Crime and Community*, pp. 45–66 and Stewart, *Urban Politics*, pp. 61–4. On the relationship between the town council and the session more general, see Stewart, *Urban Politics*, esp. chapters 1 and 2.

47 On the topic of women, gender, and the covenants, see Alasdair Raffe, 'Female Authority and Lay Activism in Scottish Presbyterianism, 1660–1740', in Sarah Petrei and Hannah Smith (eds), *Religion and Women in Britain, c. 1660–1760* (Farnham: Ashgate, 2014), pp. 59–74; Alan James McSeveney, 'Non-Conforming Presbyterian Women in Restoration Scotland: 1660–1679' (PhD thesis, University of Strathclyde, 2005); Louise Yeoman, 'A Godly Possession? Margaret Mitchelson and the Performance of Covenanted Identity', in Langley, *The National Covenant in Scotland, 1638–1689*, pp. 105–25; David G. Mullan, 'Women in Scottish Divinity, c. 1590–1640', in Elizabeth Ewan and Maureen

M. Meikle (eds), *Women in Scotland, c. 1100–c. 1750* (East Linton: Tuckwell Press, 1999), pp. 29–41; Laura Doak, 'Militant Women and "National" Community: The Execution of Isabel Alison and Marion Harvie, 1681', *Journal of the Northern Renaissance*, 12 (2021), n.p.; Michelle D. Brock, ' "She-Zealots and Satanesses": Women, Patriarchy, and the Covenanting Movement', in Mairi Cowan, Janay Nugent, and Cathryn Spence (eds), *Gender and Identity in Scotland, 1200–1800: Power, Politics, and Faith* (Edinburgh: Edinburgh University Press, 2024).

1

Clergy and covenants

The pursuit of further reformation during the seventeenth century, divine providence notwithstanding, was fundamentally about people and power. While Scotland may have technically become protestant in 1560, the subsequent decades entailed considerable debate and controversy, even as the kirk reached a general theological and disciplinary consensus that could be rightly held up as a Reformed success story. As historians have long observed, the Scottish Reformation was a winding and uneven process, a transformation that required constant reaffirmation at both the local and national levels.[1] One of the key mechanisms for instantiating and reinforcing the aims of the Reformation in its early days was the swearing and subscribing of confessions – namely, the Scots Confession of 1560 and the Negative Confession of 1581, which themselves built upon on an emotive tradition of making bonds and taking oaths. This history, infused with far older stories of the Israelites striving to uphold their covenant with God, offered important blueprints for the covenanting revolution in Ayr and across the country.[2]

While the National Covenant drew on a long and complex history of texts and rituals, its own composition was occasioned by the controversy surrounding a specific work: the Book of Common Prayer. When Charles I and his infamous archbishop William Laud sought to introduce – or, as many in Scotland saw it, impose – religious innovations upon kirks across the country, most Scottish clerics saw this as an egregious abuse of power. Worse, to presbyterian observers, the imposition of the episcopal liturgy threatened to push Scotland's ecclesiastical establishment down a slippery slope towards Catholicism. 'Popish, atheistical and English': the king's prayer book was condemned before it was even officially introduced to Scottish parishes in the summer of 1637.[3] Protests against the prayerbook soon proliferated, and Ayr was one of seven burghs in Scotland that petitioned the Privy Council for its removal early that autumn.[4] The famous incident at St Giles, in which Jenny Geddes purportedly hurled a stool at the bishop who attempted to read from the unwelcome text, was a dramatic harbinger of things to come.[5] In the coming months, opponents of episcopal 'innovations' continued to organise, and in late February 1638, the National Covenant was formally adopted and subscribed by leading clerics and statesmen in Edinburgh and rapidly distributed across Scotland.

The questions dominating Scottish discourse in this weighty moment also preoccupied Reformed communities throughout the Atlantic and European worlds: who had the right to exercise spiritual authority? What was the proper relationship between church and state, and between local, national, and international protestant interests? Of course, these questions were centuries old and had existed at the heart of the Reformation itself, but they came to a head again towards the middle of the seventeenth century amid increased religious factionalism, polemical print culture, and warfare. South of the border, English puritans, having gained significant representation and influence in the House of Commons, increasingly challenged royal initiatives deemed ungodly and unlawful.[6] The situation in England was, as we shall see, intimately bound up with the Scottish rebellion against the crown's attempted control of the kirk in the Bishops' Wars of 1639 and 1640. Meanwhile in New England, the so-called antinomian controversy – a contentious theological debate over salvation, how it was achieved, and who had the authority to offer spiritual assurances – coalesced around the figure of Anne Hutchinson, who was tried for heresy in autumn of 1637 and banished from the colony in spring 1638.[7] In continental Europe, the Thirty Years' War continued to rage, driven by an ever-shifting blend of confessional divisions and dynastic struggles. Though the fighting was far away, the plight of the godly felt near indeed. Many Scottish men fought as mercenary soldiers in the war, and throughout the long and bloody conflict, Scottish congregations collected money to support their protestant brethren in continental Europe.[8] The upshot of these overlapping and interlocking conflicts was the perception among many of Scotland's religious leaders that their faith was under assault by a wide range of enemies; accordingly, getting their own house in order was of utmost importance. The National Covenant thus ought to be viewed as both part of an ongoing project of further reformation and a response to a perceived context of national and international crisis.[9]

Though the National Covenant was purposefully ambiguous about both ecclesiology and the remit of the monarch in spiritual affairs – it was, primarily, a rejection of all things 'popish' and a commitment to further reformation – some parishes were resistant to making what could be viewed as act of rebellion against the king.[10] Ayr was at the opposite end of the spectrum. It took up the covenant early and with enthusiasm, which was little surprise given the town's history of embracing presbyterianism and rejecting perceived royal overreach. The pump was primed in 1638 for a zealous embrace of covenanting, though this would depend on the personal influence and commitment of the town's clergy as much as the assent of its parishioners. Ayr ultimately had the right leadership at the right time to become a covenanting hotspot, especially through the tumultuous years and controversies of civil war. But it nearly did not.

Administering the National Covenant

When the people of Ayr swore to uphold the National Covenant on 8 April 1638, the sharer of such an important document should have been William Annand, who had been minister of the parish kirk of St John the Baptist since 1625. An enthusiastic supporter of Charles I, he had been imposed by the king on the reluctant burgh, and by the late 1630s, his episcopal leanings had earned him considerable contempt from his parishioners.[11] A visitor to the kirk reported hearing numerous complaints that Annand 'doth so violently press the ceremonies, especially the kneeling at communion'; kneeling to receive the Eucharist was a hotly contested issue, and the strictest presbyterians found the practice unacceptably Catholic and decidedly unbiblical. Apparently on Easter 1634, as soon as he went to the communion table, 'the people all left the church and departed, and not one of them stayed, only the pastor alone'.[12] In March 1635, the session minutes note that a communion was given in the town, and Annand 'kneeled quhen he took it him self'.[13] The tone of the clerk reads as censorious – neither he, nor many other members of the community, felt comfortable countenancing such behaviour.

The position of minister was one that, ideally, carried with it respect as well as the power to discipline.[14] Annand would soon learn, however, that a cleric's place in a given parish also depended to a considerable extent upon the assent of the parishioners – and this he never really had to lose. Things went from bad to worse in August 1637, when he preached in defence of the new prayer book at a meeting of the Glasgow synod, which, according to minister Robert Baillie, resulted in his being assaulted by 'some hundredths of inraged women, of all qualities'.[15] In the months following the swearing of the National Covenant in Ayr, Annand was often away from the parish. After facing intense questioning about his 'maintaineing saints dayes, and many poynts of erroneous doctrine' from the General Assembly meeting in Glasgow (which also heard unfavourable testimony from members of his own congregation), he was formally deposed that December.[16]

During the time of Annand's absence, the parish was largely served by its second minister, Robert Blair. He made it a point to unsubtly reject the 'popish' practices of Annand, and the session minutes describe how, in July of 1639, he administered communion 'according to the institution of chryst, without superstition as before'.[17] This revealing description, included by reader and clerk William Smith, made clear the dominant position. Blair's time in Ayr was short-lived, however, and he was transferred – much to his chagrin – to St Andrews in September of 1639.[18] John Fergushill, an experienced minister who had been serving in nearby Ochiltree for the previous two and a half decades, took up the empty post that November. By this time, he had already earned a reputation for hardline presbyterian views. William Adair, who had been admitted as assistant minister in late October 1639, joined him in his work.[19] Fergushill and Adair were somewhat of a package deal, as two months prior to Fergushill's appointment, Blair had announced that both had been recommended by the General Assembly to take the clerical reins in the town.[20] The two served together until Fergushill's death in 1644, after which Adair began his nearly forty-year stint as Ayr's first, and sometimes sole, minister.

We will return to Fergushill and Adair shortly, but this ministerial timeline, far from being an irrelevant chronicle of personnel changes, helps to explain the ways in which the religious leadership of Ayr attempted to fashion the town into a covenanted community and why they were so successful in doing so. First, it illustrates that even prior to the swearing of the National Covenant, Ayr had a laity invested in defining (if not always following) godly behaviour in a particular way, which would become increasingly central to the culture of covenanting there. The commitment of a significant number of parishioners to presbyterian interpretations of religious practice was made manifest in their rejection of Annand. Of course, this was not cut and dry: even as Annand received considerable local as well as national rebuke for his support of kneeling and use of the prayer book, the session requested that he 'return to the kirk' and cited his absence before the presbytery, before eventually disavowing him.[21] This does not mean that members of the session or the wider community approved of Annand's actions, but rather reflects the sheer necessity of having more than one minister – Blair was already second in command by this time – in a town of its size. As Baillie noted of Annand, 'the towne of Aire dealt much with him; bot in vaine: so they at last gave in complaint of his miscarriages, with a resolution never more to receave him within their pulpit'.[22] When he was finally deposed, his former parisioners offered no protest, and an implicit rebuke of his ministerial style is evident in the general acceptance of the subsequent ministers. Fergushill and Adair both had impeccable presbyterian credentials, which they defended even at considerable personal cost.

Second, the turmoil surrounding Annand as well as his absence from the parish during this time complicated the actual swearing of the National Covenant, making its administration into a process as much as an event.[23] The covenant was initially read to the parishioners on 11 March 1638 by reader Smith, after which he asked all 'the haill inhabitantis to be [present] on Tuesday nixt after sermon for subscryving the same'.[24] The same day, a fast was ordered for the next sabbath by Annand, who was still hanging on to his post. The session minutes report that on Sunday 18 March, the fast had begun and the covenant was 'red again hands halden upe to stand be the same'. This, oddly enough, was not the official swearing, but a practice run of sorts; it would be another three weeks before the official communal subscription.[25] On 5 April, guest preacher James Bonar, minister at nearby Maybell, 'made a relation publictly of the houll proceding of the commissioners anent the covenant, and desired that solemlye on the Sabbath they' – meaning the congregation – 'wald conven to renewe the same'.[26] Finally, on 8 April, following morning and afternoon sermons by James Cunningham, moderator of the presbytery of Ayr, on verses of Psalm 119, the covenant 'was red and men women and all bouth younge and old held upe their hands ordourlie by thare rowmes [rank] and that conscientiously'.[27] Everyone in the town was to participate in a way that at once recognised the social order and invited involvement in an unusually egalitarian way.

This month-long process of preparing the congregation to swear the National Covenant without the direction of a man who, however controversial, had been their minister for over a dozen years had several lasting effects on the community. Most obviously, the lag time between the initial reading and explanation of the covenant and its actual administration would have meant that parishioners had longer to ponder and discuss its content and meanings, should they choose to do so. Additionally, the fact that Annand never returned to the parish after 19 March, just a week after the covenant's initial reading and three before its official swearing, made explicit the connection between his failings as a covenanter and his removal from the parish. In this way, adherence to a specific interpretation of the covenant – and inclusion in the community were wedded from the outset. Additionally, Annand's departure, combined with the fundamentally ambiguous nature of subscription to the National Covenant itself, meant that the subsequent two ministers – Fergushill and Adair – would be the primary architects of the religious identity and practical piety of this covenanted community.

Covenanting clergy

Minister John Fergushill was born in 1592 to a prominent Ayr family. His father had served as provost of the town – an administrative role akin to mayor – and his mother hailed from the influential Kennedy family. He had a somewhat circuitous path to the ministry, beginning his studies in Edinburgh before leaving for a protestant academy in Montauban in southern France during an outbreak of the plague in Scotland.[28] The young Fergushill was uncertain whether he wanted to follow in his father's footsteps by pursuing a career as a merchant or if the ministry was his true calling. The pull of the kirk won out, and he finally finished his theology degree at the University of Glasgow.[29] After a few years as minister of Ochiltree, he made a name for himself in 1618 through his vocal opposition to the Five Articles of Perth, a set of alterations to worship imposed by James VI and I, which, among other stipulations, required kneeling at communion ceremonies. Fergushill memorably deemed the articles 'scandalous, unexpedient, destroying the thing which we were building'; he was never a man to mince words.[30]

Fergushill's commitment to defending the presbyterian structure of the Scottish kirk was shared by the man who became Ayr's 'colleague minister' – a second, usually more junior clerical role in larger parishes. The events of William Adair's early life remain largely unknown to us, but according to the marker on his gravestone, he was seventy at his death in 1684, meaning he would have been born in 1614. His family, the Adairs of Kinhilt, traced their lineage back to Ireland, having settled in Dumfries and Galloway sometime in the late fourteenth century. Adair's father, William Adair of Kinhilt, is described in various sources as a 'Portpatrick laird', and William the younger was the product of his father's third marriage, meaning that any significant inheritance went to his older half-brother Sir Robert Adair, a prominent Scots planter in Ulster as well as an important military and political leader in covenanted Scotland.[31] Our Adair also appears to have been a close relative, likely the uncle, of minister Patrick Adair, who became a central figure in the history of Irish presbyterianism.[32] As befitting the second son of a middling landed family, Adair was an officer in the army before he became a man of God.[33] His military service is obscure and must have been relatively short-lived; he was a student in the mid-1630s and an expectant minister at the presbytery of Ayr in early 1638 when the National Covenant was signed. In all likelihood, he simply trained with the army in anticipation of service in one of Scotland's many regiments involved in the Thirty Years War, either just before or after university, before moving onto his clerical career. But as we shall see, his experience in military service, however limited, would come in handy for the covenanters in the coming decades.

A few clues to Adair's educational background exist. His limited papers include notes on philosophy and theology, many of them in Latin, composed primarily between 1633 and 1635 while he was, according to the archive catalogue, 'a student under Alexander Hepburn, and afterwards at the Edinburgh Academy' – meaning he studied at the University of Edinburgh.[34] In a testament to how some things never change, Adair's schoolboy notes include copious amounts of doodles, including lions, geometrical shapes, and a curious rendering of a completely nude man, interspersed amid the dense observations on ancient philosophy. This collection is, unfortunately, the beginning and end of our traces of Adair's educational background – Hew Scott's *Fasti* does not list him as having a postgraduate degree, and Adair is not listed as one of the Edinburgh graduates in 1636, as we might expect – but it is enough to demonstrate that he had received the basic classical training expected of the post-Reformation Scottish clergy.[35] Beyond this, he clearly had talent. According to James Stirling, minister of Barony from 1699 to 1737, Adair 'was in his youth reckoned a very eminent man for piety and learning, and a good gift of preaching, and had a more than ordinary gift of prayer'.[36]

Adair married twice, first in July 1651 to Janet Boyd, daughter of theologian and committed presbyterian Robert Boyd of Trochrig. This marriage was short-lived due to her untimely death, and he married Janet Kennedy in the final month of 1653.[37] His second marriage was a long time in the works. According to a story recounted by Robert Wodrow, Adair visited Robert Cunningham, minister of Holyrood, on his deathbed in Irvine in spring 1637. The dying man asked him to 'be kind to his dear wife', Janet Kennedy, after he was gone. Adair apparently decided at some point that the best way to honour his deceased friend and show this requested kindness was through marriage. After the death of his first wife, Adair proposed to Kennedy, who expressed surprise, even amazement, that 'such a well-favoured and handsome young man, of such reputation for piety and parts' wanted to marry to a widow like herself who already had multiple children. She even reportedly said that if her late husband were alive, he 'would very readily have given one of his daughters to him, if he had any desire that way'. Of course, this recounting reveals as much about early modern gender norms as it does about the relationship between the Adair and Kennedy, but after prayer and consultation with friends, she accepted his proposal as a 'very strange and wonderfull kind Providence come to her door'. They were married and had a child named after his father. Adair 'shewed great respect' to Kennedy 'for she was a most excellent woman', and he was reportedly 'a most loving father to all her children'.[38]

Despite the obscurity of Adair's pre-Ayr life and ministerial training, we have ample understanding of the religious atmosphere in which he was brought up, as well as his general theology. When he was a very young boy, the central drama in the Scottish kirk was over the aforementioned Five Articles of Perth. This controversy was the fertile ground in which the covenanting views of the generation that came before him were planted. Though the debates over the Five Articles occurred twenty years prior to those that fuelled the composition of the National Covenant and ensuing Bishops' Wars, they involved a similar set of debates over religious practices and the acceptable limits of royal authority in shaping spiritual affairs. For

Adair, who grew up as these controversies unfolded, and Fergushill, who cut his teeth as a loud voice firmly on the side of hardline presbyterianism, these long-standing debates over spiritual authority and purity would prove constants during their time at Ayr. Most of Adair's sermons are not extant, but the ones we do have, composed at various points between 1647 and 1656, reflect a typical Reformed theology centred on the supreme power of God, the immutability of divine will as expressed through the Covenant of Grace, the inherent corruption of human nature, the importance of godly obedience and duty, and the redeeming love of Christ.[39]

All evidence suggests that Fergushill and Adair had a harmonious partnership, sharing a singular vision of godliness. They sought to further reform the already-Reformed kirk of Ayr in various ways, as illustrated by amendments to the parish's communion rituals. The session minutes note that their first communion together, held in May 1640, was conducted 'verie orderlie and decentlie' – that is, in a manner free from the superstitious rituals practised by their predecessor. In the summer of 1641, the men ended the prior practice of collecting donations at the communion tables, which they deemed 'as smelling of papisticall offerings'; from now on, any monies would be collected at the church door.[40] Moreover, any community members who had failed to take the National Covenant or pass examination by the ministers on the 'heads of the Faith' – essentially, the basics of Reformed theology – would be barred from receiving the sacrament.[41] There was little room for deviation, but at the same time, Fergushill and Adair remained committed to bringing errant parishioners back into the godly – meaning, in their minds, the covenanted – fold.

When the new ministers took over preaching at the burgh's parish church in the autumn of 1639, one of their first tasks was to track down parishioners who had yet to swear the covenant. That October, for example, just a week after Adair began his post, William Ritchie was called before the session for his 'negligence in subscribing the Covenant'.[42] In response to their questioning, he 'affirmed that he had not subscrybed it with his hand bot had done it with his hart, and that he was willing to swear and subscryve the same when they pleased'. The session pressed Ritchie as to whether he had taken the so-called 'Black Oath' while in Ireland, a 1638 royal directive that required adherents to reject the covenant and upheld support for episcopacy.[43] Ritchie held firm – he had not done so and 'nather was ever mynded so to do' – and expressed resentment that such a thing would even be in doubt.[44] Satisfied, the session told him to go to the minister's chamber with a few other elders that afternoon to subscribe the covenant. Ritchie's language of swearing in his heart, if not yet by his hand, suggests that though he had not sworn the document, he knew something of its content, which enjoined subscribers to commit with their 'whole hearts' and for 'all the days' of their lives 'to adhere unto and to defend the aforesaid true religion'.[45] Even if Ritchie was just making excuses here – though his indignation suggests that he was rather sincere – he clearly had some sense of the emotional 'heart work' inherent to the corporate project of covenanting.[46]

Ritchie's case notwithstanding, the number of those in Ayr who had not taken the National Covenant in 1638 was actually very small. The more substantive issue at hand over the coming years was the parishioners who had acted in ways contrary to the aims of the covenant(s). Overt deviance of their oaths was rare, but there were exceptions, such as that of Bryce Walker, a local craftsman charged in November 1641 with committing 'diverse and sundrie misbehaviors … contrair to the Covenant of Scotland' while he was serving a soldier in a Scottish regiment stationed in England earlier in the year.[47] The most significant of these charges was his 'speaking slanderouslie amongst papists' – possibly meaning royalists rather than actual Catholics – by spreading rumours about his regiment's presbyterian chaplain, a minister in the presbytery of Irvine. After thorough questioning and Walker's insistence he had already made proper and repeated repentance at Irvine, the Ayr session let the issue drop.[48] What is most interesting here is the framing of Walker's 'diverse and sundrie misbehaviors' not as simply errors deserving of disciplinary actions, but as direct violations of the National Covenant. This would become a conflation central to the making of a covenanted community.

War comes to Ayr

The aftermath of the National Covenant coincided with the beginnings of a complex, decade-long period of war that spanned Charles I's dominions.[49] In early 1639, the king raised an army and marched towards the border to quell the rebellion in his northern kingdom but was quickly foiled by the strength of the covenanting army and lack of English enthusiasm for war against the Scots. There was a half-hearted attempt at peace, followed by another short period of warfare and negotiation, which only strengthened the dominance of the covenanting regime over the machinery of government.[50] The king's wars with the Scots required fiscal support from an increasingly strident English Parliament that he had not summoned in the eleven years of his so-called 'personal rule'. Meanwhile, in Ireland during the autumn of 1641, a group of native Irish insurgents rose up against the repressive English regime, a deeply complex attempted coup that quickly turned bloody. The violent deaths of protestant settlers, including women and children, soon became fodder for copious amounts of propaganda and inspired a panic over 'popery' throughout Britain.[51] It was an incredibly volatile situation that by the summer of 1642 had boiled over into a civil war between the royalist forces and the parliamentary army.[52] The Wars of the Three Kingdoms had begun.

The early days of war occasioned new challenges for Ayr. Worship was, in some cases, disrupted, and in others it was directed by the spiritual expediencies of combat. In May 1639, for example, Robert Blair told the congregation to prepare themselves for communion the next sabbath, but a note later added to the record explained that the service was 'delayed because of the armies that went to the border'.[53] Fasts were held for the safekeeping of the army, and thanksgivings celebrated in honour of victories and periods of peace.[54] National news of the conflict was reported to the congregation, too, recorded in small snippets in the session minutes. 'Upon fryday the 12 of june 1640', for example, parishioners learned that 'the towne of Edinburgh assailed the castle with shott of canon on all quarters'.[55] In the margins of the meeting notes from 21 July 1644, the clerk explained that an intimation had been made by visiting minister William Scott – Adair was in Ireland at the time – 'of a solemne thanksgiving for the victorie in England the 2 of july 1644 against Prince Rupart', the much loathed royalist commander and nephew of Charles. I.[56] Many of these messages should be viewed as pieces of national political propaganda as much as news reports. For example, in October 1644, the General Assembly asked all of the parishes within the presbytery of Ayr to announce the excommunication of Nathaniel Gordon, a prominent colonel in the royalist army, deeming him and his associates 'unnaturall countrymen' who had a hand in bloodthirsty acts committed by those 'infesting and invading this kingdome in the northe'.[57] For the men and women the burgh, this announcement would have only reinforced a message they had been hearing for years: to be a full member of the community, be it local or national, adherence to the covenants was essential.

The war thus came to Ayr in bits of news and rituals performed in hope of victory and peace, but above all, it came through the movement of people. Local communities had to supply large numbers of Scottish men for the war effort and equip them for fighting, making the burden of war fiscal and social as much as martial.[58] Along with the presence of soldiers quartered in the town, which would become a regular feature of urban life over the coming decades, the beginning of war coincided with an influx of religious refugees from Ireland. In January 1642, scores of Irish men, women, and children, as well as a few Ayr natives who had been living in Ireland, arrived in the town after fleeing the violence occasioned by the rebellion in Ulster the previous October.[59] Ayr had very old connections to northern Ireland, not just in terms of geography but also people: for many centuries, families from Ireland intermarried with Ayrshire families (and vice versa), and during the seventeenth century, the town provided a constant stream of settlers to the plantations in the northeast.[60] As such, the southwestern port was an obvious place of refuge for those seeking relief for their present destitution. On 21 February, for example, the session gave thirty shillings to a 'creple woman from Irland and her 5 bairnes' and a dollar to one 'Mr Mirk minister from Irland'.[61] This uptick in charity placed considerable strain on the town's resources, already strained by the war effort, but Fergushill and Adair were far more concerned with making sure that both lay and clerical incomers who intended to stay in Scotland could prove themselves loyal covenanters. Indeed, over the coming year, more than fifteen of the new arrivals came voluntarily before the kirk session to crave forgiveness for swearing the so-called 'Black Oath' and to make public repentance accordingly.

Responses to the influx demonstrated that in some cases, the kirk leaders lacked confidence in the commitment of these refugees to the covenanted cause, especially ministers seeking clerical work in Scotland. Yes, most were, broadly speaking, presbyterians, but the National Covenant had exposed new fault lines in the faith; those from Ireland were generally welcomed in the west of Scotland and given necessary aid, but they were not immediately trusted.[62] Take the case of Adam Ritchie, a minister who had fled from County Antrim and sought forgiveness in March 1642 for his actions against the covenant there. He asked the session for the opportunity to 'make declaration publictlie for taking the yrish oath … and for communicating and using of superstitious rites and ceremonies used in the sacraments thair', and explained that he had done so 'against the light of his conscience'.[63] The session was apparently moved by Ritchie's display of 'unfeigned repentence' – sincerity of contrition was of utmost importance – and ordained him to appear before the pulpit the next sabbath to declare his sins to the congregation. In terms of adherence to the covenant, the requirements for communal inclusion applied, at least theoretically, in equal ways across the social spectrum. In September 1643, for example, the session heard the case of Margaret Lafrey, a servant to a local magistrate who appears to have arrived with the refugees the previous year. She was, like minister Ritchie, 'appointed to give signs of repentance for swearing to the Irish oath', and because she had not yet done so, 'to sweir the Covenant of Scotland publicklie'.[64]

Such public displays of repentance and regret for taking the Black Oath were not only necessary for communal inclusion and increased trust; they also provided the ministers and the session with an opportunity for messaging to the congregation the importance of adherence to the covenant, whether at home or abroad. Knowledge of what precisely what was said in sacred space by refugees from Ireland is mostly lost to us, but we can imagine the affirmations and laudations of the covenant that would have likely attended their confessions, either from Ayr's ministers or the repenting parties. Moreover, when struggling refugees such as Bessie Burr and Elspeth Moncur confessed 'publicklie thair sinne in taking that godless oath in Yrland' before a June communion celebration, the whole congregation could see first-hand the providential bad luck that could befall anyone who violated or, worse, rejected, the National Covenant.[65]

This message was further amplified by those like Gavin Rob, an Ayr native 'laitlie come from Irland', who appeared voluntarily before the session to confess that while he was 'frie of the yrish oath', he was still 'trubled in conscience' for some of his behaviour abroad. Specifically, he felt deep sorrow for having for his 'kneilling at the sacrament, and for countencing of other hearing of the service book' – one old and one comparatively new bugbear for presbyterian purists. Rob asked the session 'that he might be permitted to give signes of publict repentance befor the congregation'.[66] The minister and elders, after consultation with the presbytery, ordained him to do just this the following sabbath day. And they would have been foolish to deny him, for here was an opportunity to make an example of someone who, though he had not rejected the covenant outright, had violated its implicit mandates and felt deeply troubled for having done so. The responses from Ayr's religious leaders to the refugees from Ireland, especially those who had taken the Black Oath, demonstrate that membership in a covenanted community, while carefully circumscribed, was not as brittle as might be imagined. Those who sinned across the Irish Sea were given personal and performative opportunities for inclusion, just as the ordinary sinners in Ayr would be throughout their lives.

Acts and intimations

Even amid the need to enforce the National Covenant and grapple with the fallout from the beginnings of war, long-running disciplinary challenges continued to preoccupy the session. Pursuing those who had explicitly violated the covenant, either by failing to take it or swearing a counter-oath, was critical to building a unified communal allegiance to covenanting, but so too was addressing the more quotidian moral crimes in the town. Indeed, to do so had been mandated by the text of the National Covenant itself, which in the final paragraph reads 'we therefore faithfully promise, for ourselves, our followers, and all other under us, both in public, in our particular families and personal carriage … to be good examples to others of all godliness, soberness and righteousness, and of every duty we owe to God and man'.[67] From the outset, there existed a set of guidelines, albeit relatively vague ones, for the moral conduct of a covenanted community.

Of course, promising to behave and doing so were two different matters, and the swearing of the National Covenant was not a social light switch, nor was it expected to be such. In the years immediately following its subscription, Scots continued to engage in sundry acts of fornication, adultery, slander, sabbath-breaking, and so on, just as they had for centuries. On the last day of May 1642, for example, Janet Waddell, servant to a local timberman, reported – or, in the words of the session record, 'confessed' – that John Lauchlan 'did wrestle and strugle with her upon the hill and did lay her downe, and was above hir, and thrust in his knies betwixt her legs'. Both she and Lauchlan maintained that there had been no 'carnal copulation', and as this was a clear case of assault without any actual fornication, only he had to perform public repentance.[68] In July 1643, the session summoned William Watt, a tailor who had previously confessed to fornication with Bessie Smyth, for his 'mocking of his public repentance by refusing to mak confession' when called to do so in front of the congregation.[69] That August, Alexander and Matthew Reid appeared before the session for their drunken brawling, which had ended in a bloody sword fight. The two do not appear to have been brothers; Matthew clarified that he had not been intoxicated, as accused, but that he had been provoked by the said Alexander's calling his mother a witch.[70] On the surface, then, the impact of covenanting on the day-to-day conduct of the people of Ayr had been minimal; clearly, there was no behavioural sea-change. This is unsurprising, given that, as we have seen, the Scots had been in a formally articulated covenant with God since at least the Negative Confession of 1581, if not the Scots Confession of Faith twenty years prior.[71] Yet a number of shifts, subtle at first but quite revealing upon further inspection, did occur in the ways that the clerical leadership responded to and reframed communal (mis)conduct in the decade following the National Covenant.

One of these shifts emerged primarily through the making of 'intimations' in which the minister used the language of mutual obligation to steer his flock back towards the godly – that is, the covenanted – path. Intimations were generally routine declarations from the pulpit, such as announcement of new practices of poor relief, an impending visitation from members of the presbytery, or most often, fasting and preparation for an upcoming communion.[72] In the first year of their collective tenure, for example, Fergushill and Adair 'made intimation' of the keeping of four fasts, all tied to prayers and thanksgivings for Scotland's ongoing involvement in the early rumblings of the Wars of the Three Kingdoms.[73] But in the years after the swearing of the National Covenant, intimations were increasingly used by the ministers to lay out new moral mandates or enforce older ones that were evidently being ignored. Their contents reflect the priorities of Ayr's religious leadership and the ways in which the town's ministry attempted to convey to the congregation the expectations of a covenanted community. Between 1639 and 1643, Fergushill and Adair issued over twenty specific acts and directives for communal reform from the pulpit, many of them noted as 'new intimations' even if they replicated older policies. By comparison, between 1634 and 1638, there was only such behavioural act issued – in June, two months after the National Covenant was sworn.

These intimations ran the gamut of godly concerns. In January 1640, the ministers addressed a long-standing moral nuisance when they ordained that 'no drinking or night watching to be after ten houres at evin according to the ancient actes of the session' and 'no playing in the night tyme be at cardes or dyces and tables' (the session would later lament, in 1641, that 'sundrie persones young and old' had been flagrantly violating this act).[74] In April of 1641, a directive was given 'for reserving the Sabbath day and that no person strangers or inhabitants be found wandering after preaching on the streits'.[75] A fuller keeping of the Lord's Day was, of course, a very old priority for the kirk, but the insistence that parishioners return immediately to their homes after church for the reading of scripture and the conducting of familial worship was designated as 'new' by the session. The anxiety about communal comportment apparent in this rule was further reflected two months later, when the session lamented the 'abuse and scandalous behaviour of sundrie men and women of this place' such as 'walking upon the strits, and drinking in taverns' late into the night, which was 'contrair to former laudible acts'. As such, the elders 'all in one voyce' deemed those engaging in 'the foirsaid unchristian and scandalous misbehaviours in all tyme coming' to be under risk of censure by the kirk; the warning was to be announced the next sabbath day.[76] The language of 'all time coming' frequently attended these intimations and reflects that while there was often a nod towards to the Reformation project of earlier generations, the covenanting movement was equally driven by a desire to shape the community's future.

Such intimations were not merely policy announcements; they were also enforceable and binding acts, often containing threats of punishment. In December 1640, for example, the session issued a 'new intimation' meant to counter concerns about religious ignorance and disregard for ministerial authority. After discussing 'the great negligence and misregard' of those who refused 'to present themselves befor the minister to the examination' of their religious knowledge before communion, they ordained that the guilty parties be 'severlie censured by the session according to the gravitie of their offense'.[77] The teeth behind this act seem relatively dull compared to one issued in the summer of 1643, when the session determined that another 'new intimation' should be made by the minister explaining that whenever children and servants were caught breaking sabbath, their parents or masters would likewise be made to answer to the session for their negligent oversight. Those unable to pay the associated fines were to be put to the 'common wark of the town for a day without any wages', and all were 'to satisfie the kirk also as Sabbath breakers' alongside their children and servants.[78] Such acts reflect the extent to which covenanting was seen as a communal project requiring both individual vigilance and shared responsibility from across the social spectrum.

Intimations directed at curtailing the actions of women were especially common in the years immediately following the swearing of the National Covenant. Of the roughly twenty behavioural acts issued between 1639 and swearing of the Solemn League and Covenant in November 1643, at least seven were specifically aimed at local women, while none were directed explicitly at men. While some of these intimations addressed reports of scandalous conduct by 'sundrie young women in the town' – sex work, it seems, was a persistent issue – more quotidian female behaviour within the kirk was a particular concern.[79] Take, for example, two 1640 acts: in March, the session determined that a new intimation be made 'against women that wear plaid on thair heads in tyme of preaching'; in December of that year, 'women who intrude themselves in saits which ar appoynted for men to sait in' were the target of censure.[80] These were, apparently, ongoing issues, as both of these acts would be reiterated and elaborated upon later in the decade. As we shall see in subsequent chapters, the disruptions of war, the influx of strange men into the town, and the general perception of disorder led to greater scrutiny of women's words and actions.

In isolation, one is tempted to wonder what these acts and intimations actually had to do with the covenants, beyond reflecting the general desire for a godlier community. But the major benefit of reading the session minutes in their entirety over years and even decades is the ability to discern patterns and layered meanings. While most intimations did not explicitly mention the covenants, the ones that did demonstrate a clear conflation of godly behaviour and covenanting, and a commitment to enforcing the former in service of the latter. The richest example comes from 8 August 1643, a few months before the community would collectively swear the Solemn League and Covenant. On this day, the ministers and session spent the bulk of their meeting 'gravelie considering and taking to heart' the many scandals of 'diverse inhabitants of this paroche … both sexes, old and young'. Among other things, they lamented the town's 'neglect of the worship of God morning and evening', the many conflicts 'betwixt man and wyfe', the 'disobedience of children to their parents' and 'infidelitie of servants to their masters', and the 'open flyting banning swearing and blaspheming of gods name'. All of these things, the session affirmed, were manifestly 'contrare to our sworne Covenant and Christian profession'. The solution, they determined, was to assist 'the ministers in thair great charge' by carving the town into nineteen divisions assigned to the oversight of specific elders and deacons, to whom the inhabitants should report information about any deviant activities on the part of their neighbours. The whole plan, along with the manifold sins that had occasioned it, was to be explained to the congregation the coming Saturday after the sermon of preparation for communion alongside an intimation specifying that 'reverence and obedience' should be given to the elder and deacon of every division, 'under the paines of the censure of the Kirk'. This act, like those before it and many to come, was 'to stand as ane order in all tyme coming within this congregation'.[81]

The lamenting of the community's manifold sins and the devising of plans to counter them were not novel actions, nor were they remotely unique to Ayr. What was distinct to the post-1638 period, however, was the framing of all of these sins as 'contrare to our sworne Covenant' as well as break of 'Christian profession' in the session minutes. We do not know the exact words said to the congregation when this intimation was made from the pulpit, but given the commitment of Adair and Fergushill to an expansive interpretation of the covenant's remit, it is likely that behavioural sins were explicitly noted as breaches of covenanted duty. And of course, not all agreed with either this interpretation or the corresponding disciplinary actions. On 18 September 1643, for example, the session summoned local tailor George Grier for his 'uttering of contumelous speeches' against the recent act 'maid for visitation of the town by elders and deacones', which he had called 'ane novation'. He was also charged with spewing 'imprecations and cursed speiches' against Adair. For his 'unnatural and unchristian miscarriage', he was sentenced to public repentance and a meeting with the civil magistrate.[82] Tellingly, Grier's complaint of 'ane novation' appropriated the language of the staunch presbyterians, who opposed any innovations to worship that deviated from their interpretation of the true Reformed religion. This specific framing was, as far as the records reveal, an isolated incident, but it suggests the degree to which the language of covenanting could and did permeate the local discourse of dissent.

At their core, intimations were simply announcements of enforceable acts that provided the minister and session the opportunity to address communal problems on an ad hoc basis. But the context in which these announcements were delivered is at least as critical as their content for understanding the religious culture of communities within the covenanting heartlands. Here, intimations served as formative episodes of communication between the minister and the entirety of his flock. While the main power and purpose of the pulpit revolved around the delivering of sermons and administration of discipline, announcements of new godly initiatives and directives for future conduct also served a vital purpose in shaping a covenanted community.

Indeed, it might be that parishioners understood the covenants themselves as adjacent to this genre, read as they were from the pulpit to lay out – indeed, to mandate – a shared godly path for the people of both Ayr and Scotland's broader 'imagined national community'.[83]

The Solemn League and Covenant

In the early to mid-1640s, this imagined community was expanded by a new chapter in the long relationship between Reformed protestants on both sides of the border. When the covenanters rebelled against the king, they found common cause with the English parliamentarians, a group whose religious sentiments in some cases overlapped considerably with their Scottish brethren, especially when it came to vehement anti-popery. Though differences of opinion on ecclesiastical polity would, eventually, sever their alliance, in the early days of the war they shared the conviction that Charles I had badly overstepped his authority in matters sacred and secular. In autumn 1643, the composition and administration of the Solemn League and Covenant formalised this alliance, adding to English parliamentary forces the manpower of the Scottish army.[84] This document was more direct in its rejection of episcopacy than its 1638 counterpart, though ideological flexibility and ambiguities regarding the powers of the monarch remained. It asked its adherents on both sides of the border to, among other things, commit themselves to the eradication of 'poperie, prelacie, superstitione, heresie, shisme and profainnes' in defence of the Reformed cause.

By the time of the swearing of the Solemn League and Covenant, the people of Ayr had spent the previous five years hearing about the twinned needs of further reformation and adherence to the National Covenant. They had witnessed their religious leaders crack down on deviance while also issuing forgiveness and protection to both neighbours and strangers who had sinned during their time in Ireland, so long as they were willing to repent and swear the National Covenant. The centrality, then, of covenanting to communal inclusion and godly living in Ayr was already ingrained by 5 November 1643, when minister John Fergushill 'read and explained [to the congregation] the League and Covenant drawn up betwixt the kingdomes of England Scotland and Ireland'. The next Lord's Day, he announced, the 'whole people then present suld be solemnilie sworne to adher' to the new Covenant 'in all tyme coming'.[85] Moreover, after the public swearing of the Solemn League and Covenant by the congregation, the ministers, magistrates, and town councillors were, 'for exemple to others', to publicly subscribe the same, followed by the members of the session and the deacons of the crafts.[86] The swearing of this covenant mirrored the language of earlier intimations and reflected the hope that the moral mandates of the covenants would last long after members of the present session and congregation were gone. The understanding of godly conduct and allegiance to the covenants as overlapping, mutual endeavours was further reinforced by the specific language of this new covenant, which asked its swearers to strive to eradicate not only the threats from popery and prelacy, but also 'whatsoever shall be found to be contrary to sound doctrine and the power of godliness'.[87]

The year after the administering of the Solemn League and Covenant was a difficult one for Ayr. In the spring of 1644, Adair, by now an important player in the Scottish clerical world, was dispatched to Ireland to help administer the new covenant there.[88] On 4 June, the presbytery lamented the 'present sickness' of Fergushill, who later that month 'departed this lyfe'.[89] Adair, still in Ireland when his colleague died, received a letter from an increasingly distraught session that August, 'calling him to his charge and ministerie with all possible diligence, by reason of our present desolation'.[90] In his absence the congregation was served by guest clergy sent from the presbytery, but the yearning on the part of the town for the return of their minister during an uncertain time is apparent. Adair came home to Ayr at the end of September of 1644, though there would be no colleague minister to help him in his charge for another decade. It was a fitting expression of hope amid turmoil that, in this tumultuous year, the first Ayrshire-owned vessel to make a transatlantic voyage left from Ayr to Barbados seeking tobacco. The ship, owned by local merchant Robert Wallace, was optimistically called the 'Blessing'.[91]

Over the coming years, and often in connection to the turmoil of wartime mobility, the town attempted to enforce moral behaviour and fashion itself as a sort of covenanted city upon a hill.[92] Particular concerns included women of the town being seen 'scandalouslie to go about the shippes of strangers' docked at the port, 'wanderers throw the streits upon the lords day, siters under stairs ydlie after sermon', and 'young ones playing on the streits and blaspheming the name of god'.[93] Sometimes discipline was delayed by the absences of the guilty parties due to military service. In December 1643, for example, an emergency meeting between Fergushill and 'many of the brethren of the session' was held to deal with the repeated indiscretions of John McCalmont, an elder, who was a three-time fornicator. However, as he was 'presentlie out with the armie', the session deferred his punishment of standing in sackcloth until he returned.[94] The General Assembly's adoption of the Directory for Public Worship, drawn up in Westminster in early 1645 in an effort to harmonise religious practices in England and Scotland, encouraged further disciplinary efforts from local clergy.[95] The Ayr presbytery met with all ministers and ruling elders in its jurisdiction that March and exhorted them to enact a list of practices that amounted to 'diligence in thair callins'; the few who did not follow suit were suspended from their positions. Ministers across Scotland were now clearly expected to tow the covenanted party line.[96] In January and again in March of 1646, the presbytery asked its ministers to double down on their efforts to ensure that their parishioners adhered fully to the Solemn League and Covenant, and to bar any who complied with 'the publict enemies of this kirk and state' – meaning royalists – from taking communion.[97] Adair, ever on brand, was the first to report his diligence in assuring compliance in his parish.[98]

Of course, compliance was easier promised than procured. As the decade progressed, the session continued its efforts to assure that all the townsfolk had sworn the new covenant. In autumn 1645, for example, it came to the attention of Adair and the session that 'sundrie persons' in their jurisdiction 'had not subscrybit the Covenants'. They appointed that an intimation should be issued the next Lord's Day warning 'the not subscrybers' to appear before the session to remedy the problem. Clearly, not all parishioners were happy with the increasingly emphatic efforts to enforce the godliness mandated by not one but two covenants. On 3 August 1646, local blacksmith John Lachland was cited for 'uttering unchristian inprecations' against two of the elders. When questioned, he confessed that he had said that neither 'God nor the turkes' take the sacrament and that when his ticket was taken from him in response, he had replied 'I cair not for your communion'.[99] Worse, perhaps, was the case of a stabler that same day who had absented himself from the Lord's Supper and spoken 'contempouslie of the Covenant'; unfortunately we do not know precisely what he said, but it must have been serious, for he was referred upwards to the presbytery for punishment.[100] The occasional 'not subscriber' and the more general persistence of behaviour 'contrare to our sworne Covenant' should be viewed less as a reflection of failure on the part of minister and session to successfully enforce behavioural reforms and more as a product of an increasingly zealous religious leadership grappling with the realities of controlling the conduct of a sizeable burgh during a time of social and political upheaval.

The making of a covenanted community

The swearing of the National Covenant and the Solemn League and Covenant, against the backdrop of the beginnings of war, constituted a critical chapter in Ayr's, as well as all of Scotland's, history. But what exactly made the town a covenanted community? At one level, the question seems obvious: it was a community that had sworn the National Covenant in 1638. And yet, this definition does not actually tell us much about the meanings and effects of the covenants beyond a formalised and relatively superficial level, nor does it capture the ongoing experience of covenanting. The case of Ayr, particularly in the years surrounding the administration of the covenants, offers four additional defining factors that reveal how the covenanting project could and did shape local, communal identities across Scotland.

First, a covenanted community required clerical and lay leadership that were explicitly committed to upholding the dictates of the covenants. There were, of course, substantive and sometimes dramatic debates over precisely what those dictates were, especially by the late 1640s. But at the parish level, those debates generally mattered little in terms of the daily experience of covenanting, so long as local leaders maintained a relatively united front in matters of discipline and worship – this unity that would be dramatically tested in Ayr, but not until after the Restoration. Second, in a covenanted community, allegiance to the covenant(s) was necessary for communal inclusion for both locals and newcomers, though not everyone in Ayr swore the covenants willingly or immediately understood the seriousness of the oaths before them.[101] The communal necessity of swearing the covenants was also made apparent during the eighteen months that Ayr received dozens of refugees from Ireland, whose access to permanent residence as well as immediate relief was predicated upon a public swearing of the covenant and denouncing any counter-oaths. Third, a covenanted community was one in which godly conduct was implicitly and explicitly framed, usually from the top down, as both an individual and collective obligation of covenanting. In Ayr, as we have seen, this was done through policies issued from the pulpit, in which the minister articulated the behavioural expectations for his flock. The last criteria was perhaps the most important: a covenanted community was one in which a 'covenanting ethos' – the sense of obligation to the covenants and an interpretation of quotidian sins as breaches of the covenants – was internalised, tested, and ultimately shaped by the congregation. The crises of the coming decades would test this ethos, and the personal and corporate identities it engendered, in myriad ways.

Notes

1 On the process of reform in Scotland, see, for example, Margo Todd, *Culture of Protestantism in Early Modern Scotland* (New Haven: Yale University Press, 2002); Michael Graham, *The Uses of Reform: 'Godly Discipline' and Population Behavior in Scotland and Beyond, 1560–1610* (Leiden: Brill, 1996); John McCallum, *Reforming the Scottish Parish: The Reformation in Fife, 1560–1640* (Aldershot: Ashgate, 2010). For a local study of the Reformation in Ayrshire, see Margaret Sanderson, *Ayrshire and the Reformation: People and Change, 1490–1600* (East Linton: Tuckwell, 1997).

2 On this longer history of covenanting, see Jane Dawson, 'Covenanting in Sixteenth-Century Scotland', *Scottish Historical Review*, 99 (December 2020), 336–48.
3 Quote is from Mark A. Kishlansky, *A Monarchy Transformed: Britain, 1603–1714* (London: Penguin, 1997), p. 132.
4 Laura A.M. Stewart, *Urban Politics and the British Civil Wars* (Leiden: Brill, 2006), p. 229. The other burghs represented in these petitions were Cupar, Dumbarton, Irvine, Lanark, Stirling, and Culross.
5 Laura A.M. Stewart, 'Geddes, Jenny', in Elizabeth Ewan, Rose Pipes, Jane Rendall, and Sian Reynolds (eds), *The New Biographical Dictionary of Scottish Women*, 2nd edn (Edinburgh: Edinburgh University Press, 2018), p. 158. For a discussion of the involvement of women in the early covenanting movement, see Michelle D. Brock, ' "She-Zealots and Satanesses": Women, Patriarchy, and the Covenanting Movement', in Mairi Cowan, Janay Nugent, and Cathryn Spence (eds), *Gender and Identity in Scotland, 1200–1800: Power, Politics, and Faith* (Edinburgh: Edinburgh University Press, 2024).
6 For a useful overview of the vast scholarship and debates on the causes of conflict, see Tim Harris, 'Revisiting the Causes of the English Civil War', *Huntington Library Quarterly*, 78:4 (Winter 2015), 615–35.
7 Michael P. Winship's work is a very helpful starting point on Hutchinson and the conflicts in 1630s and 1640s New England. See Michael P. Winship, *The Times and Trials of Anne Hutchinson: Puritans Divided* (Lawrence: The University of Kansas, 2005) and *Making Heretics: Militant Protestantism and Free Grace in Massachusetts, 1636–1641* (Princeton: Princeton University Press, 2002).
8 On Scottish soldiers and the Thirty Years War, Steve Murdoch and Alexia Grosjean, *Alexander Leslie and the Scottish Generals of the Thirty Years' War, 1618–1648* (London: Routledge, 2014) and Steve Murdoch (ed.), *Scotland and the Thirty Years' War* (Leiden: Brill, 2001).
9 On covenanting as part of a longer process of Reformation, see Alasdair Raffe, 'Confessions, Covenants and Continuous Reformation in Early Modern Scotland', *Études Épistémè*, 32 (2017), n.p.
10 Laura A.M. Stewart, *Rethinking the Scottish Revolution: Covenanted Scotland, 1637–1651* (Oxford: Oxford University Press, 2016), chapter two.
11 Hew Scott (ed.), *Fasti Ecclesiae Scoticanae*, vol. III: Synod of Glasgow and Ayr, new edn (Edinburgh: Oliver and Boyd, 1920), p. 6.
12 William Brereton, *Travels in Holland, the United Provinces, England, Scotland, and Ireland, 1634–5* (London: Chetham Society, 1844), p. 121.
13 National Records of Scotland (hereafter NRS), Ayr kirk session minutes, CH2/751/2, fo. 254r.
14 On clerical ideals, see Michelle D. Brock, 'Exhortations and Expectations: Preaching about the Ideal Minister in Post-Reformation Scotland', in Chris R. Langley, Catherine E. McMillan, and Russell Newton (eds), *The Clergy in Early Modern Scotland* (Woodbridge: Boydell, 2021), pp. 15–31.

15 Robert Baillie, *The Letters and Journals of Robert Baillie*, 3 vols, ed. David Laing (Edinburgh: Bannatyne Club, 1841–2), *Letters*, i, 20–1.
16 Alexander Peterkin (ed.), *Records of the Kirk of Scotland Containing the Acts and Proceedings of the General Assemblies* (Edinburgh: Peter Brown, 1843), pp. 45, 164, and 181.
17 CH2/751/2, fo. 316r.
18 Transfers from one parish to another, usually at the behest of the regional presbytery, were common and expected parts of a clerical career, especially as demands and dynamics of the ministerial role could vary in different communities and change over time. For more on clerical journeys, see Brock and Langley, *Mapping the Scottish Reformation*, www.maps.mappingthescottishreformation.org (accessed 2 January 2024). Blair is described as 'being most unwilling to remove from Ayr, where the Lord had begun to bless his labours, and to go so far from his Christian friends and acquaintance'. William Row, *The Life of Mr Robert Blair*, ed. Thomas M'Crie (Edinburgh: Wodrow Society, 1848), p. 156.
19 CH2/751/2, fos. 319r, 320r, and 322r.
20 CH2/751/2, fo. 319r.
21 CH2/751/2, fo. 294v.
22 Baillie, *Letters*, i, p. 89.
23 Neil McIntyre and Jamie McDougall have also noted the ad hoc nature of the subscription to the National Covenant throughout Scotland and the ensuing ambiguities this created. See Neil McIntyre and Jamie McDougall, 'Reframing the Covenant: *A Solemn Acknowledgment* (1648) and the Resubscription of the Solemn League and Covenant', *Seventeenth Century*, 37:5 (2022), 733–56, at 736–7.
24 CH2/751/2, fo. 292r. A man of numerous talents, Smith is also listed as the town's musician.
25 CH2/751/2, fo. 292r.
26 CH2/751/2, fo. 292v.
27 CH2/751/2, fo. 293r. In February 1640, Smith was asked by the session, at the direction of the Ayr presbytery, to record in the session minutes both a copy of the National Covenant and an attendant declaration from the General Assembly in Glasgow declaring bishops and episcopacy to be unlawful. See CH2/751/2, fos. 325v–30v.
28 Robert Wodrow, *Collections Upon the Lives of the Reformers and Most Eminent Ministers of the Church of Scotland* (Glasgow: Maitland Club, 1845), pp. 37–8.
29 *New Statistical Account of Scotland* (Edinburgh: W. Blackwood and Sons, 1845), vol. 5, pp. 114–15.
30 Quoted in Laura A.M. Stewart, ' "Brothers in Truth": Propaganda, Public Opinion and the Perth Articles Debate in Scotland', in Ralph Houlbrooke (ed.), *James VI and I: Ideas, Authority, and Government* (Aldershot: Ashgate, 2006), pp. 151–68, at p. 151.
31 Andrew Agnew, *The Hereditary Sheriffs of Galloway* (Edinburgh, 1893), p. 450. There is some confusion, it should be noted, about Adair's parentage,

and he is sometimes erroneously listed as the son of Sir Robert Adair of Kinhilt. See, for example, Robert Wodrow, *Analecta; or, Materials for a History of Remarkable Providences* (Edinburgh: Maitland Club, 1842), vol. 3, p. 72. For a useful history of Robert Adair, see John R. Young, 'Scotland and Ulster Connections in the Seventeenth Century: Sir Robert Adair of Kinhilt and the Scottish Parliament under the Covenanters', *Journal of Scotch-Irish Studies*, 3 (2013), 16–76.

32 Robert Armstrong, Andrew R. Holmes, R. Scott Spurlock, and Patrick Walsh (eds), *Presbyterian History in Ireland: Two Seventeenth-Century Narratives* (Belfast: Ulster Historical Foundation, 2016).

33 Archibald Mackenzie, 'Church from the Reformation till the End of the Eighteenth Century', in A.I. Dunlop (ed.), *The Royal Burgh of Ayr: Seven Hundred Fifty Years of History* (Edinburgh: Oliver and Boyd, 1953), pp. 104–21, at p. 110.

34 Ayrshire Archives, Acc 483, 'Papers of William Adair' (c. 1633–1656), vols I and II. Many thanks to David McOmish for his guidance in piecing together Adair's educational background. See also David McOmish, 'A Different View of Innovation and International Knowledge Exchange from Classroom Notes: The University of Edinburgh, 1604–1650', in Danilo Facca and Farkas Gabor Kiss (eds), *Practices of Teaching and Studying in Renaissance Europe* (Berlin: De Gruyter, forthcoming).

35 Jack C. Whycock, 'Ministerial Education in the Scottish Reformation', in Ian P. Hazlett (ed.), *A Companion to the Scottish Reformation* (Leiden: Brill, 2021), pp. 367–94.

36 Wodrow, *Analecta*, vol. 3, pp. 72–3.

37 CH2/751/3/1, fos. 171r and 335r; Ayrshire Archives, ATO/42/1/34, 'Contract of Marriage Adair and Kennedy'.

38 Wodrow, *Analecta*, vol. 3, p. 73.

39 Ayrshire Archives, Acc 483, Papers of William Adair (c. 1633–1656), vols I and II.

40 CH2/751/2, fo. 354r.

41 CH2/751/2, fo. 344v.

42 CH2/751/2, fo. 321r.

43 Chris Langley, 'Sheltering under the Covenant: The National Covenant, Orthodoxy and the Irish Rebellion, 1638–1644', *The Scottish Historical Review*, 96:2 (October 2017), 137–60, at 138.

44 CH2/751/2, fo. 321r.; Langley, 'Sheltering under the Covenant'.

45 Samual R. Gardiner (ed.), *The Constitutional Documents of the Puritan Revolution, 1625–1660*, 2nd edn (Oxford, 1899), p. 132.

46 Louise Yeoman, 'Heart-Work: Emotion, Empowerment and Authority in covenanting Times' (PhD thesis, University of St Andrews, 1991); Nathan Hood, 'Corporate Conversion Ceremonies: The Presentation and Reception of the National Covenant', in Chris R. Langley (ed.), *The National Covenant in Scotland, 1638–1689* (Woodbridge: Boydell, 2020), pp. 21–38.

47 CH2/751/2, fo. 360r.

48 CH2/751/2, fo. 360r.
49 On the role of Ayrshire during this period, see Sharon Adams, 'The Making of the Radical South-West: Charles I and his Scottish Kingdom, 1625–1649', in John R. Young (ed.), *Celtic Dimensions of the British Civil Wars* (Edinburgh: John Donald Publishers, 1997), pp. 53–74; William Makey, *The Church of the Covenant, 1637–1651: Revolution and Social Change in Scotland* (Edinburgh: John Donald Publishers, 1979), esp. pp. 165–78.
50 For an overview of the establishment and dominance of the covenanting regime, see, for example, David Stevenson, *The Scottish Revolution, 1637–44: The Triumph of the Covenanters* (Newton Abbot: David and Charles, 1973); Laura Stewart, 'Fiscal Revolution and State Formation in Mid Seventeenth-Century Scotland', *Historical Research*, 84 (2011), 443–69; Stewart, *Rethinking the Scottish Revolution*, esp. chapters 4 and 5; John R. Young, 'The Scottish Parliament and the Covenanting Revolution: The Emergence of a Scottish Commons', in Young, *Celtic Dimensions of the British Civil Wars*, pp. 164–84.
51 On the Irish Rebellion and its impact on the British Isles, see K.J. Lindley, 'The Impact of the 1641 Irish Rebellion upon England and Wales, 1641–5', *Irish Historical Studies*, 18 (1972), 143–76; and Eamon Darcy, *The Irish Rebellion of 1641 and the Wars of the Three Kingdoms* (Woodbridge: Boydell, 2013).
52 For an introduction of the road to and course of British civil wars from a three kingdom's approach, see, for example, Mark Fissel, *The Bishops' Wars: Charles I's Campaigns against Scotland, 1638–1640* (Cambridge: Cambridge University Press, 1994); Jane Ohlemeyer (ed.), *The Civil Wars: A Military History of England, Scotland and Ireland, 1638–1660* (Oxford: Oxford University Press, 1998).
53 CH2/751/2, fo. 314r
54 See, for example, in 1641, CH2/751/2, fos. 340r, 349r, 357r.
55 CH2/751/2, fo. 337v.
56 CH2/751/2, fo. 422r.
57 NRS, Ayr presbytery minutes, CH2/532/1, p. 176.
58 On the challenges and expenses of war within the burghs, see Laura A.M. Stewart, 'Military Power and the Scottish Burghs, 1625–1651', *Journal of Early Modern History*, 15 (2011), 59–82.
59 On religious refugees from Ireland to Scotland, see John R. Young, 'Escaping Massacre: Refugees in Scotland in the Aftermath of the 1641 Ulster Rebellion', in David Edwards, Pádraig Lenihan, and Clodagh Tait (eds), *Age of Atrocity: Violence and Political Conflict in Early Modern Ireland* (Dublin: Four Courts Press, 2007), pp. 219–41; and Langley, 'Sheltering under the Covenant'.
60 See John R. Young, 'Scotland and Ulster in the Seventeenth Century: The Movement of Peoples over the North Channel', in John R. Young and William Kelly (eds), *Ulster and Scotland, 1600–2000: History, Language and Identity* (Dublin: Four Courts Press, 2004), pp. 11–32.
61 CH2/751/2, fo. 366r.
62 Langley, 'Sheltering under the Covenant', esp. 140–1.
63 CH2/751/2, fo. 366r.

64 CH2/751/2, fo. 403r.
65 CH2/751/2, fo. 372r.
66 CH2/751/2, fo. 366v.
67 Gardiner, *The Constitutional Documents of the Puritan Revolution*, p. 134.
68 CH2/751/2, fo. 371v.
69 CH2/751/2, fo. 397v.
70 CH2/751/2, fo. 400v.
71 Dawson, 'Covenanting in Sixteenth-Century Scotland'.
72 For intimations on poor relief in Ayr see, for example, CH2/751/2, fos. 383v and 386r.
73 See CH2/751/2, fos. 323r, 335r, 340r, 343r, 349r, 354v, and 357r. See also Chapter 3, this volume.
74 CH2/751/2, fo. 355r.
75 CH2/751/2, fo. 334v.
76 CH2/751/2, fo. 337r–v.
77 CH2/751/2, fo. 344v.
78 CH2/751/2, fo. 399v–400r.
79 CH2/751/2, fo. 374v.
80 CH2/751/2, fos. 333r, 344v. This intimation also had precedents issued from the pulpit in October 1638 and April 1639, and was reissued in 1644 (fo. 428r).
81 CH2/751/2, fos. 402r-v.
82 CH2/751/2, fos 404v–405r.
83 This phrase is Laura A.M. Stewart's, 'Authority, Agency and the Reception of the Scottish National Covenant', in Robert Armstrong and Tadhg O' hAnnrachain (eds), *Insular Christianity: Alternative Models of the Church in Britain and Ireland, c. 1570–1700* (Manchester: Manchester University Press, 2013), pp. 89–107, at p. 91.
84 For a three kingdom's approach to administration and impact of the Solemn League and Covenant, see Kirsteen M. MacKenzie's *The Solemn League and Covenant of the Three Kingdoms and the Cromwellian Union, 1643–1663* (London: Routledge, 2017).
85 CH2/751/2, fo. 408r.
86 CH2/751/2, fo. 408r.
87 Gardiner, *The Constitutional Documents of the Puritan Revolution*, pp. 268–9.
88 On the administration of the Solemn League and Covenant in Ireland by Adair and others, see R. Scott Spurlock, 'The Solemn League and Covenant and the Making of a People in Ulster', *Scottish Historical Review*, 99 (2020), 368–91.
89 CH2/532/1, p. 159; CH2/751/3/1, fo. 420r.
90 CH2/751/2, fo. 423r.
91 Tom Barclay and Eric J. Graham, *The Early Transatlantic Trade of Ayr, 1640–1730* (Ayr: The Ayrshire Archaeological and Natural History Society, 2005), p. 13.
92 Ayr was not alone in this communal self-fashioning during the turmoil of the early 1640s. Laura Stewart has discussed how 'in the first flush of zeal for the new Covenant, with preparations for war going ahead on both sides, Edinburgh

was self-consciously styling itself as the new Jerusalem'. See Stewart, *Urban Politics*, pp. 81–2.
93 CH2/751/2, fos. 457v, 428r.
94 CH2/751/2, fo. 410v.
95 On the dissemination and reception of the Directory in Scottish parishes, see Jamie Murdoch McDougall, 'Covenants and Covenanters in Scotland, 1638–1679' (PhD thesis, University of Glasgow, 2017), esp. pp. 71–8. McDougall suggests, and I agree, that there 'was a widespread understanding, at least amongst the clergy, that observing the forms of worship advocated in the *Directory* was a covenanting obligation' (p. 77).
96 CH2/532/1, p. 194.
97 CH2/532/1, pp. 236–7 and 246.
98 CH2/532/1, p. 246.
99 CH2/751/2, fo. 459r.
100 CH2/751/2, fo. 459r.
101 As the records demonstrate, as late as November of 1645 the session was still trying to chase down those who 'had not subscrybit the Covenants' and intimating from the pulpit that the 'not subscrybers' should appear before the session with haste. See CH2/751/2, fo. 448r.

2

Plague

In late September 1647, the local clerk in Ayr opened the town council minutes with an ominous inscription: 'The fear of the Lord is the beginning of wisdom: he that wanteth let him seek of God.'[1] Drawn from Proverbs, his words captured both the alarm and the aspirations of that fateful autumn. The month prior, after ravaging much of western Scotland, the plague had travelled south and arrived in Ayr with impeccably bad timing. The burgh was, as we have seen, in the midst of navigating the increasingly complicated waters of a multi-faceted civil war. Minister Adair was already overstretched, having served as sole pastor of the large congregation since the death of John Fergushill three years prior. As the pestilence's first causalities were reported, he became increasingly convinced that God was justly punishing his flock with diverse 'signs of his anger' for their moral laxity and backsliding.[2] Acutely aware of the plague's potential for devastation, Adair decided that to avoid further wrath, the townsfolk must repent accordingly – not through the usual means of fasting, humiliation, and prayer, but with a week-long mass confession involving dramatic meetings, sermons, and thanksgivings.[3] This remarkable series of events, recorded in meticulous detail in the kirk session book, illustrates an exceptional protestant response to one of early modernity's most unexceptional crises.

The peril of plague was omnipresent in pre-modern towns, and especially in those like Ayr that stood on the sea. In these coastal communities, every ship, sailor, and stranger could be a potential carrier, though God's permissive will was believed to be the primary vector of disease. Critically, seventeenth-century men and women not only understood much about this challenge but also anticipated it. Thanks to both word of mouth and the printing press, they knew when the shadow of pestilence drew near after sweeping through regions in their own countries and beyond. In London, for example, city officials had been printing and distributing bills of mortality since 1603.[4] While the public flow of information by print came more slowly to Scotland, news of plague found other channels in the kirk, in collective memory, and on the street.[5] By the 1640s Scots would have certainly heard stories about the devastation wrought by previous bouts of disease and adjusted their expectations and responses accordingly. Familiarity may have bred contempt, but it did not diminish dread, for the coming of plague was yoked in early modern minds to other manifestations of providential wrath. 'Fear of the Lord', as the inscription in the town council minutes read, was thus not simply an understandable reaction but a recommended recourse for communities navigating their way through such disasters.

This was not the first time that Ayr had faced plague, nor was it the worst they had seen of the scourge. More than forty years prior, in the summer of 1606, the disease came and raged for six months, killing upwards of 2,000 people according to some accounts.[6] While this number is quite unlikely – the burgh's population was then probably no more than 3,000 – the outbreak had caused great suffering and loss of life.[7] At the time, John Welsh, son-in-law of John Knox and a towering figure of the early seventeenth-century kirk, was minister. As he put it in a pre-fast prayer, the Lord had been 'pleased to visit this sinfull town with the seikness of the pest justlie deserved for the sinns thereof'.[8] Fear of catching the plague was so great that during the height of its wrath, the session did not meet at all, only to be reconvened 'after the Lord's rod was removit' later in the year.[9] According to the Lord Chancellor of Scotland, John Campbell, rather than live under the threat of the disease, 'the most of the peple fled, and the townes almost left desolate'.[10]

Now, it seemed, the scourge had returned. The 1647 outbreak that struck Ayr was part of a larger period of plague that devastated many regions of Scotland between 1644 and 1649, leaving social upheaval, economic disruption, and severe depopulation in its wake.[11] In Edinburgh, for example, the disease arrived in 1644, carried by soldiers who had been stationed in plague-ridden Newcastle.[12] Ayr also had its first brush with this particular phase of the disease in late 1644, and the records of the kirk session note that in January of the following year, a fast was held for the 'removal of the plague'.[13] The town was then, as it would be in 1647, luckier than much of the country in the 1640s, where perhaps as much as one-fifth of the urban population perished in less than half a decade.[14]

Amid this loss of life, the Scottish people continued a long tradition of attributing the plague to the will of an omnipotent God. The most common responses involved a combination of collaborative civic and spiritual measures: town councils enforced enclosures and quarantines, while ministers and kirk sessions oversaw the administration of godly discipline, communal fasts, and prayers.[15] Local leaders broadly understood that natural causes were at play, but they also believed that behind them was the divine hand directing the targets, duration, and severity of the disease.[16] Plague was first and foremost a punishment that demanded repentance, the rituals of which reiterated both human depravity and ultimate reliance on God. As such, Adair's conclusion in 1647 that the pestilence had been invited by human sinfulness and that the townsfolk should atone accordingly is entirely unsurprising; indeed, medieval Europeans had long made public repentance as a means to alleviate or prevent disease.[17] What is surprising, though, is how he turned his vision of godly confession into practical plan involving, to varying degrees, the whole congregation of Ayr. This remarkable response to the plague reveals both the religious expectations of the community and the extent to which allegiance to covenants could prove a powerful social adhesive and mandate for action in the face of existential threats. It also reveals how confessional specificities – in our case, a covenanting, Reformed ethos – might direct responses to early modern evidence of divine wrath.

Pestilence and penitence

The first signs of trouble appeared in late summer. The town council noted that the 'infection of gods visiting hand by the plague of pestilence' had appeared at the house of a local timberman, who caught it from a visitor to Ayr, spread it to those he interacted with, and died shortly thereafter.[18] As was the usual protocol, the town was placed under a general quarantine, and throughout the autumn, all inhabitants were asked to stay indoors and visitors to keep out. Exceptions were made, as we might expect, for churchgoing on the sabbath, as well as essential work and errands. Some of these measures might strike us as familiar, as in the case of William Dyett, a local blacksmith who was permitted by the council to work his croft alongside his son so long as they kept to themselves and stayed always 'betwixt the hous and the smiddie' in an example of early modern social distancing.[19] Others appear stranger but nonetheless explicable, such as an October act that prohibited the pastoring of various livestock of Ayr on the hills on the outskirts of town for fear that their movement 'may prove for spreading of the infection'. The act noted that any cattle, sheep, or other beasts found in grazing there would be seized and 'brought in for the common use', slaughtered, and 'givin to the hospital' for feeding the poor and infirm.[20]

In accordance with these preventative measures, the kirk session did not meet between 30 August and mid-September.[21] When the minister and elders reconvened on Monday, 13 September, they noted that the divine hand lay 'sore and heavy upon this town and congregation' and contextualised the present outbreak as one among a number of 'diverse rods of [God's] wrath' that had been brought down on the community in the previous months.[22] Among the recent challenges were the inability to recruit an assistant minister, the loss of ships and goods at sea, the capture of three Ayrshire children by pirates, and 'the slaughter of two companies of their young men in the bloodie wars'.[23] It would be misleading to caricature the mid-seventeenth century as a time of unceasing chaos and threat, but the 1640s were especially turbulent, not only in Scotland but throughout the early modern world. The British civil wars raged on, albeit intermittently, enveloping all parts of the island as well as Ireland in a complex and, at times, violent conflict that disrupted social and religious life.[24] European and Atlantic waters became increasingly dangerous as the Barbary corsairs – referred to as 'Turks' – regularly captured Scottish ships and sailors for ransom, leading kirk sessions across the country to, on various occasions, raise money for the deliverance of Ayr seamen.[25] Throughout, Adair's duties left him overworked and overburdened, as repeated attempts in the years after John Fergushill's death to bring an assistant minister to the parish proved futile.

The 'grievous plague of pestilence' was, therefore, only the latest and most frightening portent, a 'terrible messenger of the Lords wrath breaking in' that could not be ignored.[26] Given the gravity of the situation, on the previous day's sabbath Adair had outlined a drastic course of action, one which drew on older rituals of repentance but reframed them according to the needs and priorities of a covenanted community. As with most things in Reformed congregations, events began with a sermon. Adair's text that September morning was Zechariah chapter 12, verse 12, which began, 'And the land shall mourn, every family apart'.[27] Part of a larger prophecy on the destruction and eventual rebuilding of Jerusalem, this passage emphasised the necessity of repentance that was at once corporate and individual, communally expressed but singularly felt. Using this verse as a godly guide to alleviating the suffering caused by the sinfulness of the town, the minster and members of the session – fourteen elders and fourteen deacons – made themselves examples by confessing their 'transgressions and sinfull shortcomings' before the congregation following the sermon.[28] In their words, 'they thought it expedient to goe before the people over whome the Lord had given them charge, and to be exemplarie in repentance as they have been exemplary in their sinnes'.[29]

As it turned out, their sins were many. The session confessed to a laundry list of transgressions, including general 'carnalitie, laziness and unfaithfulness', insufficient care for 'the godly poor', 'little hungering and thirsting for the salvation of the souls of the people, but being rather snares unto them' and not upholding the 'covenant of union made up betwixt those united nations for union and Reformation of Religion', referring to the Solemn League and Covenant of 1643.[30] These errors they admitted and lamented as a group, but the minutes note that each member of the session also made individual confession, with 'some bringing forth histories of their by past lyfe'.[31] Alas, such histories were not recorded, an omission that suggests the prioritisation of the communal over the individual, at least for the prying eyes of posterity. Still, this was evidently a powerful moment and likely a rare one, as the spiritual leaders of Ayr got down in the confessional dirt by recounting the manifold sins of their past and present. This proved an essential act of not only encouragement for the rest of the congregation to follow suit, but permission to do so; if the minister and elders willingly articulated their sins in public, without (or perhaps despite) fear of communal reproach, so too could everyone else.

After closing their confessions with collective prayer, the session recommended with 'much earnestness and care' that the town council and all the various crafts and societies of the town meet with the minister over the course of the next few days to contemplate their sins and to follow the session's example of public, communal repentance. Each group was to share their confession with the entire congregation and record the proceedings 'in their own books and in the sessione book' in hopes that future townsfolk might find direction in 'turning from [God's] fierce wrath when it is kindled against them'.[32] This sense of legacy looms large over the whole affair, as the confessions were explicitly intended not only to alleviate suffering in the present, but to provide guidance for subsequent generations of equally fallen inhabitants. In this way, they served a similar purpose to the covenants – at once statements of religious fidelity and prescriptions for future behaviour.

The sermon by Adair and the ensuing confession by the town's leading lights proved a powerful incentive to action, as the next day the town council followed their lead. The council's confession echoed much of the session's, which is unsurprising given significant overlap in personnel between the two groups.[33] They lamented their general failure in governing, as they put it, 'this poore Towne', and went on to 'beseech God of his infinite favour in the midst of wrath to remember mercie'.[34] The following day, Wednesday, 15 September, eight groups – hammermen (metal workers), coopers (barrel-makers), squaremen (masons), weavers, glovers, cordinars (shoemakers), wakers (fullers of wool), and tailors – met collectively in the kirk. From the pulpit, Adair explained to them 'how God had begune to streik them by Land with the plague of pestilence as weil as he had stricken the sailors and merchants by sea'.[35] He exhorted them to follow the good example of the session and council by making, in company of their fellow craftsmen, genuine confession over the coming days. Godliness, Adair insisted, was the most crucial profession of all, and his audience should set about 'the great craft and trade of unfained faith and repentance' straight away.[36] The audience then broke into individual groups, most meeting in the kirk itself, the cordinars and wakers in the kirk deik (a ditch just south of the kirkyard), the weavers in the hills near the kirk, and the glovers in the house of their guild deacon.[37] Guided by 'the desire of their pastor' and the aid of members of the session, they made and, at the hand of the session clerk, recorded their confessions.[38]

The statements made by the professions are quite varied in terms of content and language. The squaremen began by citing their 'covetousness in their calling and unfaithfulness, Swearing, Blaspheming the holie name of god'.[39] The glovers recognised their 'fleing back from God in the houre of temptations' as a cause of the present crisis.[40] The wakers noted their 'tipling and drinking to our hurt and hinderance in Gods service' (drunkenness was, apparently, a widespread problem).[41] The hammermen spoke of failures of individual responsibility in their meeting, during which 'everie man for himself in particular did vow and promise to lead ane more circumspect lyfe in holiness and sobrietie in all tyme coming'.[42] Some groups made direct appeals for divine relief, such as the weavers, who beseeched 'the great god for his dear sone, Jesus Christ his sake to tak away and remove our sinnes and this heavie visitation of pestilence which is presentlie amongst us in this burgh'.[43] This first wave of confessions thus ranged in content from quotidian breeches of godly conduct such as drinking and neglecting family worship to more internal moral failings such as doubt or general unfaithfulness.

Later that afternoon, Adair met with the merchants and sailors together, telling them that seafaring men faced unique 'hazards and dangers' and thus relied even more heavily on the mercy and providence of God. He admonished their spiritual carelessness and told them they must learn to better resist 'all winds of temptations and tyde of sinne and corruption' so that they may 'show themselves profitable members in the commonwalth of Israel', framing Scotland generally, and Ayr specifically, as a place of God's chosen people.[44] The use of 'winds', 'tydes', and 'profit' in addressing a mariner audience was, of course, purposeful; theology could be complex and cumbersome, and by drawing upon the language of their economic lives, Adair imbued his words with greater meaning and relatability. This spiritual admonition had a civic imperative, too: they were, as Adair put it, the 'chiefe part of the towns flourishing'.[45] A populous burgh as well as an important port, Ayr relied on commercial activities via the sea that would have been seriously impaired by the plague. Indeed, in the community's attempts at quarantine, travel to and from Ireland, England, Europe, and the West Indies to trade in goods ranging from salmon to wine would have ground to a halt.[46] When the actions of the sailors and merchants invited the wrath of God, the entire town suffered.

The ensuing confession of the merchants revolved around taking advantage of the opportunities of their chosen careers, valuing wealth over godliness, along with 'lieing, Swearing, drukennes in bargans making for the love of the gaine of this present evill worlde, forgetting that their calling wes to serve god and the commonwealth'.[47] Most surprisingly, their recorded confession notes that some of the merchants 'acknowledged their atheism', specifying 'that for a long time they lived and knew not whither their was ane god or no, estiming two pennies of gaine more than the siking of god his word'.[48] Explicit expressions of genuine doubt about the existence of God were very rare in the seventeenth century, and this was almost certainly a statement of behaving as if there might be no God, rather than a statement of true agnosticism.[49] Regardless, its inclusion in the confession illustrates a context in which doubt could be acceptably articulated – even if that articulation was directly prompted by the minister, as may have been the case.

Of all the confessional statements, that of the sailors is the longest, listing over fifteen distinct and sometimes salacious sins. After prayer by the minister, the sailors had huddled together as a group in the choir of the kirk, where each of them 'stood up upon his feet and one after another made particulare confession of his sinnes and wickedness befor the majestie of the great God and in presence of the people their assembled'.[50] More than any other group, the confession of the sailors revolved around the particular necessities and temptations of their profession – one that, even now, connotes a life of adventure, danger, and occasional debauchery. Many revealed that while abroad, they had fallen into 'much drunkenness and whoredom' with 'some both maried and unmaried persons'.[51] Some of them admitted that in their travels they did 'verie much incline to that idolatrous workshop of the masse', meaning their participation in popish rituals while in Catholic regions abroad.[52]

Perhaps most sensationally, the sailors confessed to 'their ungodlie and unlawfull gaine by alluring and carying of children to the West Indies', a reference to the captivity and selling of destitute children into indentured servitude in the American colonies, a short-lived but shameful practice in some coastal Scottish communities during the turmoil of the mid-century wars.[53] Like the merchants, they also cited their 'aitheisme unbeliefe and that plague of the hardness of the heart among all of them to abound'.[54] While most groups lamented general deficiencies of faith, only the merchants and the sailors confessed to more specific failings of belief. This may have been a product of these men having encountered belief systems other than their own during their travels, or the transgressions that occurred unabated during their prolonged absence from the kirk while abroad. Indeed, the sailors explicitly recognised the spiritual danger in missing regular religious service and drew up an agreement at the end of their confession stating that even if they were at sea, they would meet at least once a month for 'mutual edification and earnest prayer to God in their calamities'.[55] If any sailor missed such a meeting for reasons other than urgent business, he should be 'readie to give the true reasons of his absence at the next meiting'.[56] The sailors' confession, then, like many others, was not simply a recounting of previous transgression, but a plan of accountability for spiritual growth and godliness.

On Thursday, 16 September, the minutes report that 'the whole people of the town this day conveined in the kirk (god in his mercie so permitting) being in great heaviness and fear' to hear the minister give a lecture on chapters nine and ten of the book of Ezra.[57] The lengthy oration revolved around the Israelites' restoration of the temple and their quest for spiritual absolution and reformation through confession of previous trespasses. Essentially, this was a scriptural affirmation of the course the town had taken in the preceding days and a blueprint for any confessions yet to be made. After his lecture, Adair read the confessions of the abovementioned crafts, noting the 'parallel betwixt the scriptures and their practise' and 'opening up how such sins did deserve such judgements' as the plague had wrought.[58] And yet, he felt that the town had still failed to grapple with the full extent of their failings, because, as he put it, 'manie were in such transgressions as had deserved the present wrath inflicted and it could not be the work of one day'.[59] Hearing this, the people 'readily obeyed the minister' by further dividing themselves into groups, based again on profession, to make communal confessions over the next few days. The minutes note that Thursday's religious exercises went on from 'morning to 5 at night'.[60] One can only imagine how all-consuming – not to mention exhausting – this must have been for a town increasingly isolated in response to the plague, even for the women and children not named as present in making the actual confessions.[61]

The next day, still more groups, including the land labourers, baxters (bakers), gardeners, candlemakers, and notaries, officers and messengers of the town, gathered together in the kirk on a day of 'very tempestuous weather'. From the pulpit, Adair spoke about the tangible, earthly consequences of their sinful ways. Preaching on Ecclesiastes chapter five, he explained how

> for the wickednes of a people a fruitfull land is turned into barrennes, the heavens gloomes and utters by storms displeasure, the face of the mother earth looked barren wrinkled and old and when God refuses to hear the heavens, the heavens refuse to hear the earth and the mother earth lyk a grieved and perplexed woman losses the milk of corne wine and oyle and refuses to draw out her breast being dry unto such sinfull children as hath abused the comforts thereof.[62]

This was not a formal sermon delivered to the whole congregation, but rather a specific message tailored especially to those who worked the land and whose livelihoods depended on its harvests. For the hearers, Adair's words not only emphasised the potential severity of the plague, but also the culpability of the townspeople in inviting the current crisis. Through the covenants, they had made a promise to God, but their iniquities had broken that promise, and they were left desolate and vulnerable.

Over the coming days, the remaining groups met individually and recorded their own confessions. Their words echo much of what had been said by the others, which they had heard the previous day: the 'labourers and travellers and communitie of the towne' – a group that would have likely included some of the less privileged members of Ayr, such as servants and the poor – admitted their 'drunkenness and idle living and companieing one with another which causeth vanitie and prophanitie to abound in all sorts'.[63] The baxters confessed that when 'we should have made use of the preaching we went to drink ... and had no more care of that we heard nor if it had not been preached at all'.[64] The officers of the town were especially detailed in lamenting their past drunkenness, recalling how they been 'oft and diverse tymes overtaken' with drink, which, as they put it, 'is a doore to all other ... such as filthines of the flesh swearing lieing blasphemie tuzlying and swaggering sudden and fearfull imprecations and passions'.[65] They expressed collective hope that they would soon 'becometh true penitent sinners' and promised to 'turne not with the dog to the vomite nor with the sow to the pudle againe', a colourful reference to 2 Peter 2:22.[66]

By the next sabbath day, 19 September, the men of Ayr had been engaging in public confessions for the previous six days. At least eighteen different groups, some along with their servants, had made public statements of repentance, which were again 'red and reported' before the congregation.[67] The minutes note with approval that the collective actions of the town resembled the creation story, 'for at the beginning theirof their wes great confusione throw the darknes of trouble and fear ... then God said let there be light'.[68] As the days progressed, greater righteousness and mercy had begun to appear 'both among the people in their exercises and also in the work of gods providence in his ordering of the affliction'.[69] The town had, therefore, followed not only the course prophesied in Zechariah 12:12, but also mirrored the striving and enlightenment in the book of Genesis. Genuine as the sentiments of the confessions may have been, they had also been scripted, both by the minister and by scripture itself.

News of what had transpired in Ayr travelled quickly through the channels of church governance in the region. On 22 September, the brethren of the regional presbytery, which at the time oversaw twenty-five parishes, promised to ask their congregations to donate spare foodstuffs and goods to Ayr and to 'remember the said towne in their prayers'.[70] On 5 October, elder Hew McKail relayed 'the whole proceeding' to the Synod of Glasgow and Ayr – the highest presbyterian body in the southwest. He reported back to the session that 'the whole assemblie declared themselves to be much satisfied and refreshed with the course that wes taken', and that the synod had appointed other ministers in the region to pray 'both in privat and public' for the continued deliverance of Ayr.[71] The synod also exhorted the people of Ayr, who had 'begune well', to 'continue laboring to grew more and more spirituall and sincere in all such godlie exercises'.[72] The response to the plague would not, they hoped, be a flash in the pan, but rather an impetus for further reform.

The communal confession concluded, Adair spent the remainder of the fall and winter mostly absent from Ayr due to his active involvement in the Scottish kirk's brewing ecclesiastical controversies. It was not until he returned the following spring that a formal thanksgiving was held in honour of the deliverance from the plague, which had continued to concern the town through December 1647. In the end, mercifully, fewer than forty people had died. From the pulpit on 3 April 1648, Adair listed eight reasons for which the community ought to not only offer thanks but continue their 'search for further light and reasons of the lords praise'. Perhaps most important, the plague, through its encouragement of the town's collective displays of repentance and revival, had acted as 'phisick to work upon consciences and to bring out by confessiounes and prayer manie fostered corruptiounes and the plague of the heart'.[73] Moreover, God was to be thanked for allowing the whole process to occur by providing 'constant protectione securitie and libertie to meit in his house', despite the ever-present threat of contagion.[74] Adair noted that 'the number removed by the Judgement was so few while the danger of the infectioune was as great ... as when the same plague of pestilence did sweep away two thousand souls and above out of this towne', a reference to the devastating plague of 1606.[75]

While the numerous preventative measures enacted by the town council, such as restricting movement of people and livestock, surely played a large role in mitigating the disease, Adair attributed this collective deliverance to their work of confession and repentance.[76] He reminded the congregation that of all those who 'associated themselves to the blissed work of solemne humiliatione confessions prayer and purpose of reformatioune, not one was removed or takin away by that Judgement', save one of them who, he hastened to add, 'it is much doubted whither he dyed of that disease or not'.[77] The mercy showed by God had both social and economic manifestations: 'he opened our doors, removed our feares, filled our streits, removed our desolationes, restored our traffick by sea, our treads, markets and comerce by land, turned our mourning into dancing' – the last bit being a direct quote from Psalms rather than any tacit approval of dancing on the part of the minister.[78] Borrowing from Isaiah 61:3, he told his audience that, thanks to their collective actions and divine pity, the Lord 'hath given unto us beautie for ashes'. In short, the efficacy of the course taken by the people of Ayr – and indeed, by the minister and the session – was beyond doubt. True repentance had borne all manner of fruit.

Interpreting the records

What had happened during this fateful week in Ayr was, in many ways, singular. The people of the town came together over the course of seven days in a rare and remarkable display of public repentance that was meticulously recorded for future generations. It was, at its core, the performance of a religious identity that had been carefully fashioned over the previous decade by Ayr's spiritual and civil leaders, as well as an expression of how much the broader community had embraced and contributed to this identity. But, like all historical events recorded with an eye to the future, little in this response to the plague is self-evident or can be taken at face value.

To understand what took place in Ayr and why it matters, we must begin with several interpretative issues. First, this whole episode was, from start to finish, run by men organised according to male professions, raising the question of the participation and influence of the congregation as a whole. Women and children only explicitly appeared in the confessions when members of a craft cited lack of attention to family worship or some sort of sexual impropriety. Of course, one cannot know what took place privately in the homes of the tradesmen; indeed, women of all social stations likely engaged in personal introspection or even their own private confessions. But what is clear is that the public response to the plague was a mostly masculine performance from start to finish.

This is particularly striking given that, as we have seen, the women of the town were explicitly noted as having sworn, though not necessarily signed, the National Covenant of 1638.[79] The reason for the absence seems not to have been that women were seen as somehow less responsible for the onset of the plague, but rather because the organising principle of the mass confession was economic, revolving around a sphere of life in which women were less formally engaged. An additional factor may be that the town – or at least, the town's leadership – was preoccupied with the failure of men to lead their wives, children, and servants in proper family worship, something mentioned in all but three of the eighteen confessional statements. In a fundamentally patriarchal society, correction of spiritual error and laxity, as well as economic woes, must begin with the male heads of households.[80]

The content of the confessions also raises the critical question of the extent to which we can read the statements of the various societies as genuinely felt expressions of repentance rather than products of communal pressure or the persistent prodding of Ayr's influential minister. Despite the uniqueness of many of the confessions, the consistency with which certain reported sins appear suggests that Adair had fed the craftsmen some specific language, either indirectly through his own preaching or more directly in meetings with them. Most groups, for example, confessed to general spiritual laxity such as 'their wandering of mynd' during sermons, neglect of family worship, excessive drunkenness, and acting 'evill example one to another' – all moral failings that had long been concerns of the Scottish kirk and were certainly familiar to the townspeople of Ayr.[81] And certain sins, such as vanity, 'atheism and unbelief of hart', and carnality, were reoccurring themes in Adair's sermons; clearly, some parroting of his language took place in these confessions.[82]

Beyond citation of specific failings, most of the groups lamented their sinfulness in terms that reflected the teachings of Reformed protestantism. Some echoed common sermonic refrains about innate human depravity, such as the coopers, who confessed 'the seeds of all the sins, for which God at any tyme hes plagued or condemned his creations, to be in us'.[83] Along similar lines, the squaremen acknowledged that 'their hearts were given to all licentiousness, for which sinnes sake they profess themselves most worthie of everlasting torments'.[84] While these may have been genuine statements of apprehension and expectation, regular admonitions from the pulpit about their 'naturall hearts' and 'corrupt nature' doubtlessly influenced the content and composition of the confessions.[85] Of course, that Adair and the session elders were deeply concerned with the sins named by many of the societies in response to the plague does not preclude the truth or sincerity of such sentiments. Indeed, it seems that the consistency in some of the confessional language points to the extent to which covenanting zeal had been absorbed and even shaped by the laity. If they could not meet the rigorous standards set by Reformed discipline, they certainly knew what these standards were, why they mattered, and what would befall their community if they failed to, as Adair put it, 'believe als weill as to obay the morall law'.[86]

Local history is especially key to understanding the swiftness with which the town responded to Adair's admonitions and provides clues to the sincerity of the words of repentance spoken before God and congregation. When pestilence came again to Ayr in 1647, the terror of 1606 clearly loomed large in the town's collective memory. Moreover, the plague had been ravaging Scotland since 1644, and reports of the devastation it wrought would have informed the rapid and fearful reaction to the reappearance of the disease in Ayr for the first time in four decades.[87] In this context, there seems little reason to doubt the sincerity of the townsfolk's confessions in the face of an existential threat. At the very least, the swift and collective action of the congregation suggests confidence in the potential efficacy of the course set out by Adair. In simplest terms, the people of Ayr followed the directives of their minister because they believed doing so could save lives.

Moreover, in their response the townspeople drew upon the history of sacramental festivals of fasting, communion, and conversion that had developed in the southwestern part of Scotland in the decades prior to 1647. During the 1620s in particular, ministers in the southwest began to hold large, revivalist festivals revolving around the Lord's Supper. The communion festivals served, in Leigh Eric Schmidt's words, to 'enhance the popular pull of Presbyterianism, its Word, and its sacraments' in a region already acknowledged as an incubator of religious fervour.[88] While the mass confession at Ayr seems to have been an atypical, if not singular, response to a crisis, many of its features – duration, level of community engagement, role of sermons, and involvement of the minister – were shared by these sacramental festivals. In particular, the commencement of the mass confession with a powerful sermon by minister Adair provided a crucial parallel with Lord's Supper revivalism, recalling the similarly affective preaching of John Welsh, Robert Bruce, and most famously, John Livingston.[89] The history of dramatic, communal events being held in the area by fervent presbyterians thus provided a blueprint for the townsfolk to follow in future moments of crisis. In turn, the meticulous recording of the events and confessions of 1647 by the session clerk could serve as a scheme for any subsequent episodes of mass repentance.

The local history of past plagues, established patterns of revivalism, and covenanting zeal thus compose the backdrop for understanding why the townspeople of Ayr so willingly participated in an all-consuming mass confession. Yet such an event would have likely never occurred without two additional factors: the centrality of the minister to his community and the culture of covenanting that had been painstakingly established by Ayr's religious leadership and embraced by many of its people over the previous decade. Without doubt, Adair was a manifestly compelling, persuasive, and tenacious figure. His sermon on Zechariah was, along with the force of his personality and position, capable of stirring the town into mass confession. The response to the plague also illustrates the power of the pulpit as both a spiritual and physical force – provided it had the right inhabitant – that could incite early modern Scots to action.[90]

By the mid-seventeenth century, ministers throughout Scotland had long used the pulpit to convey religious knowledge and spiritual edification to their parishioners through sermons, lectures, fasts, and prayers.[91] In Ayr's response to the plague, this clerical platform became a forum for orchestrating the whole affair. Nearly every confession began with some sort of description of the minister standing at the pulpit and motivating his parishioners to speak, act, and repent. In prefacing the recounting of their manifest sins, several groups included phrases like 'the minister from the pulpit showed to them' and 'the minister having from the pulpit discoursed to them'.[92] None of these referenced sermons, but rather personalised directives dispensed from the pulpit to the people. Of course, phrases in the minutes such as 'they willingly embraced the overtour presented to them by the minister' or 'the people readily obeyed the minister' are interpretations by the session's longtime clerk, Robert Law, and ought to be treated with a good dose of caution.[93] Still, the scale and swiftness of the town's collective reaction to the plague and the exhortations of Adair demonstrates the motivational clout of the pulpit, and the man who occupied it, beyond the time of the sermon. The pulpit at Ayr was thus the centre of communal as much as sacred space.

If, taken as a whole, the mass confession demonstrates the persuasive power and authority of speaking from the pulpit, the confessions of the various groups also demonstrate the challenges of sufficiently hearing and obeying the appeals made to them by the minister. Many of these echo the ongoing disciplinary issues faced by the kirk session in the previous decade. As the tailors put it, some of them were guilty of 'slipping by carelesslie many a Sabbath day by sleiping in tym of preaching'. These in-pew naps were apparently a common issue, and Ayr would have perhaps benefited from a strategy used in Perth in which a kirk officer would patrol the back of the church wielding a staff that could be used to rudely awaken anyone dozing when they should have been listening.[94] Similarly, the labourers confessed that while they 'were in the kirk', they had not been 'faithfull and carefull hearers of the word of god'.[95] The messengers of the town were even more explicit, lamenting their half-hearted hearing of the word of god as their thoughts were 'miscaried by the devil' to the 'transitory things of the worlde' during sermon time.[96] When these individuals and groups confessed their failure to keep the sabbath and heed the word as they ought, they articulated not only an understanding of the importance of sermons and attendant religious exercises, but also the challenges inherent in the most fundamental practices of godliness.

Covenants and confession

Above all, the confessions of 1647 illustrate the entrenched expectations for godliness within a mid-seventeenth-century Scottish community. The process of swearing two national covenants, and likely other covenants at the individual level, informed these expectations and made them collectively and personally binding. From the outset, when minister John Fergushill presented the Solemn League and Covenant to his congregation in 1643, he intimated that 'the whole people then present should be solmenlie swore to adher unto the same in all time coming'.[97] Swearing a covenant of any sort was not a singular act, frozen in time, over and done with. It was, instead, a statement of allegiance and a promise of future fidelity and behaviour. Indeed, in his remarks of thanksgiving in April 1648, Adair framed the entire affair around the tradition of covenanting, calling the collective confessions 'a testimonie to Christ his cause and covenant and to the lyfe and power of godliness'.[98] Here, as we have seen before, godliness and allegiance to the covenants – ideas that at once encompassed specific documents, personal action, and biblical precedent – were explicitly conflated, bound together practically and theologically. This episode thus affords historians specific insights into what it meant to ordinary Scots to swear, before God, minister, and congregation, the National Covenant of 1638 and the Solemn League and Covenant of 1643, and how these acts informed ongoing words and deeds.

All but one of the groups that made public confession at Ayr explicitly mentioned their break of one or more covenants as a cause of the plague, making it the most oft-cited sin in the eighteen confessions.[99] The town council, for example, admitted early in the proceedings their 'break of Covenant with God, in special the Solemn League and Covenant betwixt the Kingdomes', citing the agreement of 1643 as just one component of a larger band they had made with God.[100] The coopers explicitly named the documents to which they had subscribed, collectively recognising that they had 'sworne ane National Covenant, also the covenant of the three Kingdomes', but had not 'soe wiel advysed nor keiped what we have sworne as we should'. They were, therefore, 'guiltie both of rash swearing, and also for the breach of all the contents of them, and most speciallie the not reforming of our lives'.[101]

The 'laborers and travellers' were perhaps the most specific in their confession, citing not only their 'break of our solemne covenant which we swore and did protest befor god and his children', but also elaborating on 'that particular break of our league with our neighbour nation Ingland and our not being willing to assist them in bodie and means as also our litell affection to god and his children'.[102] This is a remarkable statement from what would have been the least educated group of men in Ayr. Here they were not repeating the words of any other craft's confession, but rather identifying their specific understanding of the Solemn League and Covenant and their deviation from its mandates. Their articulation of the importance of solidarity with English parliamentary forces is noteworthy and likely reflects some of the conversations and admonitions that must have been ongoing in Ayr in the months leading up to the intense ecclesiastical controversies of the late 1640s.

Other groups spoke about break of covenant without clear reference to a specific document, but with an equally powerful understanding of the requirements of a covenanted life. After listing moral failings such as neglect of family worship and excessive drink, the wakers categorised all of these sins as products of their betrayal of the covenant that they had made, for 'all which is also the break of that Solem Covenant mad with God'.[103] The tailors spoke in even broader terms, confessing to their 'break of our covenant with our god in not leading ane holie and sober lyfe as we did sweare with our heartes and subscribe with our hands', referring to a comprehensive idea of a shared covenant that required fidelity from not only the hand but also the heart.[104] For these groups, swearing the covenants entailed allegiance not only to a national, political cause, but also to a range of daily acts of godliness – an understanding informed by the clear and consistent messaging from the minister and session over the previous near-decade. Perhaps most tellingly, when the sailors confessed to their practice of 'that idolatrous workshop of the masse' while abroad, they elaborated that 'the first thing that caused them to quit it was the swearing of the covenant in this land'.[105] Whether this was a true statement or one made to appease the minister is impossible to know with certainty. Regardless, such an admission further demonstrates that allegiance to the covenants entailed an expectation of covenanting as a purifying ritual in practical terms.

One of the most striking and consistent aspects of the confessions is a general recognition that the responsibility of covenanting and godliness was at once personal and collective. When Adair and members of the session stood before the congregation to make their confession as exemplars of the community, they spoke 'all and every one of them, the Minister with the elders and Deacons, and they with him'. The rhetorical emphasis on words and phrases like 'with', 'each other', 'in presence of the rest', and 'every one of them' set the stage for a broader communal display of individual contrition and collective responsibility. Other professional societies used similar language during the subsequent days. The hammermen, for example, 'confessed their faults one to ane other, and prayed one for another'.[106] Despite the collaborative nature of their confession, the minutes note that they also came forward 'everie man for himself, and in particulare confessed himself to be the first ondrawer of the Judgements upon himself and this place by reason of that his break of covenant with his god'.[107] Men of the cordinar craft took into consideration 'their manifold sinnes and provocations comitted by them and ilk one of them in their persones and callings against almightie god'.[108] As the coopers put it, they had convened to 'to confesse and acknowledge everie man his owne particular failings', including acting as 'evil example one to another'.[109] Not only were the townsfolk responsible for monitoring their own behaviour, they were also accountable to others, be it the minister, fellow craftsmen, loved ones, or the town at large. Ayr was, of course, a community of communities – guilds, families, the congregation, and so on – but as sworn covenanters, they were also part of a collective project of further reformation.

The men who participated in the mass confession at Ayr thus intended the records they composed to serve as statements of shared commitment in the face of the plague. But the meticulous chronicling of the events also testifies to their future-oriented purpose. While kirk session clerks across Scotland often omitted details about events presumably deemed mundane or unimportant, the response to the pestilence was, from Adair's opening sermon in September 1647 to his words of thanksgiving in April 1648, recounted in unusual detail across a variety of records. This suggests that the leaders of Ayr envisioned the records of the confession as guides for future generations of townsfolk, in hopes that they would embrace and carry forward the example set in 1647. From the beginning, Adair and the session recommended that each craft and society of the town make a 'relatione of their proceeding' that would be then written 'in their own books and in the sessione book for the use of posterity in the like cases the like course may be taken by them for turning to the Lord in their calamitie'.[110] This commitment was most eloquently expressed by the coopers, who explained at the end of their confession that they 'thought merit to registrat in our craft book for ane example to our own posteritie, knowing that whosoever hides his sinnes shall not prosper, but who confesseth them shall find mercie'.[111] Here one finds an explicit statement of both the thought-process behind the recording of events at Ayr and the importance of self-surveillance and confession to godly life.

That the mass confession at Ayr survives in remarkable detail in the kirk session minutes, and is corroborated by entries in the presbytery minutes, the town council book, and the mariner's minute book, is therefore no accident. Rather, the meticulous recording of such an event should be viewed as a purposeful act on the part of Adair and other local leaders to fashion Ayr as a covenanted town *par excellence*, not just for the present, but for posterity. This was at once a reaction to an immediate crisis and a continuation of a process that began in 1638, both of which reveal much about local dynamics of faith and identity in Ayr and in covenanted Scotland more broadly. If we define 'covenant' in expansive terms, as so many in Ayr seem to have done – as a binding promise to God and a statement of allegiance to the Reformed cause, sworn in word and recorded in writ – then we might even view the mass confession as a covenant in and of itself. As the confession of the glovers put it, 'we all with one consent have humbled our selves and beseech the god of all mercie for Christs sake to give us grace to stand to this our oath before God and grant us true repentance of all our transgressions.

At Ayr the yeire and day forso we have all subscribed with our hands'.[112] As a communal act that involved oral oaths and written subscription, the group confessions of 1647 replicated the swearing of the covenants of 1638 and 1643 and would have been all the more meaningful for it.

The response to the plague of 1647 also made manifest the centrality and function of confession to covenanting in particular and within Reformed theology in general. The diaries, personal covenants, sermons, and kirk session records of post-Reformation Scotland all point to confession as an integral part of, and even a precondition for, true repentance and godliness. The goal of the Reformed kirk in Scotland was never to eliminate sinful behaviour – an impossibility thanks to the innate depravity of elect and reprobate alike – but to ensure that people had the language and, as important, the space necessary to confess their sins with sincerity and zeal. Though the act of confession was not sacramentally enshrined within protestantism as it was within the Catholic church, it was clearly a durable part of practical divinity.[113] For the covenanters in particular, the swearing of various personal and national covenants carried certain expectations, including admission of failures to live up to those expectations. In turn, the medium of confession revealed the sinfulness of individual hearts and of the wider community, reinforcing the need for mutually binding agreements – that is, covenants of all sorts – to keep the godly in line. Thus at the local level, for both the minister and the laity, covenanting and confession acted as two sides of the same coin.

Moreover, if plague could provoke confession, then for protestants the disease itself could help purge unclean souls by, as Adair put it, working as a 'phisick ... to bring out by confessiounes and prayer manie fostered corruptiounes and the plague of the heart'.[114] Indeed, seventy-five years later, Cotton Mather, the prolific puritan turned naturalist, unknowingly echoed Adair when he encouraged his Boston readers to view smallpox as 'an Emetic, as to make us Vomit up our Sin, with a penitent Confession of it'.[115] More work remains to be done on Reformed responses to plague and to what extent confessional specificities such as providentialism determined these responses.[116] But for the men and women of Ayr, the pestilence had clearly proved a cleansing fire, forcing purity through divine destruction.

Conclusion

Ayr's collective response to the plague demonstrates that to swear the Covenants of 1638 and 1643 was to make a lifelong promise, twice-over, to God and one's community. Such an act entailed a tremendous amount of individual and corporate responsibility, not only in the immediate context, but to future generations. Certainly, the mass confession detailed here, a product of the persuasive power of Adair and the religious temperature of southwestern Scotland, provides a dramatic example of exercising this responsibility. Yet despite its unique nature, this episode demonstrates the tremendous potential of covenanter identity to motivate and mobilise whole communities in response to existential threats. By confessing *en masse* to their sins and promising personal reform, the townspeople of Ayr were not simply performing good protestant behaviour. Under Adair's guiding hand, they were also expressing and reshaping their own expectations of what it meant, in practice, to be in covenant with God, community, and country. This case reveals that to live a covenanted life entailed participation in the ongoing moral reformation of one's town, profession, family – and oneself. While the plague may have dissipated by the end of 1647, the people of Ayr faced equally acute trials over the coming decades. Their 'city upon a hill', like their own transgressive hearts, would require constant vigilance and self-examination.

Notes

1 Ayrshire Archives, B6/18/2, Ayr Council Book, 1647–1669, fo. 26r. Inscription comes partly from Proverbs 9:10.
2 National Records of Scotland (hereafter NRS), CH2/751/3/1, Ayr kirk session records, fo. 31r.
3 Parts of this chapter were originally published in Michelle D. Brock, 'Plague, Covenants, and Confession: The Strange Case of Ayr, 1647-8', *Scottish Historical Review*, 97:2 (2018), 129–52. These events are also mentioned, in brief, in Annie I. Dunlop (ed.), *The Royal Burgh of Ayr: Seven Hundred Fifty Years of History* (Edinburgh: Oliver and Boyd, 1953), p. 278; Sharon Adams, 'A Regional Road to Revolution: Religion, Politics and Society in South-West Scotland, 1600–50' (PhD thesis, University of Edinburgh, 2002), p. 160; John H. Pagan, *Annals of Ayr in the Olden Time, 1560–1692* (Ayr: Alex Fergusson, 1897), pp. 72–4; Joseph D. Shearer, *Ayr and its People: 1428 to the Time of Burns* (Ayr: n.p., 2004), pp. 61–4.
4 See, for example, Stephen Greenburg, 'Plague, the Printing Press, and Public Health in Seventeenth-Century London', *Huntington Library Quarterly*, 67:4 (December 2004), 508–27.
5 On the history of print in Scotland, see Alastair J. Mann, *The Scottish Book Trade, 1500–1720: Print Commerce and Print Control in Early Modern Scotland* (East Linton: Tuckwell Press, 2000).
6 On the plague of 1606–7, see Dunlop, *The Royal Burgh of Ayr*, pp. 275–8 and John F.D. Shrewsbury, *A History of Bubonic Plague in the British Isles* (Cambridge: Cambridge University Press, 1970), pp. 289–93.

7 In his history of Ayr, John Strawhorn suggests that the population of sixteenth-century Ayr was probably around 1,500–2,000, and likely approaching 3,000 by the later seventeenth century. See John Strawhorn, *The History of Ayr: Royal Burgh and County Town* (Edinburgh: John Donald Publishers, 1989), p. 78.
8 Dunlop, *The Royal Burgh of Ayr*, p. 275.
9 Dunlop, *The Royal Burgh of Ayr*, p. 277.
10 John P. Collier (ed.), *The Egerton Papers* (London: Nichols and Sons, 1840), pp. 406–7.
11 On the general impact of the plague in Scotland from 1644 to 1649, see Michael Flinn (ed.), *Scottish Population History* (Cambridge: Cambridge University Press, 1977), pp. 133–49; Robert Oram, '"It Cannot He Decernit Quha Are Clean and Quha Are Foulle": Responses to Epidemic Disease in Sixteenth- and Seventeenth-Century Scotland', *Renaissance and Reformation / Renaissance Et Réforme*, 30:4 (2007), 13–39, esp. 21–2; E. Patricia Dennison, Gordon DesBrisay, and Lesley Diack, 'Health in the Two Towns', in E. Patricia Dennison, David Dicthburn, and Michael Lynch (eds), *Aberdeen before 1800: A New History* (East Linton: Tuckwell Press, 2002), pp. 70–108; and David Stevenson, 'The Burghs and the Scottish Revolution', in Michael Lynch (ed.), *The Early Modern Town in Scotland* (London: Routledge, 1987), pp. 182–7; and Shrewsbury, *A History of Bubonic Plague*, pp. 426–32.
12 Laura A.M. Stewart, *Urban Politics and British Civil Wars: Edinburgh, 1617–1653* (Leiden: Brill, 2006), pp. 69–70; Michael Lynch, 'Introduction: Scottish Towns 1500–1700', in Lynch, *The Early Modern Town in Scotland*, pp. 1–15, at p. 18.
13 CH2/751/2, fo. 431r.
14 Flinn, *Scottish Population History*, pp. 133–49.
15 On social and economic responses to the plague in Scotland, see Karen Jillings, *An Urban History of the Plague: Socio-Economic, Political and Medical Impacts in a Scottish Community, 1500–1650* (London: Routledge, 2018); Charles F. Mullet, 'Plague Policy in Scotland, 16th–17th Centuries', *Osiris*, 9 (1950), 435–56; Dunlop, *The Royal Burgh of Ayr*, pp. 273–8; and most recently, Oram, 'It Cannot He Decernit Quha Are Clean and Quha Are Foulle'. For a discussion of public fasting in response to calamitous events such as plague epidemics, see Alec Ryrie, 'The Rise and Fall of Fasting in the British Reformations', in Natalie Mearns and Alec Ryrie (eds), *Worship and the Parish Church in Early Modern Britain* (Farnham: Ashgate, 2013), esp. pp. 97–103.
16 Jillings, *An Urban History of the Plague*, pp. 39–41.
17 See, for example, discussions of public repentance in Philip Ziegler's classic work, *The Black Death* (London: Collins, 1969), esp. a discussion on pp. 86–96 about Flagellents in Germany. See also John Aberth, *From the Brink of the Apocalypse: Confronting Famine, War, Plague, and Death in the Later Middle Ages*, 2nd edn (London: Routledge, 2010), chapter 3.
18 B6/18/2, fo. 26v. This description of the origins of the 1647 plague come from the council minutes on 11 October; unfortunately, the minutes are not extant from before late September 1647, so it is difficult to know an exact start date

to the plague, which is not mentioned in the kirk session minutes before 13 September.
19 B6/18/2, fo. 27r.
20 B6/18/2, fo. 27r
21 CH2/751/3/1, fo. 30r–1r.
22 CH2/751/3/1, fo. 31r. Excerpts from the kirk session at Ayr during the time of the plague are also transcribed in Edinburgh, National Library of Scotland (hereafter NLS), Wod. Qu. LXXXIII, fos. 68v–103r. Page numbers cited here are from the original kirk session minutes.
23 CH2/751/3/1, fo. 31r.
24 On the disruptions caused by the British civil wars, see Chris R. Langley, *Worship, Civil War and Community, 1638–1660* (London: Routledge, 2015).
25 Tom Barclay and Eric J. Graham, *The Early Transatlantic Trade of Ayr, 1640–1730* (Ayr: The Ayrshire Archaeological and Natural History Society, 2005), 11. On the more general problem of piracy in the region during an earlier period, see Scott Carballo, 'Piracy, the State, and the Burghs of Southwest Scotland, 1560–1603', in Allan Kennedy (ed.), *Deviance and Marginality in Early Modern Scotland* (Woodbridge: Boydell, forthcoming).
26 CH2/751/3/1, fo. 31r.
27 The full verse reads: 'And the land shall mourn, every family apart; the family of the house of David apart, and their wives apart; the family of the house of Nathan apart, and their wives apart.' Any subsequent bible verses are quoted from the King James Version (KJV). Here Adair was drawing inspiration from *The Order and Doctrine of the General Fast*, appointed by the General Assembly of the Church of Scotland Edinburgh, 15 December 1565 (London, 1603).
28 CH2/751/3/1, fo. 31v.
29 CH2/751/3/1, fo. 31v.
30 CH2/751/3/1, fos. 31v–31r.
31 CH2/751/3/1, fo. 31v.
32 CH2/751/3/1, fo. 32v.
33 Of seventeen members listed in the council records on 22 September 1647, nine are also members of the session. See B6/18/2, fo. 26r.
34 CH2/751/3/1, fo. 32v.
35 CH2/751/3/1, fo. 33v.
36 CH2/751/3/1, fo. 33v.
37 The social prominence of the various professions may have partly informed their meeting places, though convenience, spatial constraints, and the need to maintain some degree of social distance were probably more decisive factors, as there is not a clearly discernible pattern.
38 CH2/751/3/1, fo. 34r.
39 CH2/751/3/1, fo. 35r.
40 CH2/751/3/1, fo. 36r.
41 CH2/751/3/1, fo. 36v.
42 CH2/751/3/1, fo. 34v.

43 CH2/751/3/1, fo. 35v.
44 CH2/751/3/1, fo. 37r.
45 CH2/751/3/1, fo. 37r.
46 On the economic history of Ayr and the importance of its port, see T.C. Smout, 'The Overseas Trade of Ayrshire, 1660–1707', *Ayrshire Archaeological and Natural History Collections*, 2nd series, vol. 6 (1961), 56–80; Barclay and Graham, *The Early Transatlantic Trade of Ayr*; Hugh McGhee, 'The Harbour', in Dunlop (ed.), *The Royal Burgh of Ayr*, pp. 197–211; John Strawhorn, *History of Ayr: Royal Burgh and County Town* (Edinburgh: John Donald Publishers, 1989), chapters five and seven.
47 CH2/751/3/1, fo. 138r.
48 CH2/751/3/1, fo. 37v.
49 For a general history of 'atheism' in early modern Europe, see Michael Hunter and David Wooton (eds), *Atheism from the Reformation to the Enlightenment* (Oxford: Oxford University Press, 1992) and Alec Ryrie, *Unbelievers: An Emotional History of Doubt* (London: William Collins, 2019).
50 CH2/751/3/1, fos. 38v–39r.
51 CH2/751/3/1, fo. 39r.
52 CH2/751/3/1, fo. 38v.
53 CH2/751/3/1, fo. 39r. See also Shearer, *Ayr and its People*, p. 64 and David Dobson, *Scottish Emigration to Colonial America, 1607–1785* (Athens, GA: University of Georgia Press, 2004). For local studies on the forcible indenture of people, particularly servants and children, from the British Isles, see, for example, Timothy J. Shannon, 'A "Wicked Commerce": Consent, Coercion, and Kidnapping in Aberdeen's Servant Trade', *The William and Mary Quarterly*, 74:3 (2017), 437–66 and John Wareing, "'Violently taken away or cheatingly duckoyed": The Illicit Recruitment in London of Indentured Servants for the American Colonies, 1645–1718', *London Journal*, 26:2 (2001), 1–22.
54 CH2/751/3/1, fo. 38v.
55 CH2/751/3/1, fo. 39v.
56 CH2/751/3/1, fo. 39v.
57 CH2/751/3/1, fo. 39v. A lecture was a longer exposition, a larger chunk of scripture intended primarily to inform rather than instruct.
58 CH2/751/3/1, fo. 40v.
59 CH2/751/3/1, fo. 40v.
60 CH2/751/3/1, fos. 39v–40v.
61 On the closing of ports and ceasing of trade and travel, see Shrewsbury, *A History of Bubonic Plague in the British Isles*, esp. pp 289–93. Though he doesn't discuss the plague of 1647, Shrewsbury does detail some of the quite costly actions taken by the town to control the much more severe plague of 1606-7. For general social and economic responses to post-Reformation plagues, see Oram, 'It Cannot He Decernit Quha Are Clean and Quha Are Foulle', and Jillings, *An Urban History of the Plague*, esp. chapter 2.
62 CH2/751/3/1, fo.41r. For a recent treatment of responses to the weather in other Scottish towns, see Margo Todd, 'Weather, Finance and Urban Religious

Dissent in Early Modern Scotland', in Arthur der Weduwen (ed.), *Reformation, Religious Culture and Print in Early Modern Europe: Essays in Honour of Andrew Pettegree*, vol. 1 (Leiden: Brill, 2002), pp. 64–82.

63 CH2/751/3/1, fo. 43r.
64 CH2/751/3/1, fo. 43v.
65 CH2/751/3/1, fo. 43v. The confession of the officers is marked in the minutes as having been recorded five days later, on 22 September; it was read to the congregation on the Thursday thereafter.
66 CH2/751/3/1, fo. 43v. The actual verse of 2 Peter 2:22 is 'But it is happened unto them according to the true proverb, the dog is turned to his own vomit again; and the sow that was washed to her wallowing in the mire'.
67 The eighteen listed groups are, in order that they appear in the records, the minister with the session, the town council, hammermen, coupers, squaremen, weavers, glovers, cordinars, wakers, taylors, merchants, sailors, 'labourers, travellers, and communitie of the towne' (who confessed as one group), baxters, fleshers, candlemakers, 'notaries and messengers and officers' (who confessed as one group), and scholars. Servants joined in confession with their masters in the shoemaking and shipping businesses, and they may have participated alongside other crafts or as part of the general 'communitie of the towne', though on this the records are unfortunately silent. Puzzlingly absent from the records of the confession are the brewers, especially given that the session was deeply concerned with drinking on the sabbath and drunkenness more generally. My guess is the brewers met alongside another group to make confession – perhaps the fleshers or the bakers – but were not listed as an individual body.
68 CH2/751/3/1, fo. 44v.
69 CH2/751/3/1, fo. 44v.
70 NRS, Ayr Presbytery Records, CH2/532/1, p. 315.
71 CH2/751/3/1, fo. 44v.
72 CH2/751/3/1, fo, 44v.
73 CH2/751/3/1, fo. 60r.
74 CH2/751/3/1, fo. 60v.
75 CH2/751/3/1, fo. 60v.
76 Quarantine and other preventative measures discussed in town council minutes, B6/18/2, fos. 26r–27v.
77 CH2/751/3/1, fo. 61r.
78 CH2/751/3/1, fo. 61v; Psalms 30:11.
79 On the gendered aspects of taking the covenants, see Laura A.M. Stewart, *Rethinking the Scottish Revolution: Covenanted Scotland, 1637–1651* (Oxford: Oxford University Press, 2016), esp. pp. 112–15; Laura A.M. Stewart, 'Authority, Agency and the Reception of the Scottish National Covenant of 1638', in Robert Armstrong and Tadhg Ó Hannracháin (eds), *Insular Christianity: Alternative Models of the Church in Britain and Ireland, c.1570–c.1700* (Manchester: Manchester University Press, 2013), 94–7; Jamie Murdoch McDougall, 'Covenants and Covenanters in Scotland, 1638–1679' (PhD thesis, University of Glasgow, 2017), pp. 55–60.

80 Janay Nugent, 'Reformed Masculinity: Ministers, Fathers and Male Heads of Households, 1560–1660', in Lynn Abrams and Elizabeth Ewan (eds), *Nine Centuries of Man: Manhood and Masculinities in Scottish History* (Edinburgh: Edinburgh University Press, 2017), pp. 39–57.
81 CH2/751/3/1, fos. 34r, 38v, and 34v, respectively.
82 Ayrshire Archives, Acc 483, Papers of William Adair (c. 1633–1656), vol. I, n.p.
83 CH2/751/3/1, fo. 36r. See, for example, Samuel Rutherford's words in 'Sermon V' of *The Trial and Triumph of Faith* (Edinburgh, 1645), which read that 'Satan findeth his own Seed in us by Nature'.
84 CH2/751/3/1, fo. 35r.
85 See, for example, sermons given by Adair in March and October 1647. Acc. 483, vol. I, n.p.
86 Acc. 483, vol. 2, n.p.
87 Flinn, *Scottish Population History*, pp. 133–49.
88 Leigh Eric Schmidt, *Holy Fairs: Scotland and the Making of American Revivalism* (Princeton: Princeton University Press, 1989), p. 22. As Schmidt points out, this early Scottish revivalism borrowed, paradoxically, from the communal Catholic festivals and holy days that the post-Reformation kirk had sought to dismantle.
89 Schmidt, *Holy Fairs*, pp. 21–8.
90 On the importance of the word and ministry in Reformation Scotland, see Margo Todd, *Culture of Protestantism in Early Modern Scotland* (New Haven: Yale University Press, 2002), chapters 1 and 2; John McCallum, *Reforming the Scottish Parish: The Reformation in Fife, 1560–1640* (Aldershot: Ashgate, 2010), especially chapters 1 and 4; Chris R. Langley, Catherine McMillan, and Russell Newton (eds), *The Clergy in Early Modern Scotland* (Woodbridge: Boydell, 2021).
91 On preaching and spiritual edification in the reformed tradition, within and beyond Scotland, see, for example, James Thomas Ford, 'Preaching in the Reformed Tradition', in Larissa Taylor (ed.), *Preachers and People in the Reformations and Early Modern Europe* (Leiden: Brill, 2001); Michael Lynch, 'Preaching to the Converted?', in A. MacDonald, Michael Lynch, and Ian Cowan (eds), *The Renaissance in Scotland* (Leiden: Brill, 1994), pp. 307–14; Peter McCullough, Hugh Adlington, and Emma Rhatigan (eds), *The Oxford Handbook of the Early Modern Sermon* (Oxford: Oxford University Press, 2011); Mary Morrissey, 'Scripture, Style and Persuasion in Seventeenth-Century English Theories of Preaching', *The Journal of Ecclesiastical History*, 53 (2002), 686–70; Bruce Gordon, 'Preaching and Reform of the Clergy in the Swiss Reformation', in Andrew Pettegree (ed.), *The Reformation of the Parishes* (Manchester: Manchester University Press, 1993), pp. 63–84.
92 See, for example, references to the pulpit in CH2/751/3/1, fos. 33v, 37r, and 41r.
93 CH2/751/3/1, fos. 31r and 40v.
94 CH2/751/3/1, fo. 37r. Todd, *Culture of Protestantism*, p. 40.
95 CH2/751/3/1, fo. 41v.

96 CH2/751/3/1, fo. 43v.
97 CH2/751/2, fo. 409r.
98 CH2/751/3/1, fo. 60r.
99 The only group that does not explicitly cite their break of covenant as a major sin are the 'schollers', who made the shortest, and last, confession on September 18. CH2/751/3/1, fo. 44r.
100 CH2/751/3/1, fo. 33v.
101 CH2/751/3/1, fo. 34v.
102 CH2/751/3/1, fo. 42r. Exactly what the labourers meant when they confessed to their failure in assisting England in 'bodie and means' remains unclear. This may be a reference to unwillingness to enlist in or serve the covenanter army in some capacity, or to contribute to a collection fundraising for the army, during the conflicts of the previous year.
103 CH2/751/3/1, fo. 36v.
104 CH2/751/3/1, fo. 36v.
105 CH2/751/3/1, fos. 38v–39r.
106 CH2/751/3/1, fo. 34r.
107 CH2/751/3/1, fo. 34r.
108 CH2/751/3/1, fo. 36r.
109 CH2/751/3/1, fo. 34v.
110 CH2/751/3/1, fo. 32v.
111 CH2/751/3/1. fo. 35r.
112 CH2/751/3/1, fo. 36r. Unfortunately, I have only been able to track down the mariners' minute book. There is no reason to doubt, however, that the other crafts also recorded their confessions or general summaries of the events of 1647 in their own books.
113 For a helpful discussion of the emotional role of confession in protestant practice, see Alec Ryrie, *Being Protestant in Reformation Britain* (Oxford: Oxford University Press, 2013), esp. pp. 55–9.
114 CH2/751/3/1, fo. 60r.
115 Cotton Mather, *The Angel of Bethesda*, ed. Gordon W. Jones (Barre: American Antiquarian Society, 1972), p. 7.
116 On Mather and the theology of inoculation, see Robert Tindol, 'Getting the Pox off All Their Houses: Cotton Mather and the Rhetoric of Puritan Science', *Early American Literature*, 46:1 (2011), 1–23.

3

Saints and sinners

On 28 August 1650, a very busy kirk session worked through a backlog of cases that had languished while William Adair, still lone minister of the parish, had been 'absent at the Armie' for the previous three weeks.[1] Towards the bottom of the docket that day, following a complex case involving blasphemy and drunkenness, was the case of Janet Campbell, accused of 'the sin of filthiness' with Andrew Karr, a soldier stationed in Ayr. Campbell, who at the time of her appearance was pregnant, confessed to the charge but clarified that while 'the said Andrew had carnall deal with hir', it happened only once. When asked about where Karr was now, she said that he had died in nearby Irvine 'upon the Thursday after the first witches wer burnt'.[2] Campbell's own sin of fornication had changed the course of her life, while the sin of witchcraft, an intense outbreak of which was sweeping Scotland, informed her sense of time. Two weeks later, the session, reflecting on the many concurrent 'calamities of the Land', set apart the coming sabbath for a day of 'solemn humiliation'.[3]

Throughout the mid-seventeenth century, the increasingly zealous religious leadership of Scotland waged a war – at times, a literal one – against the calamities embodied by sin within and outwith their communities. This conflict was costly: the funds and manpower to support the Army of the Covenant, the expenses of maintaining and quartering troops, and the loss of lives on the battlefield quickly added up in towns across the country.[4] As Laura Stewart has pointed out, none of Scotland's urban inhabitants, regardless of status, had 'evaded responsibility and sacrifice' during the war effort.[5] War also sowed profound divisions within the covenanting movement. In Ayr, the collective response to the plague of 1647 had been a high point of covenanted unity, but it was closely followed by years of polarised lows. By the late 1640s, after a decade of intermittent and expensive warfare, the radical 'kirk party' had risen to power amid heated debates over how to best negotiate with Charles I while maintaining the ideals of the covenants. Adair, and the bulk of the community in Ayr, sided with the faction of covenanters who staunchly opposed any cooperation with a king they deemed impious and untrustworthy. Those who supported 'engaging' with the king were viewed, by extension, as dire threats, if not outright enemies, to the project of covenanting. Sin had always been politicised, but now it seemed existentially so, and stark yet muddled divisions would persist in dramatic fashion through the eve of the Cromwellian occupation. From the perspective of Adair and his ilk, claims to ecclesiastical and spiritual superiority carried the responsibility to clean one's own house first, but this was more easily envisioned than enacted.

The period between 1647 and 1651 suggests that the chaos of high-politics and ecclesiastical debates played an important but uneven role in how ordinary men and women experienced practices of piety in their own communities. At the height of their influence, hardline covenanters endeavoured to enforce more draconian disciplinary measures on a variously willing population and presided over one of Scotland's most intense periods of witch-hunting as part of a broader quest for moral reform. In Ayrshire in the late 1640s, dozens of residents, almost all of them women, were accused of witchcraft.[6] We do not know the fates of many of them, but the majority were likely convicted and then strangled and burned at the stake. This drive to eradicate witchcraft was not confined to the Scots; south of the border, England had witnessed its most intense period of witch-hunting during the chaos and puritan leadership of the 1640s.[7] Nor was this wartime peak unique to protestants – the crises of the early to mid-seventeenth century, particularly the Thirty Years' War, coincided with some of Catholic Europe's most deadly witch trials.[8] The story of these years is fundamentally one of community leaders attempting to impose moral order on a world that appeared increasingly disordered – an experience that, far from unique to Ayr, shaped communities throughout Britain, Europe, and the Atlantic during the conflict-ridden mid-century.[9]

Engaging the enemy?

Of all the things that must have kept Adair up at night in the years between the plague of 1647 and the Cromwellian invasion in 1651, few loomed as large as the dramatic fracturing of covenanter unity that began in early 1648. The previous December, representatives of the Scottish Parliament had signed a controversial (to put it mildly) alliance with Charles I known as the Engagement.[10] In return for the promise of Scottish military support if the English Parliament remained recalcitrant, the king agreed to confirm the Solemn League and Covenant, impose presbyterianism upon the Church of England for a trial period of three years, and generally allow for greater Scottish influence in his southern kingdom. This was, in some ways, a good deal for the Scots, but to men like Adair, it had one very fatal flaw: Charles steadfastly refused to take the covenant himself or to compel any of his subjects to do so. In their eyes, support for the covenant meant holding even monarchs to its implicit and explicit mandates for godliness, and on this point, Adair and his fellow members of the anti-engager faction remained immovable.[11] Soon, Scotland's civic and spiritual leadership were up in arms against one another.

Covenanter unity had been shattered at the national level, and in parishes like Ayr, political conflict provided the opportunity, albeit unwelcome, to further reinforce the culture of covenanting at the local level. For the minister and like-minded elders, this doubling down on strict adherence to the covenants was existential – those who deviated put the whole work of the reformation at stake. A commission for a fast, received on 17 May 1648 by the presbytery of Ayr from the General Assembly, articulated the high stakes of the situation: the fast was to be held 'in respect of the manie and great sinnes and provocationes of the people, as also how deep a revolting of the cause of god many ar come to, and what cause we have to feare the overturning of all that God has done for us'.[12] This order, to be read in every parish throughout the country, was clear in its top-down assessment of the present crisis: if the people did not turn from their sinful conduct in ways great and small, the wrath to come could dwarf even the turmoil of war and plague experienced in recent years.

These stakes would only intensify due to events that summer. In June 1648, an armed communion service organised by local ministers, including Adair, was held just northeast of the town at Mauchline Muir. Explicitly framed as a rebuke of the Engagement, the meeting was enthusiastically attended by some 2,000 people, many of whom were ordinary men and women rather than local elites. This grassroots support for a hardline interpretation of the covenants was a harbinger of things to come in Ayr and beyond.[13] Over the coming months, the divisions between the more zealous covenanters and their moderate opponents hardened amid armed conflict, much of it centred in the southwest. Adair was present at the so-called Whiggamore Raid, in which several thousand anti-engagers marched from Ayrshire and surrounding areas to Edinburgh and toppled engager control of parliament. Those participating in the uprising eventually formed the Western Association, an army whose members envisioned themselves the true defenders of the covenants.[14] By the end of 1648, then, it had become clear that, at least in the minds of the radical kirk party now dominating the national stage, support for the now-defunct Engagement would need to be dealt with at the parish level. Foxes, it was feared, were in the hen house, and any future treachery would have to be actively prevented.

When the kirk party-dominated General Assembly met in September 1648, on the heels of a major victory against the engagers (thanks, in large part, to help from Oliver Cromwell), they set about righting the ship – which also meant further deepening of the divisions in the covenanting movement.[15] As the hardliners saw it, those who had supported the Engagement had sinned grievously by rejecting the covenants and, by extension, their godly duties. They crafted a document to be distributed to every parish in Scotland, along with instructions for resubscription to the Solemn League and Covenant: the 'Solemn Acknowledgement of Public Sins and Breaches of the Covenant, and a Solemn Engagement to all the Duties contained therein, namely, those which do in a more special way relate to the dangers of these times'.[16] Ministers were to lead their congregations in a week of fasting and repentance, and then the Engagement was to be read, after which all those who had complied with it were to confess their transgressions and beg 'mercy for these sines'.[17] The affair ended by debarring all those guilty of participation in the Engagement not only from resubscription of the covenant, but from the critical ritual of communion. While the administration of the covenants in 1638 and 1643 had been explicitly inclusive, the General Assembly had now made taking the covenant – and with it, taking the sacrament of communion – conditional. As Jamie McDougall puts it, in this hardline view, 'no Engager was worthy of being part of the covenanting nation'.[18]

But what did this mean in parishes in the covenanting heartlands, where admittance to the covenant had been for nearly a decade central to spiritual as well as social inclusion? This was put to the test in December 1648, when the Ayr presbytery received the aforementioned commission from the General Assembly that directed parish ministers to hold communal renewals of the Solemn League and Covenant, while taking 'special care to purge their sessione of such as have been guiltie in that sinfall engagement with duke hamiltoune' during that summer.[19] By contrast, those on the sessions who had remained steadfast in loyalty to the parliamentary army and in opposition to the king were to be named and applauded. This order occasioned a good deal of debate in Ayr about the reasons behind support for the Engagement at the local level. Events of the final month of 1648 make clear how neat political divides, which might exist in theory, were rarely clear-cut in practice, even in the 'radical southwest'.

On 11 December 1648, Adair began questioning members of the session about their support for the Engagement. John Osborne, provost of the town and patriarch of a powerful merchant family, was first up. The minister asked whether that past summer he did 'subscribe a band obligding the town to put forth their proportion of men ... to assist the unlawfull engadgment'.[20] The previous week, ten men from the town had appeared before the session, accused of their service with engager forces. When questioned, they explained they had been 'forced and driven' as sheep to participate – this was in no way something they had done willingly, but at the orders of the town council.[21] Osborne confessed to his compliance in issuing this order, explaining that 'he had no sooner done it but he wes sorrowful for it'. With a detectable air of frustration, Adair chastised the provost for 'forcing and takeing out of their beds these poore souldieors' for such an ungodly cause. Yet Osborne maintained that this was far from his doing alone – the town council, under immense pressure from engager leaders, had voted on and approved the move. They were, as a body, in the wrong.[22]

The problem was that, as we have seen in previous years, there existed considerable overlap between the men who sat on the town council and served on the session – indeed, half of the elders were also council members. In accordance with orders from the General Assembly, they were removed from their positions. What is more, until they made satisfactory repentance for their actions, they were also debarred from the two most essential, public acts of belonging in the community: participation in the Lord's Supper and renewal of the covenant. This must have been a strange turn of events for the men accustomed to issuing orders of repentance themselves; soon, they would be judged by the remaining members of the session as well as the ordinary people in the pews. Given the complexity of the situation, Adair decided the session would reconvene the following day to 'hear the offer of repentance and satisfaction' from their recently expelled brethren.[23] The events of this meeting are worth examining at some length, given what they reveal about the relationships between the elders, ministers, and townsmen as well as the fundamental commitment to community concord even amid great division and debate.

When Ayr's rump session met the next day, 12 December 1648, they first heard from the members of the town council – those formerly on the session and otherwise – who presented a declaration of their grief for agreeing to levy men of the community in support of the Engagement. As they explained, 'in the hour of tentation', when '1500 comanders and souldours were lying open this burgh the space of twelve dayes', they heard pressing concerns from members of the community 'upon whom the said quartering wes grievous'. The presence of the engager army was taxing both the morale and the resources of the town, and its leader – the Earl of Callendar – urged members of the council to give 'oblidgment for putting out our proportion Ayr men or money', presumably so that the army could more quickly be resupplied and move on. Now, faced with punishment from the kirk's ruling body, they 'unfainedlie' renounced their previous course of action.[24]

In response, Adair presented the men with an alternative declaration of repentance, one that more fully, to his mind, constituted an adequate apology for their 'wicked course' of action, and encouraged them to sign it:

> Whee undersubscraybing being conveinced in our conscience doe from our hearts declair our unfained repentance and grief for subscribing ane unlawfull band to put out our proportion of men to the assistance of the unlawfull engagement against the kingdome of Ingland. The which subscription we abhorre, disclaime and renounce and all other degries of defecation condemned by the generall assemblie and there commissioners promising by the grace of god heirafter in tyme of tentation to adhere more firmlie to our solemne league and Covenant.[25]

It seems clear that the minister was reaching for a solution that would allow the men of the session and council – critical figures of leadership in the town – to fully take part in the essential rituals of kirk and community, but he was also invested in satisfying the dictates of higher ecclesiastical authorities. Indeed, it is notable just how often Adair specified that the course of action he was taking was according to guidance from the presbytery or the General Assembly. Still, the guilty cohort refused to subscribe the minister's offered declaration of repentance, stating that they had only acted to diffuse a difficult situation. Adair specified that Osborne and councilman Robert Gordon would be required to sign it if they wanted to be admitted to the covenant, because they had previously run afoul of the kirk in their 'former compliance with James Graham', the Marquis of Montrose and Scotland's preeminent royalist leader.[26] The two men were clearly on thin ice. But to 'eshew division and contention', Adair with the rest of the session agreed to see if the presbytery would accept the initial statement of apology from the council. In another special meeting the following day, the affair finally concluded when, after some debate about how to proceed, the men who had violated the rules 'compeared and offered to make publict and particular acknowledgment of their offenses' so that they could be admitted to a resubscription of the Solemn League and Covenant, an offer the session accepted.[27]

Tensions and tempers had been, at least for the time being, assuaged in the town, but pronounced divisions in the covenanter movement would remain. On 6 January 1649, Adair delivered a revealing sermon on the fifth chapter of Galatians in which he warned his congregation of the abounding deceits of those who would attempt to lure them away from the godly course. Voices contrary to the kirk, he warned, came 'not from God calling yow, bot from elsewhair to witt from the deceaverers, from yor owne inconstancy, and from the divill. Ergo this persuasion is to be rejected'.[28] On 23 January 1649, the Scottish Parliament made formal this rejection of those who disagreed with the hardliners by passing the Act of Classes, which excluded those who had supported the Engagement from public office and ensured the kirk party's civil as well as spiritual dominance.[29] A week later, the English Parliament executed Charles I, a shocking act that was uniformly denounced in Scotland, even among the staunchest opponents of the monarch of both British kingdoms. The kirk party's informal alliance with the parliamentarians was severed along with the king's head.

Adair indirectly but unsubtly characterised this alarming turn of events in a June 1649 sermon on the Epistle of Jude in which he warned that 'the divills ministers whill never rest' from disputing the true faith; as such, 'it is necessary to all true believers to have ware with this irreconcilably'. He also railed against those who were 'adversaries to all civill and politick government, bearing no kynd of magistracie or authoritie bot heaping together reproachfull faulty railings and scoffings against these honorable ordinances of god of which sort the fanatick anabaptists our age doeth see evin to this day'.[30] Referencing the spectre of anabaptism was a well-worn and imprecise trope, but his message to his flock was clear: 'where ther is danger of infection and contagion ... so also we are to eshew the company and to depart from such libertines given to such carnall pollutiones'.[31] Couched in his attack on the supposed 'libertines' of past and present was a clear message about the dangers of separatism running rampant south of the border. Adair's militaristic, polarised language reflected ongoing conflicts in Scotland and the British Isles, but it also portended the coming of a new chapter of warfare to Ayr.

In what was interpreted by the leaders of the new English Commonwealth as a clear pretence for war, the Scottish Parliament declared the recently deceased's son Charles II in February 1649. After many months of contentious negotiation, on 1 May 1650 the new king took the covenant, signed the Treaty of Breda, and arrived in Scotland in June. Adding kindling to the already combustible situation, in late July 1650, Cromwell's New Model Army invaded Scotland. Adair's message to his congregation throughout these months demonstrates his mounting unease about the situation. In May 1650, he told them that when his people are fearful, God reminds them to 'believ my covenant and let faith expel your feare, that so ye be not driven from yor duty'. Here Adair surely meant the covenant of grace, but to audience and minister alike, the idea of the covenant had become a totalising stand-in for the divine and earthly promises made from the days of Christ to their present days of crisis. It was meant to be both a comfort to those within its remit and an incentive to godly action. In June, Adair's remarks about the evolving political situation became more pointed. As part of a series of sermons on Psalms 89, he noted that 'kings and rulers of the earth ar to be warned of the danger of opposing of Christ and of wronging his kirk and kingdom'; moreover, fierce judgements awaited 'people following evill rulers in their sin'. Jesus, he reminded his audience, was 'Lord and King and sole governor of his kirk'.[32]

In his references to Charles II, Adair treaded lightly; in his condemnation of Cromwell later that summer, however, he dug in his heels. The leadership of the Commonwealth, he claimed, stood for 'all confusion both in church and stat' and for 'tolleration of all abominationes under pretenc of liberties of the people and libertie of consienc'; the consequence was the establishment of 'their babel and the kingdome of the divill'. The Scottish kirk, by contrast, fought for 'the doctrine discipline and government of Jesus Christ'. Perhaps most astoundingly, he told his audience that 'the divill and witches favour Cromwell and his cause' – a message that carried additional resonance at a moment when the kirk was engaging, as we will see, in an intense drive to eradicate witchcraft. Adair was travelling with the covenanter forces when he composed this particular sermon – it is dated 17 August 1650, during which time he was serving as an army chaplain at the behest of the presbytery – though it is unclear whether he delivered it then or when he returned to Ayr later that month. But his words read, at times, as a rallying of troops at a moment of hardship. He encouraged his audience, be they soldier or civilian, to 'beliv under hop and against hop yea against all imaginable difficulties' and to hold fast to the 'inevitablness of the ruine of gods enemyes and the enemies of his kirk'.[33]

Adair's increasingly vehement words epitomise the hardliner concerns about another king whose godliness seemed suspect and commitment to the covenanting project insincere, as well as the threat posed by the religious policies of Cromwell. Amid a context of anxiety verging on apocalyptic, the kirk party attempted to purge the army of anyone who did not meet their metrics for true loyalty to the covenants.[34] In hindsight, this was a massive misstep. On 3 September 1650, Cromwell's army marched north and met the covenanter forces at Dunbar on Scotland's southeastern coast.[35] The Scots were outnumbered, ill prepared, and thoroughly routed by the New Model Army. The loss was significant – thousands were killed, injured, or imprisoned – and as early as 18 September, the Ayr presbytery was exhorting their brethren to take up a collection for the 'lame and wounded souldiers'.[36] Arguably, though, the loss of morale for many covenanters was even greater. In some ways, the kirk party had sown its own fate by expelling thousands of experienced men from the Scottish army in wartime. But to men like Adair, it seemed clear that God was punishing Scotland for cooperation with a fundamentally ungodly king.[37]

By late autumn 1650, the shards that remained of national covenanter unity fractured even further as the most radical members of the movement – many of whom came from the southwest – issued a statement of protest known as a 'remonstrance', addressed to the Committee of Estates, the governing body that ruled while parliament was not sitting.[38] In it, they blamed the disaster of Dunbar on those who had supported negotiating with Charles II in the first place before having seen evidence of genuine repentance for his former acts against the covenants. Adair captured the intensity of these sentiments in some October sermon notes in which he wrote that 'unfaithfull and treacherous bretherin', in the 'tyme of Ziones calamitie', show their true colours by siding with the enemies of the kirk – which, he added, 'is very apparent in our days wherin hypocrits syd with malignants and sectaries'.[39] Tensions flared even further when, in December 1650, the Commission of the Kirk, which handled the Scottish church's public affairs, issued a series of resolutions that opened the door for those who had supported the Engagement – and even the royalist cause itself – to be allowed back into the army. The logic was that the Scottish government was morally and practically obliged to 'employ all lawful means' to combat Cromwell's army, now poised to invade the country. The radical faction that opposed such resolutions became known as 'protestors'; Adair, like many of his fellow ministers in the southwest, was among them.[40]

Often, when historians think about the fracturing of covenanter unity, they focus on prominent examples of fracas between the opposing factions.[41] And there is a good reason to do so: these conflicts were serious business. But in some – likely many – cases, communal and kinship ties complicated and at times transcended political division. Adair's own personal life, despite the bite in some of his sermons, testifies to this. In early summer 1651, he married Janet Boyd, daughter of a minister and member of a prominent Ayrshire family. Her sister, Margaret, had wed Robert Douglas in 1646; Adair, a key protestor voice, and Douglas, the leading resolutioner and moderator of the General Assembly, may have stood on opposite ideological sides, but they were bound together by marriage.[42] A letter Adair wrote to Douglas in April 1651, shortly before his marriage, exemplifies these dynamics. He had apparently written to the moderator three times before and was growing concerned that he had not received a reply. He expressed his hope that Douglas would 'spair som lytle tyme from mor weightie business' to send 'a lyn or two' to Adair and his bride-to-be. Adair then went on to say that 'Union in the Lord is heartily desired by all heir who ar accounted divyders and separtists', and he signed the letter with 'I am your loving brother'.[43] This does not read as mere convention or nicety; instead, Adair hoped to mend fences and clarify his desire for peace with an old friend and almost relative. Such mollifying impulses also played out at the local level, as evidenced by the minister, session, and town council's moves to set aside their disagreements in order to keep the communal threads from unravelling.

There was simply too much business to be done to allow things to further deteriorate.

Throughout this period, the hardline covenanters holding the reins of church and state waged an emphatic campaign against the sins that had caused Scotland so much hardship over the previous decade. Their efforts were as intense as their national dominance was short. For the community of Ayr, this campaign shaped lived experiences through three of its core components: political turmoil, which could breed confusion and reshape interpersonal dynamics; a wave of disciplinary initiatives in the parish emanating from both the local session and the national kirk; and increased attention to certain types of dramatic and highly publicised crimes. The men and women of the town were already accustomed to and variously invested in a fervent culture of covenanting, but the stakes for godliness had risen along with the most radical regime ever to control the Scottish institutions of power. Moreover, the resubscription of the Solemn League and Covenant in 1648 had clarified the strict obligations of a covenanted community, and there was little room for error. Against the backdrop of warfare, the atmosphere must have been combustible.

The campaign against sin

The sins that dominate the pages of the Ayr session minutes between 1648 and 1651 include fornication, drunkenness, blasphemy, breach of sabbath, and general scandal. Some of the women of the town seem to have been a source of particular frustration for the session, beyond regular cases of sexual scandal. Jean Wan, for example, was cited for calling Isobell Caldwell 'a drunk herlot'; Janet Boyd blasphemed that if 'there were a devill in hell shee would raise him'; a witness reported he had seen Janet Kirk 'clapping with hir hands and stamping with hir feet in the open streits' even as two members of the session told her to be quiet and go home; and John Boyle complained that his sister, Christian Boyle, had repeatedly accused him of 'pishing' in the neighbour's milk.[44] As I have written elsewhere, while covenanting offered Scottish women new opportunities for protest and spiritual creativity, the disciplinary regime it wrought was fundamentally patriarchal and disproportionately affected on women through its campaign against sexual sins and witchcraft.[45] Yet it was not only women who ran afoul of the strict dictates of the kirk. In February 1651, the session lamented that many of the young men and women of the town had been up all night 'drinking and dancing promiscuslie' at a local wedding; the groom, Alexander Osburne, had to make public repentance for his 'drinking, fiddling, and dancing' the whole night through.[46] The details of other reported sins demonstrate just how interconnected the seaside town was not only with broader Scottish affairs but also the wider world. In April 1650, for example, Janet Burns stood accused of having sex with Patrick Linton, a trooper stationed nearby. There was initially some question about the nature of the crime given that Burns had, at one point, been married to a sailor, but witnesses confirmed that he had been taken captive by the 'Turks' to Argyre some years prior, where he had died and been buried. This was thus a simple case of fornication, and Burns was sentenced to make public repentance over the course of at least two sabbath days.[47]

This was, as anyone who has perused session minutes from across Scotland will note, standard fare. Yet in this moment of political turmoil when the covenanting project was at once on the ascendant and at stake, there was an urgency to the campaign against sin – in Ayr and elsewhere – that remains palpable to modern readers.[48] This was due, at least in part, to the enthusiasm for repentance that followed the country's mid-1640s brush with plague, the rapidly changing circumstances of war, and the zealous national leadership. Indeed, the turmoil at the top of Scottish society had long local legs, and ordinary people also grappled with politicised divisions between friends and neighbours. Because participation in the Engagement was treated as a 'notorious' sin against the covenant, often situated alongside a range of more quotidian violations of norms, it was very visible to all in the community. In April 1649, for example, the session debarred from taking communion six men for 'their notour scandalls threw the unlawful engagement', ten people deemed 'grosslie ignorant' of the gospel, and five people labelled 'commom drunkards'.[49] While at the national level, the kirk party took steps to bar former-engagers from public office or service, kirk sessions hoped to elicit sincere repentance from local residents followed by full reintegration into the community. As late as February 1650, the congregation watched men like Alexander Lockhart and Robert McKinnon make public repentance for their 'lait unlawfull engagment against Ingland' and be readmitted to the covenant and, accordingly, the spiritual community.[50] The kirk session records also offer glimpses of the extent to which ordinary people were thinking about the political issues that animated national debates. Perhaps the most detailed example comes from the summer of 1650, when several witnesses accused John Geoffray of blasphemy. According to reports, Geoffray had been drinking with John Craig, a tailor, and his son, when a neighbour overheard them in 'a contest about king Christ and king Charles'. Craig had challenged Geoffray for 'his malignancie for joyning in the unlawfull engagement', to which Geoffray replied 'that he had never don Christ wrong bot Christ had don him wrong'. The session ordered the apparent blasphemer to make public repentance, and they also referred him to the magistrate for additional punishment.[51]

We can imagine the scene: two men, over drinks, start to talk politics. Things get heated, voices are raised, neighbours hear, and soon, a significant blasphemy is uttered: that Christ, or God, had erred in some way. What is telling about this episode is the image of one ordinary man chastising another for involvement in the Engagement, and the framing of the issue as 'king Christ vs. king Charles', which mirrored the view of the staunch covenanters whose influence was especially dominant in the southwest. Messages from the pulpit as well as public confessions for participation in the 'unlawful engagement' had not only been understood by parishioners; ordinary people in Ayr could also make up their own minds about the conflict and what it meant for their own covenanter identities. Of course, this could also mean the spread of erroneous opinions – that is, additional 'sins' – for the session to combat.

The chaotic period between 1648 and 1651 generated renewed disciplinary initiatives at the local level as well as from the General Assembly. At times the Ayr session's own innovations anticipated what was coming next from the national kirk – a parish to centre-of-power pipeline that is unsurprising given the dominance of radicals at both levels. In November 1648, Adair and the elders convened to 'lay to heart' the 'sundrie scandalls and scandalous cariages of divers persons old and young of both sexes' in the burgh. Complaints included: neglecting family worship, not instructing children and servants in the 'heads of religion', 'drinking unto drunkenness', neighbourly brawls, the proliferation of 'idle persons living without callings', and young women living in houses alone.[52] To combat this proliferation of further sin, the session passed an order stipulating that the congregation would be carved into nineteen divisions, each overseen by an elder and a deacon who would 'deliver the directions for familie worshipe to the families within their severall divisions and take special care that the said directions be obeyed and practiced by themselves and all the rest of the families'.[53]

If this sounds familiar, that is because this act closely echoed a similar one passed a few months prior to the subscription of the Solemn League and Covenant.[54] The difference was not in the details, but in the context. In 1643, the covenanters in Ayr and beyond had been, for the most part, united against the common enemies of popery and royalist interference with the kirk. Then, aspiration and idealism drove initiatives to reform local communities. Five years later, however, one gets a sense that the session was attempting to claw back some semblance of control by imposing disciplinary order on an increasingly disorderly body. And indeed, in the first half of 1649, the radical cohort in control of the Scottish Parliament passed a series of acts targeted at eliminating fornication, incest, adultery, blasphemy, drunkenness, swearing, and witchcraft, among others.[55] Given the divisiveness of Engagement and the attempts to maintain unity amid the recent protester–resolutioner split, the members of the Ayr session also renewed attempts to hold themselves to the highest standards possible. When one of their rank, William Mitchell, was cited in December 1650 for frequent drunkenness, the elders agreed that the next meeting day they should make 'particular inquirie among themselves concerning ther carriag and scandales'.[56] As draconian as hardline covenanters can often seem to the modern reader, they were not hypocrites: they eschewed bad behaviour and backsliding among their own ranks as much as among those under their charge.

During this period of renewal of the covenants and the passage of reformist acts, the discipline of ordinary men and women in Ayr increasingly centred on oath-taking and the making of pronouncements that obliged individuals in some way to their community.[57] Two examples are especially telling. In March 1651, the session called and accused Robert Alexander and Elizabeth Miller of fornication, an interrogation that quickly devolved into a case of he-said, she-said. Alexander admitted that he had 'put his hand to hir and fand hir over readie' but that the 'terror of god and inabilitie' had prevented him from any carnal dealing – he had been rendered impotent in that moment. Miller confirmed this story, but also explained that Alexander returned two weeks later, and over the course of their interactions, they had intercourse three times, leading her to become pregnant. Unsure who was telling the truth, the session decided that both should be 'refered to their oaths'; Alexander refused to swear to his version of events, while Miller was from the outset willing, and it was thus her word that won the day.[58] Another example of the use of oaths by the session occurred in the case of Margaret Murchie and William Logan, two parishioners who were married to other people but apparently spending an unseemly amount of time together. The minister and elders had repeatedly exhorted them to avoid each other, and while both insisted no 'act' had occurred between the two of them, they continued to be seen together, much to the exasperation of their spouses. To address the issue, the session persuaded both to 'bind themselves' by subscribing an oath that would guarantee avoidance of future scandal. In it, they acknowledged their 'our hynous sin, that wheras we, by too much conversing togidder and familiaritie' and promised before God and the session that they should 'not be found in on anothers companie, other privatlie or apairt' under pain of full punishment as adulterers.[59] In this culture of covenanting, the taking of oaths brought greater personal and communal salience to otherwise unremarkable disciplinary directives.

The search for a second minister

The impact of reformist initiatives in Ayr was somewhat impeded by Adair's involvement in high-profile national affairs that took him away from the town for extended periods of time, during which the gears of local discipline kept turning, but only just. For example, at its meeting on 9 June 1651, the session ordained six men accused of sabbath-breaking to appear again the next day 'when the minister come home' to receive their punishment.[60] When Adair was in Ayr, the session held lengthy, jam-packed meetings, playing catch up and trying to resolve long-delayed cases that had become more convoluted over time. For the townspeople, this meant that relatively quiet periods in the kirk, with few displays of public repentance and guest sermons from visiting ministers, were followed by intense bursts of public testimony, trial, and confession.

Adair's absences were compounded by Ayr's ongoing inability to attract a colleague minister to labour alongside him. In December 1647, in the wake of the town's latest brush with and deliverance from the plague, the Ayr presbytery took into their consideration the 'the weghtines and number of the charge of the paroch' and recommitted themselves to seeking a second minister for the congregation.[61] In May of the following year, the presbytery received a passionate supplication from the 'session towne counsall and communitie' of Ayr 'making mentione of the great prejudice there ministerie susteaned by want of a collegue to Mr Wm Adaire these four yeares bypast' and noting the 'great paines and diligence' all parties involved had devoted to recruiting another pastor. In hopes of a solution, the men of the presbytery set their sights on George Hutchinson, minister in nearby Colmonell parish.[62] Given the 'eminency of the place as greatnes of the charge, being the chief towne of the shyre and prebrie seat and a place of great resorte both of countrey men and stangers of all sorte', they asked that Hutchinson transport himself and his family to Ayr by the coming fall.[63] This, however, never happened – according to Robert Baillie, Hutchinson preferred to go to Burntisland or Edinburgh rather 'than to joine with Mr William Adair'.[64] During the May 1649 visitation by representatives of the presbytery – a regular practice in all parishes to ensure that religious instruction and discipline was being properly meted out – the elders reported that Adair preached satisfactorily on the sabbath and once during the week, but 'earnestly requested the prebrie to concurre with and assisten them' in the recruitment of a colleague minister.[65] This need would become even more pressing as Adair's role in national leadership grew; in July and August of 1650, for example, the minister was chosen by the presbytery to accompany the Scottish army during the ill-fated Dunbar campaign, and he was accordingly away from the town for much of that autumn.[66]

Between 1645 and 1651, the presbytery – at times with the explicit backing of the General Assembly – called at least five men to Ayr, all of whom declined; the parish would not have a second minister until the appointment of William Eccles in 1656. They had used, as a July 1648 commission put it, 'all menies possibill' to recruit a colleague, to no avail, and were in a truly 'lamentabill condition'.[67] When Adair was away, the session continued its essential work of providing poor relief, issuing bands of marriage, and hearing complaints, but discipline had to be put on the backburner without their leader present and with no obvious second in command.[68] This situation was untenable and, in the minds of the leaders of Ayr, getting ridiculous. After all, Ayr was a fairly populous and prominent burgh, a plum position for many ministers and one that had previously attracted the clerical cream of the crop. Though the recruitment challenges were likely due to a combination of the uncertainty of sufficient remuneration and the shadow of Adair's radical reputation, the leaders of Ayr attributed the difficulty, like so much else, to divine displeasure. Adair, too, took to lamenting this situation in his sermons: in one composed in the beginning of the 1650s, he reflected upon the heavy weight of his ministry, writing that 'ministers are subject to many troubles and sufferings in the preaching and for the preaching of the gospel' which may lead to them 'to ane infirme and bas externall condition'.[69] The lone minister was exhausted from a combination of daily discipline and ecclesiastical disagreement, pastoral burdens only increased by Adair's first major dealings with one of early modern Scotland's most notorious sins: witchcraft.

Witchcraft abounding

For committed covenanters, the proliferation of witches was the latest and greatest example of the abounding of sin during the chaotic mid-century. Witchcraft was, at its core, a crime rooted in relationships and reputations, accusations of sins both mundane and monstrous, many of which predated the dominance of the kirk party.[70] Ayr had its own history of witch-hunting that spanned generations: in the final decades of the sixteenth century, costs associated with the execution of several witches were recorded in the burgh's account books. These make for a cold and gruesome read. In 1595, an entry was made for 'the coals, cords, tar-barrels, and other graith [materials] that burnt Marion Grief'; in 1599, the town paid the local hangman four pounds Scots for the execution of Janet Young, first by rope and then by fire.[71] But like much of Scotland – and Britain as a whole – Ayr saw its witch-hunting heyday in the mid-seventeenth century, amid zealous lay and ecclesiastical leadership and the turmoil of war and revolution.[72]

The case of Janet Smaillie is instructive in situating the hunts of the mid-century within a wider framework of Scottish witch-hunting. In 1613, she had appeared before the Ayr session accused of 'filthie slandrous speiches towardis hir neighbouris'.[73] What she said, the records do not tell us, but if similar cases are any indication, she might have accused a man of being a thief or his wife of being an adulteress. Or perhaps her words even featured sexually explicit language or taking the Lord's name in vain. Whatever she said, it was serious: in punishment, she was hauled before the town's 'Fish Cross' – the stone marker at the centre of Ayr's bustling fish market – where a small, spiked instrument was placed into her mouth, 'according to a former act given out aganes hir'. She had, apparently, been a long-time blasphemer and general thorn in the side of the kirk. A 1621 case in the session records tells how Smaillie had repeatedly been imprisoned for 'numerous musbehauioris to sendrie persones', had been 'convicted for intending to poyson hir selff', and was eventually banished from the town.[74]

Smaillie's tragic story did not end there. She had made amends enough to be resettled in the town, but in 1630 she appeared before the burgh court for the 'oppin profession and practices of witchcraft and sorcerie', an accusation altogether unsurprising for a woman with Smaillie's sordid reputation. Her punishment – this time, anyway – was to be dragged and flogged through the town, burned on the cheek as a mark of her crime, and banished yet again, this time for 'all the dayis of her lyftyme', only to return upon 'pane of death'.[75] And that appears to be what happened. In May 1650, an old woman by the same name – and almost certainly the same woman – was in Ayr, and in jail. There she died and found no dignity in death. Adair, who presently had on his hands a rash of witchcraft cases, ordered Smaillie's corpse to be carried on a sled to the gallows and 'brunt in asches' – a belated execution for her devilish crime.[76]

Smaillie's fate, and the other accused witches of Ayr in the early 1650s, should be understood as a local chapter of a nationwide hunt that peaked between the summer of 1649 and the autumn of 1650, raging until the beginnings of the Cromwellian occupation redirected the ecclesiastical establishment's attention. Like many of Scotland's witch hunts, those in Ayr originated in reports to the kirk session and received commissions to proceed from authorities in Edinburgh who were equally concerned with eradicating the scourge of witchcraft. In the first months of 1649, the dogmatic parliament passed a dozen acts tackling a wide range of sins, including witchcraft.[77] Decisive action attended this legislative zeal, and while we have only estimates for exact numbers of executions, 1649 was perhaps the deadliest year in the history of Scottish witch-hunting.[78] As Paula Hughes notes, we ought to view the 1649–50 hunts as the culmination of 'ten years of dominance of political and religious life by Presbyterian radicals with apocalyptic visions and an impending sense that the nation's troubles resulted from the scourge of the ungodly threatening to subvert a covenanted and godly nation'.[79] The demonic pact – by this point implicit in the concept of witchcraft, at least in the minds of the elites overseeing the trials – was more than an inversion of covenants; it represented the ultimate betrayal of the covenanted community.

The first two years of the 1650s comprised a particularly intense period for witch-hunting in the burgh and surrounding areas. Moreover, this was Adair's first real brush with witchcraft, and he surely felt, in this moment of general anxiety and upheaval, that he had both a moral duty and something to prove. Several years earlier, in 1643, the presbytery of Ayr had requested a warrant to try town resident Susanna Shang for 'the sinne of witchcraft', but beyond this, the first decade of the minister's tenure had been notably witch-free.[80] This changed dramatically in the spring of 1650, when the members of the presbytery took into 'serious consideration with great greif of heart that horrible and exorable sin of witchcraft at this tyme so much abounding in the land'. Every minister was exhorted to be 'faithfull and carefull' in searching out witches in their own parishes and bringing them to justice.[81] A week later, the neighbouring Irvine presbytery, 'finding that the sin of witchraft was growing daillie' and lamenting that many 'hidden works of darkness was discovered' in its own parishes, requested the Committee of Estates grant a commission to try the said evil-doers.[82] Usually, such a request would have gone to the Privy Council, but during the 1640s the institution was diminished and largely supplanted in its duties by the Committee, a governing body greatly influenced (if not controlled) by the wishes of the radical covenanters. The General Assembly also took on an increasingly large role in the hunting of witches, working with parliament to empower the localities to root out the most egregious of sins.[83]

By early May, the intensity of the situation was apparent to the central authorities: on the first day of the month, the Ayr presbytery received record of the confessions of five women, four of them residents of the town, for 'that horrid and devilish sin of sorcery'.[84] They moved quickly to obtain a commission for their trial and punishment, and their request was followed by a letter from Adair to Robert Douglas, moderator of the General Assembly and his future brother-in-law. After beginning with reference to recent victories during the war against Cromwell's forces – victories that were soon to be very short lived – he asked that Douglas work with the Committee of Estates to get a commission to try and execute the witches of Ayr with all possible haste. The minister feared that the continuation of 'the lat malignancies and opposition of some to the work of god in this plac, hes flowed from a deiper root than the comune corription of nature'. His words suggest a double meaning, referring not only to witchcraft, but to those 'malignants' who had joined the Engagement. Satan, he implied, was clearly at work and had a myriad of weapons at his disposal.[85] Parliament granted Adair's wish for a trial on 18 May 1650, and by early June, the burgh jail held several accused witches and anticipated more to come.[86]

For the spiritual leadership of Ayr, the eradication of witches was the latest and perhaps greatest in a long line of threats to their authority, influence, and ability to guide their godly community. In the summer of 1650, as the number of accused grew, the kirk session agreed to appoint daily an elder and deacon to 'oversie' the prisoners as they awaited trial in order to 'exhort them to confessione and to pray with them to God'.[87] Long days and nights lay ahead for the session – not to mention the accused – as appointed members were to watch over the purported witches in twenty-four-hour shifts and to 'tak all paines for the furtherance of so good a work'.[88] We ought to understand the desire for confession, and the explicit involvement of the session in procuring one, not just as a means to conviction, but also as part of a broader emphasis in post-Reformation Scotland on the importance of confession for communal purity and cohesion. Indeed, many of those currently awaiting trial in Ayr's jail had already confessed to witchcraft before the town provost and other local magistrates; what the elders and minister sought, then, was not so much a confession of crime as sincere acknowledgement of sin. As evidenced by the town's reaction to the plague only three years prior or the repentance rituals that preceded the resubscription of the Solemn League and Covenant, the importance of a confession lay in its ability to keep the wrath of God at bay and the godly community intact.

Though we do not have records of what happened to those swept up in the local witch hunts of 1650, we do know the fates of three women accused the following year: Janet Sawer, Janet Slowane, and Elspeth Cuninghame. The accusations against these women began sometime in the summer or fall of 1651, and the case of Janet Sawer, which eventually involved formal testimony from many witnesses and seventeen separate charges, exemplifies both general trends in Scottish witch-hunting and the mid-century mood. Many allegations against her centred on old communal rivalries and grievances. She had been seen, for example, with her arms around the neck of a horse that belonged to a neighbour who she had often quarrelled with. Within twenty days, the horse had died.[89] The neighbour, John McConnell, did not fare much better, growing so feverish and faint 'that he was altogidder waik and unable for workeing and sumtymes knew not wher he was'.[90] Harm to horses was a particular theme of her case: she had, at some point in 1649, asked a young man to move his three horses blocking the entrance of a close, and when he refused, she yelled at him in anger. One of his horses then 'lay downe seik and eat no moir', and within a month, all were dead, though the local farrier found no evidence of 'ordinar disease of horses'.[91]

In late spring 1649, when Sawer had argued with a neighbour couple and shaken their baby in anger, the mother had cried out 'Lord save my chyld, avoyd the Sathan, doune the stair witche theife!', and Sawer fled, calling out 'many injurious words' as she did.[92] Soon after, the family faced an extended tragedy involving wounded children, a miscarriage, and impoverishment. Other charges of harmful magic are more unusual: Sawer supposedly raised a storm to destroy a ship that was stopping at Ayr en route to Barbados. The evidence? She had been seen floating in the ocean near the shore, sucking the air like an udder. Ayr's seaside location was at the heart of another charge against Sawer: that she had predicted 'haird newes' for the husband of a neighbour she had been arguing with, and in a voyage begun immediately thereafter, the man was 'taken by a pirret and keipeit in prison for ane yeir'. Her reputation for the 'devilish art' was thus clearly well-established, and it was further confirmed by Helen Girvan, a local 'confessing witch now burnt'.[93]

But perhaps most damning, especially at a time when clerical leadership was most emphatic about purity and compliance, Sawer challenged the authority of the kirk. Some years back, she had apparently cursed a searcher who found her absent from church on a Sunday and threatened to report her to the session. The following Monday he fell ill, and just before his death declared Sawer 'a devil out of hell'.[94] She had also quarrelled with William Smith, the church reader, over rent payments; despite warnings that she should 'meddell not with that man for he is a man of the kirk', she reportedly cursed him with malicious words near her home. Shortly after this, when Smith was on his way to visit Adair, he passed by the same spot where Sawer had cursed him, and a 'great pak of wooll' fell directly upon his head and 'dang him to the ground'. He met his maker soon after.[95]

Things did not bode well for Sawer, who checked all the boxes of harming neighbours, children, animals, the economy, and the church. What is more, many people genuinely felt afraid of her, and these fears were surely exacerbated by the fact that their minister increasingly railed against the dangers of witches. As we have seen, Adair explicitly connected the current Anglo-Scots war to the sin of witchcraft when he explained in June 1650 that 'the divill and witches favour Cromwell and his cause'. From Ayr's pulpit the following summer, he told his parishioners that 'witchcrafts ar a caus of gods fearce wreaths'. What was more, in his mind, the kirk's perennial fornication problem was bound up with the sin of witchcraft: 'Whoordomes and witchcrafts go communly together'. 'Witchcraft', he explained, 'is a fruit of the flesh', and the 'sin of whoordome prevailing is introductis to the others'.[96] In other words, sexual crimes were a gateway to even graver offences like witchcraft, and at the core of both we find a pronounced anxiety about 'disordered' or unbridled sexuality, especially among women.[97] Not only, then, did the actions of someone like Sawer invite corporeal and economic harm to the community through maleficium; the combination of the notably gendered offences perceived to be so prevailing in the town provoked God's deadly wrath. There was much to fear indeed.

But on 7 October 1651, for reasons still unclear, Hew Kennedy, the former provost of the town and a member of the parliamentary commission for witchcraft set up in 1650, joined with two former baillies in making 'protestationne as magistratis for [the] exoneratione' of Sawer and her fellow accused.[98] Kennedy's request was denied, and in July of the following year, a commission was granted for the trial of the prisoners. Their fates looked grim. If an October 1652 report on local witchcraft cases from William Clarke, an English statesman in Scotland, is any indication, horrific torture involving whipping, burning, and the strappado awaited them.[99] Yet it would be seven years before these women would have their days in court. A new and profound sign of God's displeasure, one that proved an even greater logistical challenge than witchcraft, had by then captured the full attention of the town and country's covenanter leadership: the Cromwellian occupation. As the Convention of Royal Burghs reported ominously in the summer of 1650, the 'unexpectit aproches of the Inglisch armies both by sea and land' posed an imminent danger to 'kirk and kingdome', 'threatning no les then the ruyne of both, except the Lord prevent the samyn'.[100] The threat was existential, and the possible deliverance was divine. Only the former seemed assured.

Notes

1 National Records of Scotland (NRS), Ayr kirk session minutes, CH2/751/3/1, fo. 135r.
2 CH2/751/3/1, fo. 138r.
3 CH2/751/3/1, fo. 139v.
4 On the financing and general provisions for war in Scotland, see, for example, Laura A.M. Stewart, 'Military Power and the Scottish Burghs, 1625–1651', *Journal of Early Modern History*, 15 (2011), 59–82; Laura A.M. Stewart, 'Fiscal Revolution and State Formation in Mid Seventeenth-Century Scotland', *Historical Research*, 84:225 (2011), 443–69; David Stevenson, 'The Financing of the Cause of the Covenants 1638–51', *Scottish Historical Review*, 51 (1972), 89–123; and Pete Edwards, 'Arming and Equipping the Covenanting Armies 1638–1651', in Steve Murdoch and Andrew Mackillop (eds), *Fighting for Identity: Scottish Military Experience c. 1550–1900* (Leiden: Brill, 2002), pp. 239–64. As Stewart points out in 'Military Power and the Scottish Burghs', the size of the armies raised and maintained in Scotland during the civil war period, as well as the length and extent of continual service, 'represented a fundamental discontinuity with Scotland's former military experiences' (at p. 70).
5 Stewart, 'Military Powers', 79. For a detailed chronicling of the losses during the war in one town, see John Barrett and Alastair Mitchell, *Elgin's Love-Gift: Civil War in Scotland and the Depositions of 1646* (Chichester: Phillimore, 2007).

6 For a summary of an ongoing debate about gender and witchcraft, see Julian Goodare, 'Women and the Witch-Hunt in Scotland', *Social History*, 23:3 (October 1998), 288–308.
7 On witch-hunting in revolutionary Britain, see Brian P. Levack, *Witch-Hunting in Scotland: Law, Politics and Religion* (New York: Routledge, 2008), chapter 4; and Malcolm Gaskill, *Witchfinders: A Seventeenth-Century English Tragedy* (Cambridge: Cambridge University Press, 2007).
8 See, for example, the intense trials in Würzburg, Bamberg, and Cologne in the late 1620s through mid 1630s, which coincided with economic and agricultural distress as well as the violence of war. For an introduction to these hunts, see Thomas Robisheaux, 'The German Witch Trials', in Brian P. Levack (ed.), *The Oxford Handbook of Witchcraft in Early Modern Europe and Colonial America* (Oxford: Oxford University Press, 2013), pp. 179–98.
9 See, for example, Geoffrey Parker, *Global Crisis: War, Climate Change and Catastrophe in the Seventeenth Century* (New Haven: Yale University Press, 2013).
10 On the Engagement and its aftermath, see David Stevenson, *Revolution and Counter-Revolution in Scotland, 1644–51* (London: Royal Historical Society, 1977); and Laura A.M. Stewart, *Rethinking the Scottish Revolution: Covenanted Scotland, 1637–1651* (Oxford: Oxford University Press, 2016), esp. chapter 6; and Salvatore Cipriano, 'The Engagement, the Universities and the Fracturing of the Covenanter Movement, 1647–51', in Chris R. Langley (ed.), *The National Covenant in Scotland, 1638–1689* (Woodbridge: Boydell, 2020), pp. 145–60.
11 For the General Assembly debate over, and ultimate opposition to, the Engagement, see Church of Scotland, *Acts of the General Assembly of the Church of Scotland* (Edinburgh, 1843), pp. 166–200.
12 NRS, Ayr presbytery records, CH2/532/1, p. 327.
13 This point is also made by Jamie McDougall, 'Allegiance, Confession and Covenanting Identities', in Langley, *The National Covenant*, pp. 71–86, at p. 83.
14 Adair was chosen by the Ayr presbytery for the Western Association army in September 1650. See NRS, CH2/532/1, p. 439 and David Stevenson, 'The Covenanters and the Western Association, 1648–1650', *Ayrshire Collections* xiii (Ayr, 1982), 147–87.
15 John R. Young, 'Scottish Covenanting Radicalism, the Commission of the Kirk and the Establishment of the Parliamentary Radical Regime of 1648–1649', *Records of the Scottish Church History Society*, 25 (1993), 342–75.
16 Alexander F. Mitchell and James Christie (eds), *The Records of the Commissions of the General Assemblies of the Church of Scotland* (hereafter RCGA), II (Edinburgh: T. and A. Constable, 1896), pp. 80–8. On the resubscription of the Solemn League and Covenant in 1648, see Neil McIntyre and Jamie McDougall, 'Reframing the Covenant: *A Solemn Acknowledgment* (1648) and the resubscription of the Solemn League and Covenant', *Seventeenth Century*, 37:5 (2022), 733–56.

17 *RCGA*, II, pp. 80–8.
18 McDougall, 'Allegiance, Confession and Covenanting Identities', p. 83.
19 CH2/532/1, p. 342.
20 CH2/751/3/1, fo. 84r. Things had clearly been contentious in the town council that autumn; in October of 1648, they had passed an act intended to encourage 'better decorum' and prevent the 'interrupting of voyces' during weekly meetings. Ayrshire Archives, B6/18/2, Ayr Council Book, 1647–1669, fo. 41v.
21 CH2/751/3/1, fo. 83v.
22 CH2/751/3/1, fo. 84r. The compelling of men to fight in the engager army happened in a range of places in Scotland, as detailed by McIntyre and McDougall, 'Reframing the Covenant', 745–6.
23 CH2/751/3/1, fo. 84r.
24 CH2/751/3/1, fo. 85v.
25 CH2/751/3/1, fos. 85v–86r.
26 CH2/751/3/1, fo. 86r–v.
27 CH2/751/3/1, fo. 86v.
28 Ayrshire Archives, Acc 483, Papers of William Adair (c. 1633–1656), vol. I, n.p.
29 *Records of the Parliaments of Scotland to 1707* (hereafter *RPS*) ed. Keith M. Brown et al., www.rps.ac.uk (accessed 2 January 2024), 1649/1/43.
30 Acc. 483, vol. I, n.p.
31 On anti-anabaptist polemics in early modern Britain, see Gary K. Waite, *Anti-Anabaptist Polemics: Dutch Anabaptism and the Devil in England, 1531–1660* (Thunder Bay: Pandora Press, 2023).
32 Acc. 483, vol. I, n.p.
33 Acc. 483, vol. I, n.p.
34 For a discussion of attempts by the kirk party to purge 'malignants' from office and tightly define communal inclusion, see Stewart, *Rethinking the Scottish Revolution*, pp. 246–55.
35 John D. Grainger, *Cromwell against the Scots: The Last Anglo-Scottish War, 1650–1652* (East Linton: Tuckwell Press, 1997), chapter 3.
36 CH2/532/1, p. 439.
37 On the providential interpretations of events at Dunbar on both sides, see R. Scott Spurlock, *Cromwell and Scotland: Conquest and Religion, 1650–60* (Edinburgh: John Donald Publishers, 2007), pp. 33–8 and Crawford Gribben, 'Polemic and Apocalyptic in the Cromwellian Invasion of Scotland', *Literature and History*, 23:1 (2014), 1–18.
38 *RCGA*, III, pp. 95–103.
39 Acc. 483, vol. I, n.p.
40 William Makey, *The Church of the Covenant, 1637–1651: Revolution and Social Change in Scotland* (Edinburgh: John Donald Publishers, 1979), pp. 80–4; Kyle D. Holfelder, 'Factionalism in the Kirk during the Cromwellian Invasion and Occupation of Scotland, 1650 to 1660: The Protester-Resolutioner controversy' (PhD thesis, University of Edinburgh, 1998).
41 See, for example, Stevenson, *Revolution and Counter-Revolution in Scotland, 1644–51* and Holfelder, 'Factionalism in the Kirk'. Chris Langley has recently

offered a counter to neat narratives of separation and division, suggesting that protestors during the latter 1650s generally tried to reform the established church from within. Chris Langley, 'Parish Politics and Godly Agitation in Late Interregnum Scotland', *Church History*, 90 (2021), 557–8.
42 Hew Scott (ed.), *Fasti Ecclesiae Scoticanae*, vol. III: Synod of Glasgow and Ayr (Edinburgh: Oliver and Boyd, 1920), pp. 162–3.
43 National Library of Scotland (hereafter NLS), Wod. Fol. XXV, 'Letter from April 17 1651, to Mr. Robert Douglas', fo. 218r.
44 CH2/751/3/1, fos. 65r, 91r, 96r, 188v.
45 Michelle D. Brock, ' "She-Zealots and Satanesses": Women, Patriarchy, and the Covenanting Movement', in Mairi Cowan, Janay Nugent, and Cathryn Spence (eds), *Gender and Identity in Scotland, 1200–1800: Power, Politics, and Faith* (Edinburgh: Edinburgh University Press, 2024).
46 CH2/751/3/1, fo. 156r.
47 CH2/751/3/1, fo. 128r.
48 On local discipline during the era and aftermath of the civil wars, see Chris R. Langley, *Worship, Civil War and Community, 1638–1660* (London: Routledge, 2015), chapter 2, and Claire McNulty, 'The Experience of Discipline in Parish Communities in Edinburgh, Scotland, 1638–1651' (PhD thesis, Queen's University Belfast, 2021).
49 CH2/751/3/1, fo. 99v.
50 CH2/751/3/1, fo. 123r.
51 CH2/751/3/1, fos. 133r–34r.
52 CH2/751/3/1, fos. 80r–v.
53 CH2/751/3/1, fo. 80v.
54 See Chapter 1, this volume.
55 See, for example, *RPS*, 1649/1/62, 118, 119, 157, 219.
56 CH2/751/3/1, fo. 149r.
57 On the importance of oaths, see Karin Bowie, *Public Opinion in Early Modern Scotland, 1560–1707* (Cambridge: Cambridge University Press, 2020), chapter 3.
58 CH2/751/3/1, fo. 165v.
59 CH2/751/3/1, fo. 201r.
60 CH2/751/3/1, fo. 177v.
61 CH2/532/1, p. 287.
62 CH2/532/1, p. 326.
63 CH2/532/1, p. 326.
64 Robert Baillie, *The Letters and Journals of Robert Baillie*, 3 vols, ed. David Laing (Edinburgh: Bannatyne Club, 1841–2), iii, p. 61.
65 CH2/532/1, p. 366.
66 CH2/532/1, p. 426.
67 NLS, MS. 3430, 'Petition to the General Assembly for planting another minister at Ayr', p. 86.
68 In the Ayrshire Archives, there is also a revealing list of all the monies paid to neighbouring ministers who filled in when Adair was away or needing assistance. See B6/39/9, 'account of what moneyes has been payit to ministers in the

tyme of the vaccancie of ane collige minister by order and act of presbiterie for serving the cuir since anno 1648', 27 January 1657.
69 Ayrshire Archives, Acc 483, Papers of William Adair (c. 1633–1656), vol. I, n.p.
70 On the history of Scottish witch-hunting, see, for example, Levack, *Witch-Hunting in Scotland*; Julian Goodare (ed.), *The Scottish Witch-Hunt in Context* (Manchester: Manchester University Press, 2002); Christina Larner, *Witchcraft and Religion: The Politics of Popular Belief* (Oxford: Oxford University Press, 1984); Lawrence Normand and Gareth Roberts, *Witchcraft in Early Modern Scotland: James VI's Demonology and the North Berwick Witches* (Exeter: University of Exeter Press, 2000).
71 George S. Pryde (trans. and ed.), *Ayr Burgh Accounts, 1534–1624* (Edinburgh: Scottish History Society, 1937), pp. 183 and 200.
72 Levack, *Witch-Hunting in Scotland*, chapter 4.
73 Ayrshire Archives, Alastair Hendry, 'Witch-Hunting in Ayrshire: A Calendar of Documents, etc' (unpublished, May 1998), p. 27.
74 Hendry, 'Witch-Hunting in Ayrshire', p. 27.
75 Hendry, 'Witch-Hunting in Ayrshire', p. 28. The commission for her trial is noted in *RPCS* 2nd series III, p. 446.
76 B6/18/2, fo. 67; Hendry, 'Witch-Hunting in Ayrshire', p. 28.
77 John R. Young, 'The Scottish Parliament and Witch-Hunting in Scotland under the Covenanters', *Parliaments, Estates & Representation*, 26:1 (2006), 53–65.
78 Christina Larner, *Enemies of God: The Witch-hunt in Scotland* (Baltimore: Johns Hopkins University Press, 1981), p. 78; Julian Goodare, Lauren Martin, Joyce Miller, and Louise Yeoman, 'The Survey of Scottish Witchcraft', https://witches.hca.ed.ac.uk (archived January 2003, accessed 23 September 2023).
79 Paula Hughes, 'Witch-Hunting in Scotland, 1649–1650', in Julian Goodare (ed), *Scottish Witches and Witch-Hunters* (London: Palgrave, 2013), p. 87.
80 CH2/532/1, p. 95.
81 CH2/532/1, p. 409.
82 Hendry, 'Witch-Hunting in Ayrshire', pp. 36–7.
83 Young, 'The Scottish Parliament and Witch-Hunting in Scotland under the Covenanters'.
84 CH2/532/1, p. 410.
85 NLS, Wod. Fol. XXV, 'Letter from William Adair to Robert Douglas, 11 May 1650', 130r.
86 *RPS*, 1650/5/6.
87 CH2/751/3/1, fo. 132r.
88 CH2/751/3/1, fo. 132r.
89 NRS, JC26/25, High Court of Justiciary, Process notes, 1658.
90 JC26/25, Process notes.
91 JC26/25, Process notes.
92 JC26/25, Process notes.
93 JC26/25, Process notes.
94 JC26/25, Process notes.

95 JC26/25, Process notes.
96 Ayrshire Archives, Acc 483, vol. I, n.p.
97 Sierra Dye, 'To Converse with the Devil? Speech, Sexuality, and Witchcraft in Early Modern Scotland', *International Review of Scottish Studies*, 37 (2012), 9–40.
98 B6/18/2, fo. 80v.
99 Charles H. Firth (ed.), *Scotland and the Commonwealth: Letters and Papers relating to the Military Government of Scotland from August 1651 to December 1653* (Edinburgh: T. and A. Constable, 1895), p. 368.
100 James D. Marwick (ed.), *Extracts from the Records of the Convention of Royal Burghs, 1615–1676*, vol. III (Edinburgh, 1866), p. 358.

4

Occupation

Ayr's port, with its easy connections to Ireland and the wider Atlantic world, had long been an advantage for its residents, enabling a wide range of economic, social, political, and religious opportunities. When the plague spread in 1647, Ayr's seaside location became a liability, as incoming ships portended disease as much as profit. When Oliver Cromwell considered where to build his citadels after the crushing defeat of Scottish forces at Dunbar on 3 September 1650, the town's coastline made it a target.[1] In the aftermath of another major loss at Worcester exactly a year after Dunbar, Ayr, like the vast majority of Scotland, came under English control, as Scottish burghs generally did not have the defensive resources and manpower to mount violent resistance to enemy forces.[2] By early 1652, the port city was transformed into a garrison town for the Cromwellian army, its infrastructure and strategic position across the Irish Sea making it the ideal location for one of Cromwell's largest citadels, while others were built in Perth, Leith, Inverness, and Inverlochy.[3] The English also hoped to keep tabs on the actions of the zealous covenanters in the area, whose unrelenting commitment to presbyterian polity and Scottish sovereignty had motivated some of the northern kingdom's staunchest resistance to the incorporating union in 1652.[4] The church of St John the Baptist, which had from the early thirteenth century been the centre of worship in the town, was incorporated into the citadel and used variously as a meeting place and an armoury for the occupying army. The parishioners moved their services to the nearby grammar school until a new church was built in 1654.[5]

The occupation disrupted the living and the dead alike.[6] In April 1652, Hew Kennedy, former provost of the town, complained to the session that the 'fortifications werking by the Englishes' had approached the location where 'his prececesors, and he, did burie their dead', and that the construction had 'casten up aleadie som of ther corps and bodies'.[7] The town council soon commenced its search for a suitable location for a new parish burial ground.[8] Luckily for the communal stability of the localities, councils and kirk sessions across the country were generally allowed to operate as they had for decades prior, despite the Cromwellian regime's initial goals for reshaping Scottish institutions.[9] The Ayr session thus functioned during the occupation much as before, though it now met in the town school, having been 'dispossest of the old kirk'.[10] Adair, who had been feeling the immense strain of service as the town's sole minister since 1644, was in January 1656 finally joined by a colleague minister named William Eccles, who had completed his trials before the Ayr presbytery the previous autumn.[11] Adair and Eccles seem to have been cut from the same cloth. Like his senior colleague, Eccles was a man of unwavering commitment to both the covenants and godly discipline – a good thing, too, because by the time he took up the post, the session had their hands more than full with new challenges posed by the presence of the occupying army.

The biggest shift in how Scots navigated the built environment of their own communities came from the sheer numbers of soldiers in their midst – an army of some 16,000 men was now stationed across the country, and the effects of their presence were felt most acutely in the burghs that had become homes to large citadels.[12] In April 1652, the Ayr magistrates nominated baillie William Cunningham to go to Dalkeith to meet with English commissioners about the 'sad condition of this burgh', the residents of which were under enormous financial strain due to the quartering of so many soldiers.[13] Relief was not forthcoming, in Ayr or elsewhere, and in 1657 the convention of royal burghs – which continued to lobby for the interests of the burghs throughout the decade – noted its intention to communicate to the Lord Protector the 'heavie prejudice susteaned be the burrowis' by the 'locall quarteringis of souldiouris'.[14] The economic burden of quartering was not merely about lodging; it also entailed provision of horses, furnishings for garrisons, the supply of 'coal and candle', and more.[15] The seemingly bottomless cost of maintaining the English army was exacerbated by the fact that the union brought with it protectionist trade policies, an uptick in unlicensed (or 'unfree') traders in the burghs, and a new excise tax – and all this after an expensive decade of war.[16] Thomas Tucker, sent by the government in England in 1656 to survey the state of Scotland's ports, reported that the condition of Ayr was 'certainly to be deplored, the place groweing everyday worse'. Only Glasgow, in his telling, had maintained its trading resilience in the recent years despite the loss of access to foreign markets.[17] While the presence of the English army across Scotland also came with new commercial opportunities for Scots – such as increased demands for domestic labour from Scottish women, provision of good and materials for garrisons, and formalised trading routes with English colonies – the perception was generally one of significant hardship, taken as further evidence of God's displeasure.[18]

The disruption of the physical landscapes and economic health of the Scottish burghs was compounded by the scale and frequency of misbehaviour cases involving the English, who remained in Scotland for the entirety of the decade. The session records from citadel communities and garrison towns from across the country reveal that on a daily basis, ministers and kirk sessions struggled to navigate the complicated interpersonal dynamics caused by their parishioners living, and at times sleeping, with members of a foreign army.[19] On top of this, the religious heterodoxy and toleration of Cromwell's forces – the occupying army contained independents, baptists, quakers, and more – threatened to destabilise the practices and hierarchy of presbyterianism.[20] We should not let the comparatively peaceful nature of the English invasion (with the notorious exception of the storming of Dundee) overshadow the material and psychological costs of occupation, which were especially great in urban Scotland.[21] As David Stevenson has put it, 'foreign conquest must have seemed merely a crowning disaster to burgh communities already town apart by war, plague and internal dissension'.[22]

The Ayr kirk session summarised the manifold challenges of these years when, in late 1657, it set aside a day for the congregation to 'morne befor the lord' for 'the great lousnes and increase of sine in this place, and the grat controversie that is against us with many other particular reasons'.[23] The occupying forces contributing to much of this 'sine' and 'controversie' may have been from a different country, but only a few years prior, many of them had fought alongside the covenanters until ecclesiological disagreements and the regicide of Charles I in 1649 dismantled the intrinsically fragile alliance. What did it mean, then, for religious leaders and ordinary Scots alike to live alongside men from another country and with different political and sectarian commitments, who nonetheless shared with them many linguistic basics, theological beliefs, and historical experiences?[24] The long martial presence in Ayr offers an ideal opportunity to expand our understanding of how the culture of covenanting functioned under immense strain, as well as recover the civilian (and often gendered) experiences of occupation. As we will see, the Cromwellian subjugation of Ayr, rather than marking any definitive failure of the covenanting revolution in the town, brought to the fore both the fragility and flexibility of its covenanter identity, which, for all its purported rigidity, proved an internalised and adaptable guide for what to believe and how to behave in times of crisis.[25]

Living, and sleeping, with the English

The presence of a copious number of strangers in Ayr, billeted with local residents and roaming the streets near the citadel, posed a range of problems for the status quo of social and religious life. Unsurprisingly, given the centrality of the institution to the town, many of these problems ended up before the kirk session. The first significant appearance of the English in the session records from the new decade came in October of 1651, when David McWalter was called for sabbath-breaking after having been found 'ryding into the toun along the bridg upon the Sabbath in tym of sermon'.[26] He explained that he had spent the morning at the nearby kirk of Galston, and 'by reason of a report of the approach of the Englishes, which put all the countrie there in a fear', his rode home to Ayr 'in heast', and was thus found out of kirk during afternoon sermon.[27] This northward march of Cromwell's army would have been expected by the session; not only did news of the Scots' failed last stand at Worcester travel fast, but Adair was deeply involved in military matters and had been with Scottish forces on and off over the previous year, including at Dunbar.[28] What was perhaps less anticipated was the extent to which English disruption of sermon attendance, a cornerstone of Reformed piety in Ayr and elsewhere, would quickly become commonplace.

Within the first months of 1652, parishioners found themselves explaining to the session at unprecedented rates why they had been absent from kirk on sabbath days. In June 1652, Mathew McCall, cited for sabbath-breaking, said the reason for his absence was that 'ther was a boat comin in where his goodes was', and when he heard 'that the soldiers was going to plunder his boat', he rushed to the docks during sermon time to see if this was true.[29] Janet Kirkland came before the session in January of the following year for sabbath-breaking and explained that the soldiers had caused her absence when they 'commanded hir to doe a business for them'.[30] In July 1653, five women, found in their houses during sermon time, described how they had been 'forced to bring in wine to the Englishes' and 'forced to stay at hom and mak the souldioures meat readie'.[31] In October of the same year, an elder reported that he had asked Cristiane Hunter why she was 'at hom upon the Lords day in tym of preaching', to which she retorted 'what is that to yow?'.[32] Called before the session to explain her obstinance, she declared that she was 'behoved to byd at hom and keep the hous because the souldiours wer in it', and that her disrespectful response to the elder was due to the 'greif and anger' caused by the 'abuse' of the Englishmen in her home. The session, recognising the great disruption currently being experienced by the parishioners, judged nearly all of these sabbath-breakers to be sincere and exhorted them 'to be cairfull of the Lords day heirafter'.[33]

Concerning as it was, involuntary sabbath-breaking proved to be the least of the session's troubles, and more serious behavioural infractions show up in the records immediately after the soldiers arrived in town. In January 1652, the session cited Agnes Murdoch and her two daughters, Isobel and Margaret, for 'lous living', and more specifically, 'scandalous miscariag with the Englishmen'.[34] Apparently, they had been heard 'piping and dancing' at midnight, and reports circulated in the town that their home was a playground of drunkenness and fornication; a fiddler who had joined their festivities 'did so play till he fell doune' of intoxication and exhaustion. Even the Englishmen who had participated in some of this scandalous behaviour declared to members of the session that 'if they wer to stay in Ayr they should burne the hous', full of sin as it was.[35] After repeated admonishments from the minister, Murdoch and her daughters 'evidenced sorrow' for their misbehaviour, confessed their 'sin and miscariag' before the session, and were 'rebuked and exhorted to live christinalie in all tym coming'.[36] This was their one warning: should they fall into the error of their scandalous ways again, they would be publicly censored and required to repent before the congregation. The women complied, and the English soldiers who threatened to burn their house did, in fact, stay in the town, though no such arson was committed.

This episode – a brief case of Scottish women accused of carousing with the occupying soldiers in ways deemed unseemly and unchristian – is among the earliest of its kind in the minutes, but far from the last. Indeed, it was a harbinger of the many challenges to come. Later in January 1652, Barbara McNeider and her daughter Gibella Wallace were called before the session for drinking and revelling with soldiers late into the night, inviting them into their home even though the men were formally quartered elsewhere.[37] The most interesting aspect of this case was that the session also cited McNeider and Wallace for 'Lous and scandalous living with the Scotish Soldiers', who, the records go on to specify, were actually a couple of 'Mosstroopers' – marauders active in the borders who made their livelihoods by attacking both civilians and parliamentary soldiers for supplies during the mid-seventeenth century.[38] Apparently, Wallace had gone north with the Moss-troopers to Dumbarton (perhaps first encountering them en route to Glasgow), and then accompanied them back to Ayr. She must have developed quite a cosy relationship with these men, for when they eventually left the town, she walked them to the 'Bridg end' just on the outskirts of Ayr and 'kissed them and gave them a pint of wine'.[39]

The community of Ayr was in the midst of navigating how to deal with the occupation, and the minutes note that Wallace had been 'very hurtfull to the toune in bringing back of the mostroupers' who had 'spoyled the hurt Englishmen that wer heir' – meaning raided their goods – 'to the great prejudice of toune'.[40] Despite the many qualms the session had with the English presence, they wanted to avoid provoking unnecessary antagonism, for the reality of occupation meant that despite the continued moral authority of local kirk sessions, Scotland was effectively under martial law. In punishment for their detrimental actions, McNeider and Wallace were barred from performing the necessary rituals that allow them to rejoin the congregation until 'their cariage after be seine to evidence repentance'.[41] This language of 'cariage', long present in kirk discipline, would become increasingly central to the session's dealings with wayward parishioners during the occupation.

As these cases attest, the session was initially very anxious to police interaction between locals and the army. It spent much of 1652 and 1653 summoning Scottish women to the court for various types of 'scandalous cariag' with the English, including 'drinking with souldiers', spending evenings 'with an Englishman alon', or just generally 'being over familier' with the town's uninvited guests.[42] Such efforts proved relatively futile, but this was less a sign of the kirk's diminished influence and more a product of the extenuating circumstance of hundreds of strange men in the town.[43] The overriding concern here was not about simple fraternisation, though this too was not ideal, but the potential for fornication or adultery. This concern is exemplified by the case of Sara McClurg, who in the summer of 1652 was caught 'lying with ane Englishman in the fields'.[44] After a long trial and the calling of witnesses, she confessed that she had gone with a soldier for a walk, and that 'hir cariage was evill favoured and scandalous and also that hir thoughtes wer not good but evill and sinfull'. She denied, however, any actual fornication with the said Englishman, though she did confess that the soldier had put his hand on her knee.[45] McClurg's confession reflects the Reformed insistence that the godly monitor not only their words and actions but also their thoughts, as well as the potential for temptation generated by an influx of young soldiers in Ayr. Here, she also articulated what would become a central challenge for women across Scotland during the occupation: the need to control one's own desires while navigating the complexity of new relationships and potentially dangerous interactions. Ultimately, the session took McClurg at her word and issued the usual prescription in such cases: to confess one's sins and repent before the congregation, which she did.

Often, however, the relations between English soldiers and Ayr women did not stop with a stroll in the fields or a hand on a knee.[46] The case of Barbara Hunter is typical and representative of a marked spike in cases of sexual immorality in the early 1650s. Called before the session in April 1653, she confessed to 'the sin of filthiness with William McJewall', an Englishman who had been in the town the previous winter but had since left for Ireland.[47] Her sentence was delayed until 'mor information and knowledge be had that the said William is a free man or not, or if the said Barbaras husband be dead or not'.[48] As often happened during the occupation, the session did not know whether to treat the case as simple fornication, if both parties were unmarried, or the more serious infraction of adultery, if not.[49] After learning that her husband had died of plague the previous year and repeatedly asking Hunter if she had any more information on McJewall, the session still could not find out whether he was single. The ministers and elders seemed to give up on Hunter for a while, but in the summer of 1654 she was summoned to the session along with fifteen other women who had similarly transgressed with English soldiers who had since left town, leaving uncertainty about the nature of their crimes, and sometimes their unborn children, in their wake. After having dealt with case after case of uncategorised 'sins of filthiness', the exasperated session rebuked the women for their 'uncleanes, inpenitencie, and cairlesnes of clearing themselves in the said scandal'.[50] The women were warned that unless 'their diligence and other signes of repentence, be maid mor manifest to the satisfaction of the sessione', they would be suspended from kirk services, and a warning would be made to the rest of the congregation 'to tak notic of such persones'.[51] The minutes note that thirteen of the women complied in their repentance, while three of them were suspended from the kirk that autumn.

Occasionally, women from other parts of Scotland who had come to town with the English either as servants or romantic companions also caused a headache for the session. In the spring of 1653, for example, it repeatedly attempted to bring Margaret Thornton, a Scottish woman who was a servant to an English officer, under the umbrella of kirk discipline. She was accused, variously, of fornication with English soldiers, drinking on the sabbath, and bidding both a town officer and the minister to 'come kise her arse'.[52] Eventually, after repeated calls and failures to appear before the session, Thornton was finally 'judged to be disobedient and also being in ane Englishman's service was judged non of oures', and the case was dropped.[53] As we will see, in these years the kirk session became very explicit about who belonged in their godly community, Scottish or not.

What of the many English soldiers who had 'fallen' with the women of Ayr? It is worth noting that, while the Scots were essentially a conquered population, Cromwell had insisted that they be treated with the respect befitting godly people.[54] Accordingly, English soldiers were instructed not to behave improperly with Scottish women, which could compromise community relations as well as their own morality.[55] The English court martial records from Dundee, for example, contain orders that 'Noe man should bee out of his quarters, nor sitt uppe drinking in their quarter after the tattoe beaten'. Soldiers were also confined to stay within one half mile of a garrison, unless given specific permission otherwise.[56] While they came fairly regularly before the Ayr session as witnesses, the Englishmen accused of sexual crimes were generally disciplined by their own superiors and presumably the English court martial. There are a few cases, for example, in which English soldiers were subject to 'publick scrudging' – that is, flogging – 'throw the streits' for committing adultery with Ayr women.[57] Only when one of Cromwell's men wanted to marry a local woman, as in the case of Matthew Aikensone, did they submit themselves to the discipline of the kirk. In March 1653, Aikensone came before the session to declare that he had been 'reduced and put out of the English service' and to see if they would grant him marriage to Janet Bell, an Ayr native. The session agreed, but only 'upon condition if he wald swear and subscribe the covenant, which he promised to doe, and soe in the presene of the session did solemlie swear to all the articles of the covenant and gave consent to the clerk to wryt for him because he could not wryt'.[58] For the next six months, Aikensone and Bell appear to have lived together as a typical couple within the congregation, before being granted a testimonial about 'their cariag since they wer maried' so that they could settle elsewhere in the country.[59] Not all Englishmen were deemed equally worthy of marriage or taking the covenant, however: in March 1654, an elder reported to the rest of the session that the man who had 'fallen with' and impregnated Jean Lowrie was 'not worthie of mariag, but a sillie feckles lad'.[60]

To offer some sense of scale, between 1650 and 1655, 168 people appeared before the Ayr session for sexual crimes, and 63 for 'scandalous carriage'; by contrast, in the previous decade from 1639 to 1649, 139 appeared for sexual crimes and 21 for 'scandalous carriage'.[61] This overwhelming number of fornication cases with the English, frequent in the early years of occupation and only occasionally ending in marriage, generated two priorities for the session that dovetailed with expectations for a covenanted community: to stave off divine wrath that might be invited by such moral misbehaviour, an old anxiety made all the more potent by the perceived punishment of the occupation itself; and to prevent issues raised by the care of children born out of wedlock to absent fathers. These concerns were not unique to Ayr, and other areas with the presence of citadels or garrisons, such as Dundee, Stirling, Elgin, and Leith, also grappled with copious sexual offenses. As a result, during the 1650s young women throughout Scotland came under increased scrutiny from the kirk and from their fellow townspeople.[62] Part of this attention was, of course, logistical; while the session occasionally reprimanded the men of Ayr for cavorting with female servants of the English army, the reality was that the town had been overrun with men who were, either officially or situationally, without wives. The quartering of soldiers also kept women of all ages away from kirk on the sabbath, as the domestic tasks of sewing, washing, cooking, and other support work fell disproportionately on their shoulders.[63]

More harrowingly, there are numerous stories like that of widow Janet Reid, who two soldiers had fought over, one saying 'will not thow let me have the whor', and Issobell Cunningham, who, when called before the session for drinking with the English, explained that 'the soldiers threatened to strick hir' because she had initially refused to partake with them.[64] The case of Amaple Donald, who in February 1655 stood accused of the 'sine of filthnes' with a stranger (the man was not known to the session, or to her), reflects the physical and emotional traumas some women faced during the upheaval of occupation.[65] Donald's 'fall' had happened six months before, when a man 'cam to hir and lay with hir' in the gorse while she was on her way to the river Doon. The man had apparently followed her to the water and 'spak nothing to hir, but strak hir and stoped hir moueth when she wald hav cryed'.[66] He had a 'cap on his head and drew it over his face that she could not know him'. At no point in this case was the term 'rape' used, though it seems clear that this is what had transpired.[67] The session's priority was to properly punish sin and prevent further social disorder, and it devoted considerable time and energy to finding out whether her attacker was a 'free man', while exhorting Donald to 'lay to heirt the hynnousnes of hir sine'.[68] While many of the more intimate interactions between soldiers and local women may have been consensual, positive, and mutually instigated (or instigated by the women), some clearly were not. At least a few of the women punished for fornication with the soldiers were, according to their testimonies, hesitant partners at best and victims of sexual assault at worst.[69] The events in Ayr offer only a snapshot of the more general experiences of Scottish women during occupation, but they suggest paths forward in rethinking the role of gender during the Wars of the Three Kingdoms and their aftermath.[70]

Discipline under occupation

Disciplinary challenges related to the occupation itself dominated the agenda of the kirk session for much of the 1650s, and cases of sex with soldiers persisted through the end of the decade. But by 1656, as the newness of so many English soldiers stationed in Ayr wore off, the kirk turned its attention back to the long-standing issues of blasphemy, drunkenness, and flyting. In May 1656, for example, James McIlveen appeared before the session for 'blasphemie in swearing by the wounds of God' and 'constant drunkenness'; apparently a man of multiple hobbies, witnesses confirmed that he was 'a great swearer and a great drunkard'.[71] The following June, elder Jon Guthrie told the session that he had heard Bessie Hunter say 'publickly in the streights' that the devil had stollen her rooster, and witnesses reported that she had asked God to 'mak my cock crall out of the bellie who hes taken him'.[72] Hunter, being found both ignorant of religion and ultimately impenitent, was not received back into the congregation despite performing public repentance. The challenge of impenitent parishioners persisted; in November 1656, the session accused Jon Dick of profaning the sabbath day by drunkenness and 'stricking and abusing his wife'. Dick appeared before the congregation, but rather than evince the appropriate sorrow for his sin, he was deemed 'ignorant and inpenitent' and was rebuked by the minister rather than received by the congregation.[73] The session also dealt with sexual crimes not involving soldiers. On 23 June 1656, Hew Kennedy the younger – who was the son of an elder – returned from Barbados and presented to the session a supplication confessing his sin of fornication with Kathrine Mason, committed just before he had commenced his travels. The session, 'being acquainted with his knowledge in the groundes of religione', sentenced him to public repentance.[74] The fate of fornicator Margaret Wilson that same summer, who was 'quintralaps in filthiness', was much harsher; the magistrates of the town banished her from the burgh for her multiple fornications in Ayr and elsewhere.[75]

None of the offences discussed thus far were unusual, except in terms of some of the parties involved. But amid the disruption caused by so many outsiders throughout the town – and critically, outsiders of a different ecclesiological persuasion – the responses of Adair and the session elders to the perceived moral offences of the community grew both more urgent and more complex. The question now was how the session could maintain its commitment to covenanting and continue to please God in the face of occupation, the evident transgressions of so many of its inhabitants, and the potential toleration brought by a religiously diverse army. In response to all this uncertainty, one might expect that the session would have simply increased the swiftness of their responses and the severity of the penalties. Indeed, the institution of the kirk session, especially when run by staunch covenanters, is often caricatured in both popular and scholarly literature as draconian and inflexible.[76] But this is not quite what happened.

Three interrelated patterns emerge in how the session grappled with the influx of offenses, especially 'sins of filthiness', during the Cromwellian occupation. First, the session became increasingly insistent that guilty parties make *sincere* confession for their sins, despite the fact that logistics of performing repentance in the town were initially disrupted by the inability of the congregation to use their old kirk.[77] In the beginning of 1652, as acts of scandalous carriage with the English began to abound, the session 'did judg it fit and expedient that scandalous persones continuing inpetitent should be keeped under process from tym to tym till ther be som evidences and signes of repentance sein in them befor they be committed to com to publick'.[78] In other words, those cited for misbehaviour who did not display satisfactory sorrow for their sins were to continue appearing before the session until deemed fit to make public repentance. Second, adjudicating sexual scandals became opportunities for the minister and elders to question deviants not only about their sins of the flesh, but also their knowledge of religion and the meaning of repentance. In practice, this meant that many of the cases dealing with sexual misbehaviour resulted not only in convictions of fornication, but in people being found 'ignorant of the grounds of religion' as well as lacking a 'true sense of their sin'.[79] When this occurred, the session also delayed assigning punishment and asked the guilty townsperson to return for regular questioning until such knowledge be adequately demonstrated. These two trends comprised aspects of a more general, third pattern in kirk discipline during these years: the increased defining and policing the boundaries of who was, and who deserved to be, a member of Ayr's covenanted congregation.

In the spring of 1655, for example, the widow Janet Chalmers was convicted of repeatedly sleeping with Richard Wildine, an English soldier. The session spoke with her numerous times, but did not allow her to make public repentance until three things happened: first, that she showed adequate 'sorrow for hir sine' and expressed genuine desire 'to be reconciled to god and his kirk'; second, that she give proof of her knowledge of 'the grounds of religion', which generally meant things like the Ten Commandments and the catechism; and last, the session could find out whether Wildine was a 'frie man', meaning unmarried. Once all these requirements were met, she could perform public repentance and be received into the congregation once again.[80] Chalmers eventually did as the session hoped. But others who remained ignorant of religion and unremorseful for their sins were deemed unfit for public displays of repentance, and instead suspended from the kirk until such time as 'the lord wirk mor effectually' in their hearts and make them 'sensible of sin'.[81] A revealing case is that of George Cassie in the winter of 1653–4. Originally from Perth and a newcomer to the parish who was working for the English in an unspecified capacity, Cassie confessed to fornication with a local woman. After initially fleeing when the session demanded he make repentance, he returned a few weeks later and produced a 'supplicatione befor the session declaring his sorrow for his sine and for his disobedience, whereby he acknowledged he deserved to be thrust out as a rotten member from the Lords people'. He professed, with tears in his eyes, 'his willingness to give all obedience' to the kirk in future.[82]

Upon receiving his entreaty, the session examined Cassie for his 'sense of his sin and the nature therof' and found him 'most ignorant even of the chief principles of religione' as well as the 'the natur of repentance'.[83] Yes, he felt very sorry for what he had done, but he did not fully understand his wrongdoing, or the theological code according to which he should feel that sorrow. From the perspective of the session and in the context of so much external pressure on the community, it was essential that congregants understand not only what they had done wrong, but how seemingly isolated sins were products of their innate and total depravity. Adair set about regularly meeting with Cassie to give him further instruction, and an elder spoke to his master to see if he could spare his apprentice 'som tym to use diligence heirin' to learn the grounds of religion.[84] In the end, though, he failed to make adequate progress, and the session, 'notwithstanding of much paines taken upon him both in privat by the minister and also in publick before the session', determined that Cassie did not 'properlie belong to this congregatione being a stranger' and decided to 'lay him by' – that is, bar him from kirk privileges.[85]

The session expressed this emphasis on religious knowledge, which it clearly felt would ensure the congregation's unity, through passage of several measures to prevent religious ignorance and theological deviance from taking root. In January 1653, at the start of the second year under occupation, the session ordained that catechisms be recited by the parishioners every sabbath during both the morning and afternoon meeting.[86] Parents were exhorted the following month to make sure to 'traine [their children] up in the fear of the Lord' and to be themselves 'diligent to acquire the groundes of religione'.[87] In August, aid to those who were 'montethlie or weiklie pensioners' or who 'resid in the hospital' was newly conditioned on proof of 'the knowledge of the groundes of religione, viz at least the Lords prayer, the beliefe and ten comandements, togidder with som knowledge of the catechism'.[88] Such additional measures were not new or unique, but they demonstrate a renewed thoroughness on the part of an already thorough session.[89] This was also the first time in recent memory that the Ayr session had conditioned poor relief on such an explicit test.[90] Moreover, prior to the Cromwellian invasion, the session certainly expected genuine acknowledgement of sin from those who had done wrong, but not necessarily as a precondition to public repentance itself. And it was not until 1652, when Cromwell's army had settled in the town, that the session started systematically interrogating many of those who came before it for their knowledge of the 'grounds of religion'.[91]

The preaching materials we have from Adair during the occupation reflect this commitment to ensuring the religious competencies of Ayr's parishioners. While the batch of extant sermon and lecture notes from 1647 to 1651 centre on the inevitable destruction of the kirk's enemies and offer thinly veiled criticism of those with whom the hardliners disagreed, writings from the mid-1650s reveal an almost 'back to basics' approach in Adair's preaching.[92] Lectures composed between late December 1654 and July 1656 cover topics such the purpose of the Old and New Testaments ('the only rule to direct us how wee may glorifie and injoy [God]'); the nature of God ('God is in himself and of his own nature imutable'); the Trinity ('ther are three persones in the godhead'); the workings of providence ('there is nothing in all his providence which is not holy he is no author of or impeller to'); and the danger of the devil ('be war of the wyles of Sathan and his craft in tentation and to stand with all the armor of god against him').[93] Adair's preaching in these years, at least what we have record of, was all very standard Reformed fare and decidedly apolitical. This likely reflects both his desire to avoid calling unwanted attention to himself as well as a genuine commitment to ensuring his flock remained knowledgeable of and committed to the fundamental beliefs and principles of the kirk.

Sincerity of repentance and knowledge of religion became pillars of discerning whether those who had transgressed deserved readmittance to the congregation, and these religious tests were part of a broader programme of policing the boundaries of Ayr's spiritual community. The programme is exemplified by the fact that during the early years of occupation, in a moment of acute crisis, far more people than before were suspended from kirk privileges, and their suspensions were read from the pulpit as warning to other congregants who might face similar temptations.[94] In the vast majority of such cases, it was not the initial crime that earned this exclusion, but continued unwillingness to repent or the inability to grasp 'the principals of religion'.[95] Newcomers to the town also faced increased scrutiny from civic and spiritual authorities alike. The session often deemed those from other parts of Scotland residing in Ayr, especially if they were in service of the English, to be 'non of ours' if they transgressed, while the town council stepped up its insistence on getting testimonials of the 'honesitie and carriage and behaviour' of those from 'forrain pairtis' now dwelling in the burgh.[96] The session took things a step further on 1 September 1656, when the elders determined that they would go through their allotted parts of the town and 'tak special notice of and mark these who live lousley and scandalouslye, and of such who live not piouslye and godlye not serving nor worshipping God in their families', with the goal of reporting such people back to the minister.[97] This moral stock-taking had an explicit purpose: to determine who should be admitted to the celebration of communion later that month.

On 15 September 1656 Adair made the following declaration before the session regarding the upcoming communion service and 'craved that the sam' be inserted into the minutes:

> Wheras it is resolved by the sessione to goe about the celebration of the lordes supper in this congregatione, and in regarde of the confusions that ar in this place, it is probable that there will not be that exactnes in admitting of persones to the said ordiance which is requisite according to the due maner and preparation of the sanctuarie. I due therfor declair that what Libertie or Latitud shall be now taken, or what deviating there shall be from the rules of Gods word and the established doctrine discipline and government, actes and consitutiones of this kirk in admitting of peoples to the lords table, that therin I am passive.[98]

He went on to explain that 'in respect of the present trubled stait the kirk', errors might be made in following the proper order in 'admission to this ordinance'. Adair wanted to make it clear that he did not approve of such errors and that the extenuating circumstances of occupation should not be used in the 'hindering of a mor exact exercise of discipline in reference to admissione to the lords table' in time to come. Underlaying Adair's statement was a recognition that the standards set in 1648, which made strict adherence to a hardline interpretation of the covenants a precondition for both resubscription of the Solemn League and Covenant and admittance to communion, might be hard to enforce.[99] He wanted no part – and no blame – in allowing such errors, but also recognised that desperate times called for desperate measures.

William Eccles, moderating that day's meeting of the session, went on to present a list of rules for the upcoming communion that adhered to the 'established doctrine, worship, discipline, government, actes, and constitutiones of this kirk'.[100] Those to be debarred from the Lord's table fell into six categories: those ignorant of the basics of religion; 'all who ar ungodlye' or are known to neglect family worship; those who absented themselves from or disrupted public worship; anyone still in the process of being disciplined but not yet received by the congregation; all those who live alone in houses and expose themselves to 'manifold snares and temptations' (this was implicitly directed at the women of the town); and all who are known to live scandalously – a rather broad category including drunkards, swearers, and sabbath-breakers, as well as 'all such as cast off the established doctrine worship and government of this kirk'. The session was to meet the Wednesday before the communion and go over the names of inhabitants of the town to make a revised list of those to be debarred from the Lord's Supper.[101] Though not mentioned explicitly in the above rules, Adair and the men of the session would have no doubt considered these transgressions as explicit violations of the mandates of the covenants. Policing admission to the ritual of communion offered a way for the session to exert control over the integrity of the covenanted community at a time when their spiritual and secular authority faced an unprecedented challenge. As Adair anticipated, the rules could not be perfectly enforced, but having them was better than nothing.

Covenanter identity in Cromwellian Scotland

What does all of this suggest about covenanter identity in Cromwellian Scotland? At the risk of stating the obvious, this was a time of great unease, due at least in part to the new religious ideas circulating in Ayr thanks to an occupying army full of independents and sectarians. This tension was made manifest in mid-June 1653, when two officers from Cromwell's army arrived unexpectedly at a meeting of Ayr's kirk session. The men 'declared they had ane ordour from Colonel Alured' – head of the regiment at Ayr – 'to sit ther in'.[102] The session had little choice but to acquiesce, but Adair asked the clerk to make note that such compliance should not be interpreted 'as if it wer approven by the sessione, or did impart any allowance of ther power or practize as favoring of Erastianisme'.[103] Moreover, he 'protested against any incroachment upon the autoritie and libertie of the kirk of Scotland', and while he could do nothing about the English presence at their meeting, he asked that they afford the session the liberty to 'exercise discipline as formerlie'.[104]

The freedom to, in Adair's words, 'exercise discipline as formerlie', was granted, but the session still struggled to maintain the appearance – paired with sincere practice – of piety, cohesion, and embodiment of the true faith in the face of competing religious factions. Covenanter identity, cultivated over the previous decade in much of Scotland and with great intensity in places like Ayr, had to be performed and recited in new ways – hence the emphasis on genuine repentance, thorough knowledge, and the need to 'walk mor christianlie and holilie' behind closed doors and, crucially, in public.[105] One woman, for example, was exhorted to avoid 'all appearance of evill and scandalous companie'; another two were warned that 'the elders have ther eyes upon them to sie how they carie themselves'.[106] As we have seen, communal performance had been central to the signing of covenants and their swearing in Scottish parishes, and the importance of unity was likewise built into the language of the original documents.[107] But over a decade later, when the covenanting regime had lost its national political power in a country occupied by the English army, the burden of practising and performing covenanter identity became increasingly localised and urgent.

Despite the manifest anxieties of Ayr's spiritual authorities, as well as the disagreements within the covenanting movement itself, the new religious ideas brought by the English proved a relatively ineffective and short-lived challenge to the town's presbyterian hegemony. The hierarchy of Ayr undoubtedly struggled with complex internal divisions surrounding the protester–resolutioner controversy of 1652–3, but these seem to have mostly abated at the parish level by 1654, likely out of necessity as much as any genuine agreement.[108] While independents, quakers, and baptists did find traction in some areas of Scotland, most hints of sectarian influence in Ayr during the occupation never evolved into genuine threats.[109] Merchant William Mure, for example, was accused in May 1653 by another townsman of having been 'rebaptised and diped in Ladie Cragies Well' – a tantalising suggestion of the influence of English baptists reportedly stationed in Ayr.[110] The accusation, however, was effectively neutralised by Mure's signed testimonial 'declaring his judgement anent the erroures of antitrinitarianisme and puedobaptisme of which he fand himself to be bruited', which prompted the discerning session to vindicate him and prosecute his libeller.[111] In a less detailed case later that year, Marjorie Taylor was rebuked for calling Margaret Shaw a 'puritan', among other names, but the session did not consider this a serious accusation of religious deviance on Shaw's part.[112]

In some cases, it is often hard to judge whether episodes of religious dissent reflected a true drift away from the presbyterian establishment, or more quotidian grievances against authority. The case of Jon Craig, a mason from Edinburgh who had been 'working with the Englishes', exemplifies this interpretive hurdle. In the late autumn of 1653, Craig was convicted of adultery with a local woman, Margaret Stevenson, and both were eventually suspended from kirk privileges because of their ongoing bad behaviour and general unwillingness to repent. In April 1654, he appears again in the records after having spoken 'villie and abominablie publicklie' against the 'holie word of god' and 'the minister of this parish', saying in particular that Adair had 'preached false doctreine'.[113] At first glance, we might wonder if Craig had been influenced by new ideas encountered during his time with the English soldiers. However, a few weeks later, he came voluntarily before the session to give them a 'supplication conteining his sorrow both for his scandal of adultrie with Margot Stevenson and his flyting of the session: and also for his great sine and comtemp both of the minister and ordinances'.[114] In it, he explained that 'that the devil hes so far prevailed as not only to mak me scandalous in my behavior … but also that he should have loused my tounge to speak reproachfullie and threattene maliciouslie the faithfull servant of god who was seiking nothing but my salvation, and drawing out of the hands of the devil'.[115] Craig went on to beg 'in the bowles of jesus Christ that not only I may be received unto my publick repentence but also that ye wold strive with God by prayer for me, that I may be delivered from the subtill snares of Satan, wherin if god prevent not, I am lyk to parish'. The minutes note that after this remarkably detailed statement, taken as sincere by the session, 'the minister for his pairt did forgive him'.[116] Craig was then scheduled to meet regularly with Adair until found satisfactorily cognisant of his sin, after which he could give public repentance and be received back into the congregation, which he did. He does not appear in the records again.

Numerous questions are raised by this episode: What led to Craig's abrupt about-face and desire to be reabsorbed into the community, one that was not actually his hometown? How much external influence was there in the crafting of such a detailed statement of repentance? What exactly was his relationship to the English army in the first place? What does seem clear, however, is that whether new religious ideas or personal grievance had compelled him to speak ill of the minister, in the end the overriding desire to be received again as a member of this covenanted community won out. Such evidence suggests that at least in the early years of occupation, the confessional unity of the town held fast, thanks not only to the vigilance of Ayr's religious leaders, but also the persistent communal resonance of covenanting.[117]

Moreover, commitment to covenanting and religious conformity did not preclude collaboration with those from divergent backgrounds. In fact, the session regularly sought out English military leaders for testimony about the character and marital status of their soldiers.[118] Occasionally, too, did individual soldiers help the session in its disciplinary goals, as in the case of the Englishman who reported finding two townsfolk in bed together on the sabbath to elders.[119] And of course, the men and women of Ayr frequently (though with varying degrees of willingness) interacted with the English, and in some cases appear to have developed relationships of trust, friendship, and even love. In short, in the context of Cromwellian Ayr, the town's leading figures, at this point nearly all hardline covenanters, ought not be understood as exclusionary extremists. Due to a combination of situational compulsion and genuine flexibility, they played the hand they were dealt and worked with their occupiers as and when necessary.[120]

Witchcraft under occupation

Our story of the Cromwellian decade in Ayr ends, fittingly, as it began: with witchcraft. In 1658, five months before the death of the Lord Protector, three women we have met before – Janet Sawer, Janet Slowane, and Elspeth Cuninghame – found themselves again in jail, awaiting trial for devilish crimes purportedly committed over seven years ago, just before Cromwell's men had invaded their town. Their delayed fates attest to the disruption wrought by the Cromwellian invasion as well as the continuity of covenanter endeavours to maintain a godly community, a task that became even more imperative during the added pressures of occupation. The Ayr witch hunts of the late 1650s also suggest how the anxiety about female bodies and behaviours over the previous decade informed pursuit of purported witches in Ayr during the 1658–9 resurgence of trials and across the country during Scotland's most intense period of witch-hunting immediately following the Restoration.[121]

During the occupation, local leaders throughout the country had the disruption of an invading army to contend with and could not afford to make pursuing witches a top priority. Moreover, seventeenth-century English judges – now largely running the legal show – were significantly more reticent than their Scottish counterparts to prosecute witches and more sceptical about the uses and efficacy of torture. Between 1653 and 1657, English commissioners in Scotland kept witchcraft prosecutions to a comparative minimum: only around a dozen convicted witches met their deaths by strangulation.[122] Yet there was large uptick in executions in the waning years of the Cromwellian period, beginning in late spring of 1658 and culminating in the accusation of over 150 witches across Scotland in 1658–9, 47 of them in the county of Ayr and 25 within the remit of the Ayr presbytery.[123] It is unclear why, exactly, English authorities allowed for such heightened persecutions after years of judicial restraint and attempts to curtain perceived excesses of Scottish law, but it is clear that at the local level, Scottish leaders felt more empowered to address what Robert Ballie described as 'much witcherie up and downe our land'.[124]

In Ayr, this meant that the days of the women accused earlier in the decade were numbered. Janet Sawer was the first of the women tried in the town tolbooth, and her detailed case featured seventeen separate charges attested by witnesses, most of them dating back to the late 1640s.[125] Among the charges of harmful magic, the fittingly numbered thirteenth charge accused Sawer of entering into a pact with Satan, renouncing her baptism, and receiving the mark of demonic servitude, found 'in divers pairts of [her] bodie by stabeing of the samen'.[126] She, like many other mid-century Scottish witches, had been a victim of the invasive and painful practices of witch-prickers who were especially active during the 1658–9 and 1661–2 hunts.[127] Sawer stood charged of threatening not only her neighbours, but also the spiritual and economic health of Ayr. The strength and number of these allegations – all of which she strenuously denied – sealed her fate: for the 'devilishe airt of witchraft Threantenings and minaceing', she was 'convict and burnt' in April 1658.[128]

A letter written by Colonel Robert Sawrey, an English officer in Ayr, vividly described the end of Sawer's ordeal:

> [Sawer] did contantly deny that she knew any thing of witchcraft, and at her death made a very large confession of her wicked life, and had good exhortations to the living, but remained to affirm that she knew nothing of witchcraft. And as I was informed by those that heard her, when the Minister was urgeing her to confesse she had these words, 'Sir, I am shortly to appear before the Judge of all the earth, and a lye may damne my soule to hell. I am clear of witchcraft, for which I am presently to suffer'.[129]

Sawrey, in reporting on the last words of Janet Sawer, made a general observation that 'the people in this country are more sett against witchcraft then any other wickedness, and if once a person have that name and come upon an Assize it's hard to get of with lesse than this poor creature'.[130] While it is likely that the colonel's words were imbued with a sense of cultural superiority and general distaste for Scottish law, there is little reason to doubt the general veracity of his account of Sawer's last days and the zeal of Scottish witch hunters in Ayr and elsewhere.

Sawer would not be the last victim in Ayr that decade; the two women imprisoned with her, Janet Slowane and Elspeth Cuninghame, were tried and executed almost a year later after a lengthy and convoluted investigation. Slowane, whose own daughter testified against her, had a trial featuring witness accounts by fourteen men and ten women, most involving allegations of cursing, threats to neighbours, magic-induced illness, trying to flee town while under suspicion of witchcraft, and general disorderly conduct. She was deemed 'guiltie of becoming of Sathans servant haveing his mark', and despite her denial of all charges, she was executed as a 'notorious witch'.[131] Cuninghame, like Sawer, faced a blend of maleficium and demonism charges. She was accused of committing disruptive and destabilising acts, many of them involving alcohol, such as bewitching a man into drunkenly beating his wife and using magical means to steal ale. Adair entered the fray as a witness and accused her of joining 'an other confessing witche' in Bordeaux, France, for a sort of demonic girls' weekend where they 'drank wyne togidder'.[132] Worse, Cuninghame had purportedly participated in a witches sabbath in which the witches 'sought the good of the fruits of the ground and fisheing af the sea from Sathan'. Like Sawer and Slowane, the court subjected her to a painful search for the devil's mark, the supposed uncovering of which sealed her fate.[133]

It had been a challenging period in Cromwell's northern kingdom, one that had only reified the commitment of men like Adair to creating and maintaining a covenanted community. Witches, as perhaps the most egregious of those who violated their covenants with God and country, would not be tolerated. When the Protectorate ended in May 1659 and Scotland's courts ground to virtual halt amid the confusion and personnel change, the leadership of Ayr would have surely agreed with the Earl of Haddington who complained that, 'becaus the laws ar now silent ... this sin becomes daylie more frequent'.[134] The sin to which Haddington referred was witchcraft, but he could have been speaking about the general unease and spiritual angst of the decade, in which an occupying army put covenanting – as a communal practice and political ethos – to a profound test.

Before leaving witches behind, it is essential to note that witchcraft was not understood, either by elites or ordinary Scots, as operating within a silo, separate from more typical sins. Instead, and especially after more than a decade of attempts by religious leaders to frame all sin as a violation of the covenants, witchcraft existed as part and parcel of perceived morass of wrong-doing – much of it profoundly gendered – that became more urgent during the occupation. This integration is illustrated by a May 1653 case in which Ayr's minister and elders conducted a lengthy investigation into a conflict between Janet Whyte and Helen Brakenrig, two residents who had used the language of witchcraft to slander one another.[135] Brakenrig claimed that Whyte had spread a rumour that she had 'witched' both Whyte and her husband.[136] Worse still, Whyte had told neighbours that Brakenrig had 'borne a bairne' to an unknown father and then buried the body in her yard, adding to the charge of witchcraft an allegation of possible infanticide. When the session called Whyte to explain her words, she confessed that she had indeed called Brakenrig a witch but insisted that she too had been wronged: she was 'daylie and hourlie molested with the sclanderous speaches of Helen Brakenrig, who not once but every tym cales me a witch'. What is more, Brakenrig had accused Whyte of 'lying with the Englishmen' – an unsurprising allegation at a time when the exasperated session had taken to punishing local women in batches for sex with Cromwellian soldiers, so widespread was the problem.[137]

There remains more to this case – including the gruesome discovery of what was deemed an 'untimely birth' in the yard of Helen Brakenrig – but for our purposes, what is noteworthy is how what began with witchcraft soon became an amalgam of the particularly gendered sins and anxieties of the period between the kirk party ascendancy in 1649 and the Restoration. As I have written elsewhere, during the turmoil of occupation, parish kirks viewed female bodies as the primary sites of, and potential vectors for, social and religious disruption.[138] This policing of women's actions and bodies was by no means a new development, but rather a long-standing feature of a disciplinary system that was heightened by the anxiety and unpredictability of the years immediately following the Cromwellian invasion. And this policing entered popular discourse, as ordinary Scots, to varying degrees, informed, shared, and reflected the anxieties of the kirk. The drive to eradicate witchcraft should, then, be understood not as an aberration from an otherwise gender-blind disciplinary programme, but rather as a core part of a gendered search for order amid disorder in covenanted communities.[139]

Conclusion

Ultimately, the actions of local religious leaders during the Cromwellian occupation cannot simply be read as attempts to control their population in a time of uncertainty, though this is clearly part of the story. What also pervades the records during these years is genuine confidence on the part of the session that the truth of their faith and the promises of their covenants with God and with each other would see the town through this difficult period. This is especially apparent in Adair's sermons, which constantly reminded his flock that the 'church of believers' would always find in Christ 'a refuge sanctuary and strong hold to them bot specially in the tyme of trouble when other strongholds are worthless'.[140] Above all, during the occupation, covenanting remained central to communal inclusion – a lesson learned by both those who supposedly subverted the covenants through deals with the devil and those who sought membership in this community of the Scottish godly.

That the handful of English soldiers seeking to marry Ayr women and become part of the parish congregation had to lay down their arms and subscribe the covenant before the discriminating eyes of the session attests to the totalising persistence of the town's covenanter identity.[141] This fact is also demonstrated by the case of William and Thomas Burges, two men – likely relatives who had been away from the town in recent years – who appeared before the session in June 1657. They had come to seek communal inclusion, but first to declare, in no uncertain terms, that

> we are frie of and doe remaine and disclame all the errors publickly profesed now in Britane, and whatsoever is contrarie to sound doctrine and the power of godlynes and doe ingag ourselves to adher to the doctrine worship discipline and government of the kirk of Scotland as its now established according to the word of god confessione of faith and covenants soe subscribeth.

The case of the Burgeses was not singular. In October 1658, Englishman William Baits came to the session seeking 'benefit of baptisme of his child' and declared in front of witnesses that he was free of the errors 'menteined by many in Brittaine' and committed to 'the word of God, confessione of faith, and covenants'. Not being fully literate, Baits marked his initials at the bottom of the declaration.[142]

By signing their names to the end of their statements – which themselves replicated older covenanting oaths – these men demonstrated the reality that to be a full member of the community clearly meant being a covenanter, and to demonstrate one's religious knowledge, sense of sin, and understanding of the directives of the kirk accordingly. This was true in 1638 and in 1643, and it remained true in the decade after Ayr, along with the rest of Scotland, had been forcibly incorporated into the English Commonwealth. In the end, at least in this community, the Cromwellian invasion seems to have done more to instantiate covenanter identity than to impede it. Yet as the end of one chaotic decade turned into another, even greater challenges for the maintenance of Ayr's covenanting ethos lay ahead.

Notes

1 Parts of this chapter were originally published in Michelle D. Brock, 'Keeping the Covenant in Cromwellian Scotland', *Scottish Historical Review*, 99 (2020), 392–411.

Occupation 115

2 Laura A.M Stewart, 'Military Power and the Scottish Burghs, 1625–1651', *Journal of Early Modern History*, 15 (2011), 59–82, at 77.
3 R. Scott Spurlock, *Cromwell and Scotland: Conquest and Religion, 1650–60* (Edinburgh: John Donald Publishers, 2007), p. xv; Tom Barclay and Eric J. Graham, *The Early Transatlantic Trade of Ayr, 1640–1730* (Ayr: The Ayrshire Archaeological and Natural History Society, 2005), p. 15. James Morris claims Ayr was the largest of Cromwell's Scottish fortresses. See James Morris, *The Auld Toon o' Ayr* (Ayr: Stephen and Pollock, 1928), p. 9.
4 On the southwest's resistance to union, despite initial English hopes to find common cause with the region's staunch protestors, see Neil McIntyre, 'Saints and Subverters: The Later Covenanters in Scotland, c. 1648–1682' (PhD thesis, University of Strathclyde, 2016), pp. 43–4, and Susan Gillanders, 'The Scottish Burghs during the Cromwellian Occupation 1651–1660' (PhD thesis, University of Edinburgh, 1999), pp. 56–9.
5 For a description of the financing and building of the new kirk, the details of which were still being worked out in 1656, see National Library of Scotland (hereafter NLS), 'Extracts from the minutes of the Ayr Town council', MS 10335, copied ca. 1820, fos. 141r–3r; and Ayrshire Archives, B6/18/2: Ayr Council Book, 1647–1669, fos. 90v–92r.
6 On the civilian and communal dynamics of the Cromwellian occupation, see Spurlock, *Cromwell and Scotland*; Allan Kennedy, 'Military Rule, Protectoral Government and the Scottish Highlands, c.1654–60', *Scottish Archives*, 23 (2017), 80–102; and Gordon DesBrisay, 'Authority and Discipline in Aberdeen, 1650–1700' (PhD thesis, University of St Andrews, 1989), pp. 20–42.
7 National Records of Scotland (hereafter NRS), CH/2/751/3/1, fo. 220v.
8 B6/18/2, fo. 88v.
9 Laura A.M. Stewart, 'Cromwell and the Scots', in Jane A. Mills (ed.), *Cromwell's Legacy* (Manchester: Manchester University Press, 2012), pp. 171–90, at p. 181. For a discussion of the logistics of kirk–army dynamics in urban areas in the 1650s, see Gillanders, 'The Scottish Burghs', pp. 227–55. On the operation of the courts in Cromwellian Scotland more generally, see Lesley M. Smith, 'Sackcloth for the Sinner or Punishment for the Crime: Church and Secular Courts in Cromwellian Scotland', in John Dwyer, Roger Mason, and Alexander Murdoch (eds), *New Perspectives on the Politics and Culture of Early Modern Scotland* (Edinburgh: John Donald Publishers, 1982), pp. 116–32. It is also worth noting the surprising stability of poor relief in some Scottish burghs during the tumultuous 1650s; see John McCallum, 'Charity and Conflict: Poor Relief in Mid-Seventeenth-Century Dundee', *The Scottish Historical Review*, 95:240 (April 2016), 30–56.
10 CH2/751/3/1, fo. 249v.
11 CH2/751/3/1, fo. 471r. Eccles was present at meetings of the session from November 1655 on, but not formally admitted to the post until the following January. For the contract for Eccles' stipend, composed on 6 November 1655, see Ayrshire Archives, B6/39/8, 'Contract between the magistrates and council of the burgh of Ayr, with consent of the kirk session and deacon convener of the crafts and Mr William Eccles'. Eccles was paid 1,000 merks per annum as

his stipend with a yearly augmentation of 2 chalders victual, 2 bolls meal, 12 bolls malt, and £50 for house rent.

12 Frances Dow, *Cromwellian Scotland, 1651–1660* (Edinburgh: John Donald Publishers, 1979), p. 8.
13 B6/18/2, fo. 87v.
14 James D. Marwick (ed.), *Extracts from the Records of the Convention of Royal Burghs, 1615–1676*, vol. III (Edinburgh, 1866), p. 483. The convention, as John Toller points out, was the only national institution to survive the Cromwellian occupation. See Toller, '"Now of little significancy"? The Convention of the Royal Burghs of Scotland, 1651–1688' (PhD thesis, University of Dundee, 2010), pp. 155–96.
15 Gillanders, 'The Scottish Burghs', p. 25.
16 For a useful summary of these policies and their effects on the burghs, which complained bitterly about the impact of English policies on trade and their economic conditions, see Gillanders, 'The Scottish Burghs', pp. 195–201.
17 Gillanders, 'The Scottish Burghs', p. 199. It is also worth noting the decline in Ayr's ships themselves; though they do not represent the overall volume of trade, it is notable that in 1638 Ayr had twenty working ships, but by 1645 this number had dwindled to six, and further to three by 1656. See Hugh McGhee, 'The Harbour', in Annie I. Dunlop (ed.), *The Royal Burgh of Ayr* (Edinburgh: Oliver and Boyd, 1953), pp. 197–211, at p. 99.
18 For discussion of the economic opportunities of the Cromwellian occupation in a Scottish burgh, the effects of which seem to have been much more positive than in Ayr, see Allan Kennedy, 'The Urban Community in Restoration Scotland: Government, Society and Economy in Inverness, 1660–C.1688', *Northern Scotland*, 5:1 (2014), 26–49, at 36.
19 I have written about these experiences through the country's urban communities in Michelle Brock, '"The Man Will Shame Me": Women, Sex and Kirk Discipline in Cromwellian Scotland', *Scottish Church History*, 51:2 (2022), 133–56.
20 On presbyterian anxiety about and polemics against the religious diversity brought by the English army, see Spurlock, *Cromwell and Scotland*, chapter 1. For an introduction to the varied religious commitments during the English Civil War, see John Coffey, 'Religious Thought', in Michael J. Braddick (ed.), *The Oxford Handbook of the English Revolution* (Oxford: Oxford University Press, 2015), pp. 447–65.
21 On the storming of Dundee, see John Robertson, *Dundee and the Civil Wars, 1639–1660* (Dundee: Friends of Dundee City Archives, 2007).
22 David Stevenson, 'The Burghs and the Scottish Revolution', in Michael Lynch (ed.), *The Early Modern Town in Scotland* (London: Routledge, 1987), pp. 167–91, at p. 187.
23 CH/2/751/3/2, fo. 517r.
24 The best study of the 1650s remains Dow's *Cromwellian Scotland*. Two useful PhD theses on Cromwellian Scotland, though neither of them engages in depth with local responses to occupation, are Kyle David Holfelder, 'Factionalism

in the Kirk during the Cromwellian Invasion and Occupation of Scotland, 1650–1660: The Protestor-Resolutioner Controversy' (PhD thesis, University of Edinburgh, 1998) and Gillanders, 'The Scottish Burghs'. Chris R. Langley's *Worship, Civil War, and Community, 1638–1660* (London: Routledge, 2015) also deals with ecclesiastical responses to the Cromwellian occupation, though at the regional presbytery and synod levels rather than in local parish communities.

25 On the occupation as marking the failure of the Covenanting revolution in Scotland, see Scott Spurlock, 'State, Politics, and Society in Scotland', in Michael J. Braddick (ed.), *The Oxford Handbook of the English Revolution* (Oxford: Oxford University Press, 2014), pp. 363–78, at p. 373.
26 CH2/751/3/1 fo. 195r.
27 CH2/751/3/1 fo. 195r.
28 Dunlop, *The Royal Burgh of Ayr*, p. 113. The session minutes also note Adair's absence during military campaigns. See, for example, NRS CH2/751/3/1, fo. 135r, when Adair's extended absence 'at the Armie' caused there to be no session meeting for three weeks.
29 CH2/751/3/1, fo. 229v.
30 CH2/751/3/1, fo. 268v.
31 CH2/751/3/2, fo. 306r.
32 CH2/751/3/2, fo. 322v.
33 CH2/751/3/2, fo. 322v.
34 CH2/751/3/1 fo. 205r. On scandal in Ayr during the 1650s as well as analysis of Reformed ideas about 'scandal', see also Alfred Johnson, 'Scandalous Ayr: Parish-Level Continuities in 1650s Scotland', in Fiona McCall (ed.), *Church and the People in Interregnum Britain* (London: University of London Press, 2021), pp. 171–92.
35 CH2/751/3/1, fo. 208r.
36 CH2/751/3/, fo. 210r.
37 CH2/751/3/1, fo. 206r.
38 For more information on Moss-troupers in a Celtic context, see Éamonn Ó Ciardha, 'Tories and Moss-Troopers in Scotland and Ireland in the Interregnum: a Political Dimension', in John R. Young (ed.), *Celtic Dimensions of the British Civil Wars* (Edinburgh: John Donald Publishers, 1997), pp. 141–57.
39 CH2/751/3/1, fo. 206r.
40 CH2/751/3/1, fo. 206r.
41 CH2/751/3/1, fo. 210r.
42 See, for example, CH2/751/3/1, fos. 215r, 225v, and 241r.
43 Susan Gillanders has suggested that the rise of fornication and drunkenness cases in Scotland might be taken as 'proof that the kirk's authority did not carry as much weight as it once had', a conclusion with which I disagree, at least in the context of Ayr. Gillanders, 'The Scottish Burghs', p. 237.
44 CH2/751/3/1 fo. 239r.
45 CH2/752/3/2, fo. 268v.

46 For examples of fornication, see cases on CH2/752/3/1–2, fos. 228r, 230r, 243r, 274r, 278v, and 282r.
47 CH2/751/3/2, fo. 287r.
48 CH2/751/3/2, fo. 287v.
49 An example of the type of testimonial sought by the session was slotted into the end of this volume of kirk session minutes. Signed by two soldiers, it attested that one William Shirralay, a drummer in Colonel Alured's regiment, 'hes bein knowen by me thes thre yeirs and upward and is now of the age betwixt eighteine and nynteine and has he seemed to me to uncapable of marriage … as hes never maried any woman to my knowledge as witness my hand at aire 17 april 1654'. CH2/751/3/2, fo. 574v.
50 CH2/751/3/2, fo. 392r.
51 CH2/751/3/2, fo. 392r.
52 CH2/751/3/2, fo. 285r.
53 CH2/751/3/2, fo. 286v.
54 On Cromwell's reluctance to use force against the Scots, whom he regarded as godly but misguided, see Gillanders, 'The Scottish Burghs', p. 3, and Stewart, 'Cromwell and the Scots', p. 178.
55 On the New Model Army's code of conduct, see Mariana Muravyena, 'Do not Rape and Pillage without Command: Sex Offenses and Early Modern European Armies', *Clio: Women, Gender, History*, 39 (2014), 53–77, at 65; Ian Gentles, *The New Model Army in England, Ireland and Scotland, 1645–1653* (Oxford: Oxford University Press, 1992), p. 120.
56 Gillanders, 'The Scottish Burghs', pp. 23–4, and Godfrey Davies (ed.), 'Dundee Court Martial Records 1651', *Miscellany of the Scottish History Society*, iii (Edinburgh: Scottish History Society, 1919), p. 12.
57 CH2/751/3/2, fos. 391r and 434v.
58 CH2/751/3/2, fo. 277r. It is unclear as to which specific covenant the session was referring to here, though it is probably the Solemn League and Covenant, being that it was the most recent document to which they had subscribed. Still, this ambiguity about what specifically 'the Covenant' refers to is a common issue, as both ministers and ordinary Scots sometimes used the term vaguely or spoke about the covenants of 1638 and 1643 in tandem or even interchangeably. See, for example, the sermon preached by Robert Douglas (a man who, admittedly, Adair and his ilk found far too moderate) at the coronation of Charles II in January 1651, which refers numerous times simply to 'this Covenant'. See Robert Douglas, *The Forme and Order of the Coronation of Charles the Second, King of Scotland, England, France, and Ireland* (Aberdeen, 1651), pp. 8–10. For a discussion of varied references to the covenants among the parishioners of Ayr, see Michelle D. Brock, 'Plague, Covenants, and Confession: The Strange Case of Ayr, 1647–8', *Scottish Historical Review*, 97:2 (2018), 129–52, at 147–9.
59 CH2/751/3/2, fo. 314r.
60 CH2/751/3/2, fo. 357r.
61 For a quantitative look at sins in Ayr, see Johnson, 'Scandalous Ayr', p. 181.

62 For a discussion of sexual offenses in other burghs, see Gillanders, 'The Scottish Burghs', esp. pp. 231–9; Langley, *Worship, Civil War, and Community*, pp. 56–60; and Brock, 'The Man Will Shame Me'.
63 For cases of women called before the session for breach of sabbath due to the presence of soldiers in their homes, see CH2/751/3/2, fos. 267v, 270r, 316r, and 322v.
64 CH2/751/3/2, fos. 349v and 319r.
65 CH2/751/3/2, fo. 443r. Given the constant stream of recent fornication cases the session first assumed he was English, but Donald reported that she thought he was a Scotsman, likely one of the many passing through the town amid the dislocation of the period.
66 CH2/751/3/2, fo. 443r.
67 On early modern Scottish definitions of rape, see Brian P. Levack, 'The Prosecution of Sexual Crimes in Early Eighteenth-Century Scotland', *The Scottish Historical Review*, 89:228 (October 2010), 172–93, at 178.
68 CH2/751/3/2, fo. 443r.
69 See, for example, cases on CH2/751/3/2, fos. 425–6v and 458r. See also Muravyena, 'Do not Rape and Pillage without Command'.
70 Works that have touched on, but not centred, the experiences of women during the 1640s and 1650s include Langley's *Worship, Civil War, and Community*; Laura A.M. Stewart, *Rethinking the Scottish Revolution* (Oxford: Oxford University Press, 2016), esp. pp. 112–15; and Jamie Murdoch McDougall, 'Covenants and Covenanters in Scotland, 1638–1679' (PhD thesis, University of Glasgow, 2017), esp. pp. 55–60. Jason White has also published a helpful recent article that explores the gendered interactions with Scottish soldiers levied to serve in the Thirty Years' War; see Jason White, 'Women, Gender, and the Kirk before the Covenant', *International Review of Scottish Studies*, 45 (2020), 27–53. For examples of the more voluminous work on women and the English Revolution, see, for example, Diane Purkiss, *Literature, Gender and Politics during the English Civil War* (Cambridge: Cambridge University Press, 2005) and Ann Hughes, *Gender and the English Revolution* (London: Routledge, 2012).
71 CH2/751/3/2, fo. 492v.
72 CH2/751/3/2, fo. 494r
73 CH2/751/3/2, fo. 500r.
74 CH2/751/3/2, fo. 494v.
75 CH2/751/3/2, fo. 495r.
76 Stewart synthesises this characterisation, and how it has informed scholarly appraisals of Cromwell's religious policies, in 'Cromwell and the Scots', pp. 172–3.
77 In April 1653, the session minutes note that 'for the interim that scandalous persones procesed who live upon the north side of the toune ar to mak their repentence in the hospitall fir the mor expeidncy of pentents'. CH2/751/3/2, fo. 288v.
78 CH2/751/3/1, fo. 205r.

79 CH2/751/3/2, fo. 364r.
80 CH2/751/3/2, fos. 452–4r.
81 See, for example, CH2/751/3/2, fos. 426r and 446r.
82 CH2/751/3/2, fo. 380r.
83 CH2/751/3/2, fo. 371r.
84 CH2/751/3/2, fo. 380r.
85 CH2/751/3/2, fo. 387r. Margaret Andersone, with whom he had slept, was first 'suspended of all church priviledges'. A note in the minutes recounts that she soon fled town, at fo. 365r.
86 CH2/751/3/2, fo. 268v.
87 CH2/751/3/2, fo. 284r.
88 CH2/751/3/2, fo. 314v.
89 On poor relief in early modern Scotland more generally, see John McCallum, *Poor Relief and the Church in Scotland, 1560–1650* (Edinburgh: Edinburgh University Press, 2018). McCallum references a few notable late sixteenth-century examples of poor relief having been conditioned on religious knowledge, similar to the case in Ayr that I have detailed here. He also notes that while that immorality and religious failings could be a reason that some of the poor might be denied relief, such explicit cases are relatively rare in the session records (at pp. 192–3).
90 It was the first time in the period beginning in 1632; I have not examined the kirk session records thoroughly prior to this date.
91 See cases on CH2/751/3/2, fos. 346r, 433r, 438r, and 443v–4r. During the occupation, the kirk session also enforced policies directed at improving the religious knowledge of children, servants, and the poor. See CH2/751/3/2, fos. 284r and 314v.
92 Ayrshire Archives, Acc. 483, vol. II. The first part of this volume is paginated for the entries composed through May 1656. They are, compared to the first volume of Adair papers, well-organised and seem to be primarily lectures, with bits of Latin, Hebrew, and Greek interspersed throughout; they may have been intended for publication.
93 Acc. 483, vol. II, 17, 42, 56, n.p.
94 At least twenty people between 1652 and 1655 were suspended, compared to almost none between 1638 and 1651.
95 Examples of this specific language can be found at CH2/751/3/1, fo. 238v and CH2/751/3/2, fo. 434v.
96 CH2/751/3/2, fos. 321r, 346r, and 368v; B6/18/2, fo. 96r.
97 CH2/751/3/2, fo. 497r.
98 CH2/751/3/2, fo. 498r.
99 Neil McIntyre and Jamie McDougall, 'Reframing the Covenant: *A Solemn Acknowledgment* (1648) and the Resubscription of the Solemn League and Covenant', *Seventeenth Century*, 37:5 (2022), 733–56.
100 CH2/751/3/2, fo. 498r.
101 CH2/751/3/2, fo. 498r.
102 CH2/751/3/2, fo. 299v.
103 CH2/751/3/2, fo. 300r.

Occupation 121

104 CH2/751/3/2, fo. 300r. This language of 'liberty' was a common feature of the goals and protestations made by hardline throughout the Scottish Revolution and into the Restoration era. See Sharon Adams, 'In Search of the Scottish Republic', in Sharon Adams and Julian Goodare (eds), *Scotland in the Age of Two Revolutions* (Woodbridge: Boydell, 2014), pp. 97–114.
105 CH2/751/3/2, fo. 346r.
106 CH2/751/3/2, fo. 352r; CH2/751/3/1, fo. 210r.
107 On covenanting as a performative act from the beginning, see Stewart, *Rethinking the Scottish Revolution*, esp. chapter 1, and Edward. J. Cowan, 'The Making of a National Covenant', in John Morrill (ed.), *The Scottish National Covenant in its British Context* (Edinburgh: Edinburgh University Press, 1990), pp. 68–89.
108 Explicit episodes of dissent and disagreement only show up a couple of times in the session minutes during occupation, the most notable regarding the ill-fated General Assembly of the summer of 1653 and the rival protester–resolutioner meetings. In both cases, the session elders uncomfortable with directives from the protesters were overruled by the minister and other elders, but they remained on the session as fully participating ministers. See CH2/751/3/2, fos. 300v and 313v.
109 On the influence of sectarian groups in Scotland, see Spurlock, *Cromwell and Scotland*, chapters 4 and 5.
110 CH2/751/3/2, fo. 291r.
111 CH2/751/3/2, fo. 291r. 'Puedobaptism' is a variant of 'paedobaptism', and here, Mur was being asked to comment on his judgement about infant baptism (it is clear from the context that the 'erroures of' is only modifying 'antitrinitarinism'). Mur went on to further clarify that 'he esteemes the baptisme of childreine of believing parents so valid that they neid not be rebaptized'. Shortly thereafter, William Mur is listed as a deacon, but I am not entirely sure if this is the same Mur, though it is very likely, as many merchants served as elders or deacons. Spurlock suggests that the citadel at Ayr was 'a Baptist hotbed' (*Cromwell and Scotland*, p. 168).
112 CH2/751/3/2, fo. 309v.
113 CH2/751/3/2, fo. 370v.
114 CH2/751/3/2, fo. 376r.
115 CH2/751/3/2, fo. 376r.
116 CH2/751/3/2, fo. 376r.
117 Stewart and Gillanders have also pointed out the limited effect had by English ideas about toleration and independency introduced during occupation, particularly in the Burghs. See Gillanders, 'The Scottish Burghs', p. 250 and Stewart, 'Cromwell and the Scots', pp. 180–1.
118 See, for example, CH2/751/3/1, fo. 237r; CH2/751/3/2, fos. 370v and 428r.
119 CH2/751/3/2, fo. 314v.
120 This is reinforced by the fact that, throughout Scotland, some of those initially most opposed to occupation eventually collaborated with the Cromwellian regime. Patrick Little and David L. Smith have detailed the participation of Scotsmen in the new parliament at Westminster in *Parliament and Politics*

during the Cromwellian Protectorate (Cambridge: Cambridge University Press, 2007), chapter 12. It is important to keep in mind, however, that as Laura Stewart has pointed out, Westminster remained an Anglocentric body, and Scottish participation therein seems to have little effect on the lived experience of occupation in the parishes. See Stewart, 'Cromwell and the Scots', p. 179.
121 I have also made this point in Brock, 'The Man Will Shame Me'.
122 Julian Goodare, Lauren Martin, Joyce Miller, and Louise Yeoman, 'The Survey of Scottish Witchcraft', https://witches.hca.ed.ac.uk (archived January 2003, accessed 23 September 2023). On English policies regarding Scottish witch-hunting, see Brian P. Levack, 'The Great Scottish Witch Hunt of 1661–1662', *Journal of British Studies*, 20:1 (1980), 90–108, at 91–3.
123 Julian Goodare et al., 'Survey of Scottish Witchcraft'. The 1658–9 hunts have been rather understudied, due to the fact that the intensity of the 'Great Scottish Witch Hunt' of 1661–2 has, understandably, dominated research into mid-century witch-hunting in Scotland. See, for example, Levack, 'The Great Scottish Witch Hunt of 1661–1662'.
124 Robert Baillie, *The Letters and Journals of Robert Baillie*, 3 vols, ed. David Laing (Edinburgh: Bannatyne Club, 1841–2), p. 436.
125 For a discussion of these charges, see Chapter 3, this volume.
126 NRS, JC 26/25, High Court of Justiciary process notes.
127 Levack argues that witch prickers are 'at least partly responsible' for the intensity of the 1661–2 hunts, as well as the large number of those convicted and executed in 1659. Levack, 'Great Scottish Witch Hunt', 99.
128 JC 26/25, Process notes.
129 Charles H. Firth (ed.), *Scotland and the Commonwealth: Letters and Papers relating to the Military Government of Scotland from August 1651 to December 1653* (Edinburgh: T. and A. Constable, 1895), p. 382.
130 Firth, *Scotland and the Commonwealth*, p. 382.
131 NRS, JC 26/26, High Court of Justiciary, process notes, 1659.
132 JC 26/26.
133 JC 26/26; Julian Goodare et al., 'Survey of Scottish Witchcraft'.
134 Quoted in Levack, 'Great Scottish Witch Hunt', 93–4.
135 On this subject, see Michelle D. Brock, 'Enemies of God?: Slander, Gender, and Witchcraft in the Scottish Parish', in Martha McGill and Alasdair Raffe (eds), *The Scottish State and the Experience of Government, 1560–1707* (Edinburgh: Edinburgh University Press, forthcoming).
136 CH2/751/3/2, fos. 378r–9r.
137 CH2/751/3/2, fos. 378r–9r.
138 Brock, 'The Man Will Shame Me'.
139 For a recent summary of historiographical debates about gender and kirk discipline, Elizabeth Ewan, 'Gendering the Reformation', in Ian P. Hazlett (ed.), *A Companion to the Scottish Reformation* (Leiden: Brill, 2021), pp. 519–21.
140 From a January 1651 sermon on the prophesy of Nahum. Ayrshire Archives, Acc. 483, Papers of William Adair, vol. I, n.p.
141 See, for example, CH2/751/3/2, fos. 277r, 395r, and 417v.
142 CH2/751/3/2, fo. 529r.

5

Restoration and rebellion

On 3 September 1658, Oliver Cromwell rapidly succumbed to complications from malaria. That his death fell on the anniversary of his great victories at Dunbar and Worchester was a fitting end for a man obsessed with providence. His son Richard, who he had appointed as next in line for the Protectorship, took the reins of power in the Commonwealth, and he was not, as he has often been caricatured, an inept or bumbling successor.[1] But he inherited a tremendously fragile settlement, one held together only by military force and the personality of his father. By May 1659, the younger Cromwell had resigned his post, and the newly reconstituted English Parliament set about restoring Charles II to the throne (he had, of course, already assumed this position in Scotland in 1650). For the people of Ayr as throughout the country, this change was initially cause for celebration. Whatever reservations they may have had about the monarch, they were not republicans and he was still their king.[2] At the dawn of the 1660s, even men like Adair expected the new regime to instate an ecclesiastical settlement that would permit the kirk's presbyterian system, centred on the covenants, to continue unmolested. Such hopes were soon dashed.

The Restoration brought dramatic change to Scotland. After 1660, the political and economic influence of the burghs eroded, and the turmoil of the next decade compounded the country's already bleak finances.[3] A litany of mostly unwelcome ecclesiastical transformations occurred within the first few years of Charles II's British reign: bishops were reintroduced – or reimposed, depending on who you asked; three of the most prominent covenanting leaders were publicly executed for treason; the Oath of Allegiance to the monarch replaced the covenants as the oaths required for public office; and one-third of the ministry was deposed. As much as possible, the new government attempted to return the Scottish kirk to the pre-1638 period, rescinding nearly all of the acts passed by either faction of the covenanter-led Scottish Parliament.[4] Most Scots conformed to these changes and did not deem acceptance of episcopacy, however begrudging, to be fundamentally contrary to the covenants.[5] And in some quarters, fealty to the covenants, as both religious practice and centrepiece of political identity, fell out of favour – after all, one could interpret the disastrous English occupation of the past decade as divine retribution for the covenanters' rebellion against Charles I.[6] But in Ayr, many parishioners held fast to their carefully cultivated culture of covenanting. The town, while certainly not monolithic or static in its commitments, quickly became a hotbed of dissent, with Adair in an increasingly precarious position.

While the general nonconformity of the southwest is well known to historians, less understood is how debate over episcopacy operated at the local level in terms of parish politics, personal piety, and communal identity.[7] While many Scots may have experienced 'little disruption' after Charles II returned to the throne, in Ayr, the Restoration hindered the exercise of kirk discipline, wrought new and at times dramatic division in the town leadership, and sparked popular rebellion.[8] The confused vacillation of government policy between moderation, repression, and looking the other way for nearly three decades between the Restoration and the Revolution of 1689 meant that the actions of the town leadership and general population were also inconsistent. Moreover, the significant levels of conformity and compromise throughout in the country and at times in Ayr should not obscure the fact that the Restoration ushered in a period of economic precarity, social upheaval, and challenges to deep-seated political and religious identities. The 1660s in the burgh were characterised, at times paradoxically, by steady attempts at adaptation and a rising tide of radicalisation – the latter less among the leadership than the ordinary men and women of Ayr.[9]

Resistance, like conformity, comes in many forms, and the decade following the Restoration was an exercise in getting creative with implicit and explicit dissent. The people of Ayr, though far from a monolith, generally rejected or resisted the reintroduction of episcopacy in these years not because of an ideological stake in ecclesiastical politics or an entrenched theological commitment, but because of their deeply ingrained covenanter identity. This identity operated differently among the various constituencies of the town, and at times it was set aside for the sake of political and economic expediency. Yet ultimately, far from having been dampened by the turmoil of the Cromwellian era, the covenanting ethos of Ayr's residents remained bound up with loyalty to their long-time minister and continued to grow and evolve alongside a burgeoning sense of their role as Scots on a national and international stage.

Episcopacy restored

Despite the fact that a handful of the most radical covenanters seriously embraced independency and flirted with republicanism, the ideas had little influence in Ayr, which resisted both the incorporating union and the introduction of religious tolerance in Scotland during the Cromwellian occupation.[10] And even though one faction of Scottish ministers had had serious reservations about the godliness of Charles II, the kirk as a whole had, as Robert Baillie put it, been 'very faithfull to our King' during 'all the English tymes' and had been as 'instrumentall as we could for his restitution'.[11] In late May 1660, the town marked the Restoration by offering 'ane solemne congratulatione in the most sutabill and decent maner' to the king for his 'returne in safty and peace to his kingdoms'.[12] In April 1661, provost William Cunningham – a man very keen to play nice with the new government – sent a letter to the council at the behest of Charles II instructing a celebration be held in the burgh the following week 'in reference to his majesties coronatione in England'.[13] Those who failed to mark the occasion appropriately would be heavily fined.

The session minutes are remarkably quiet on the Restoration itself. Discipline continued through the consequential spring of 1660, as it had during the disruption of the Cromwellian invasion. Two cases in July of that year give us some insight into the priorities of Adair, the elders, and their parishioners. On 24 July, Jon McClatchie appeared after a long absence from the community, accused of fornication with Janet Smyth – his fourth such offence. He professed 'his sorrow both for his said sine and his long disobedience in flying away from the censurs of the kirk' and presented them with an emotional supplication: 'I am sorrie that by my miscarriage and unworried walking I should have so offended the lord so often as I have … I desyr that the lord of his mercy wuld convert me, by giving me a spiritual lyfe, in opening my understanding and being and will and offectiones, for giving me spirituall obedienbce to his comandes.'[14] McClatchie, to his own mind, was an extraordinary sinner, in need of extraordinary repentance and forgiveness. As he told the session,

> I might confese that my sines stick so fast in me, that I have neid of som singular kind of washing. I pray that in tym comin I may live more soberly and qietly in the fear of the lord, and that I may not defy any farder that I may renew my Covenant with jesus Christ, for I can have no rest til I be reconciled. I desyr to be reconciled to the kirk and that ye wuld have compassione on me, for I hop in tym coming to walk in the fear of the lord mor not formerly, I desyr to be maid a freind to yrs and no more a freind to Satan.[15]

McClatchie signed his statement, and after seeking advice from the presbytery, the session decided to grant his request, but only after performance of public repentance each sabbath day until March 1661. What is noteworthy here is McClatchie's earnest desire – or at least, judged to be so by the scrupulous session – to renew the covenant (presumably the Solemn League and Covenant) in order to be reconciled to the kirk. For this errant parishioner as for Adair and the elders, covenanting continued to occupy the central place not only in their religious lives, but as the primary means through which communal inclusion and even spiritual rest could be found.

The hangover from the turmoil of the occupation also bled into the disciplinary concerns of the kirk, even after the troops began to leave the town. On 30 July 1660, Gibilla Wallace, a local woman who had married an 'Inglishman who also wes anabaptistically disposed', was called before the session for the fornication before marriage and, worse, 'having deteined her child from Baptisme thes several years'.[16] She sorrowfully confessed to both crimes, and after some investigation, it was determined that she had not been herself rebaptised but 'only ingadged by her anabaptisicall husband to keep her child from Baptisme'. Wallace was accordingly ordained to come before the congregation and 'acknowledge her sines forsaid and renounce Anabaptism'.[17] Well into the 1660s, anxieties surrounding the material and spiritual consequences of the relationships between Ayr women and English soldiers continued to weigh heavily on the minds of the session members. As late as the spring of 1664, women came before the session either accused of sex with soldiers or of their own accord, such as Margaret Wilson who in April of that year presented a supplication 'desyring the priveledg to be admitted to publick to give signes of repentenc and satisfaction of the kirk', which was granted.[18]

The legacy of Ayr's most intense period of witch-hunting also persisted after the Restoration. Even as the town was largely spared from the intensity of the 'Great Scottish Witch Hunt' of 1661–2, the rhetoric about witches permeated the language of insult into the early 1660s.[19] On 24 June 1661, for example, Jean Gilmour produced a bill against Janet McGuire claiming that she had called Gilmour 'a devil and a witch', and another woman 'a drunken vyll whoor'.[20] In September 1663, Agnes Dunschit appeared before the kirk session at Ayr to complain that Margaret McCall had 'slandered her good name' by calling her 'a rank witch' who should be 'burnt quick'. McCall had even accused Dunschit of coming to her house on a Thursday night and bidding 'her renounce her baptisme', an allegation that displayed the degree to which, by this point, the demonic pact had become part of popular understandings of witchcraft.[21] Such accusations were deadly business, especially coming so soon after one of Scotland's most intense periods of witch-hunting. If taken seriously, they had the potential to cast individuals as enemies not only of church and state, but of community and Christendom. In this case, however, the session judged McCall guilty of slander and required her confess her sin before the congregation on the next sabbath day; Dunschit's good name, at least for the time being, was preserved. Similar examples of successful countersuits for libellous witchcraft allegations can be found in session registers throughout the country, especially during and following periods of intense witch trials.[22]

During the first year after the Restoration, then, it was more or less business as usual for the kirk session, but change – most of it unwelcome – was on the horizon. By the end of 1660, the English troops had mostly withdrawn, leaving behind an abandoned citadel and, in some cases, lovers and children.[23] For the people of the town, their departure must have elicited mixed feelings. The occupation had not been easy on the community in many respects, but it had also brought new economic and spiritual opportunities (the former embraced more often than the latter), as well as new relationships.[24] Despite abundant rumours that they had been using their sermons to 'fill the people with fears of the Bishops, Books, destroying of the Covenant, setting up of profanitie', even the staunchest protestors were distrustful but initially keen to cooperate with the Restoration regime.[25] In the autumn of 1660, Adair wrote to Robert Douglas, a resolutioner (as well as the husband of Adair's sister-in-law) who had been working to ensure a smooth transition of power. In the letter dated 6 September, Adair addressed head-on reports that he had preached in a way disloyal to the king, which he attributed to misinformation spread by town provost and apparent rival William Cunningham, who had been elected earlier in the year.[26] His words give us a window into both his own view on good governance and lukewarm, if initially conciliary, feelings about the new regime.

The sermons in question had been on Psalm 92, and though we do not have a record of what Adair said that raised suspicion, the later passages of the text, such as verse seven, offer a clue: 'When the wicked spring as the grass, and when all the workers of iniquity do flourish; it is that they shall be destroyed for ever.'[27] To the best of his memory, Adair told Douglas that all he had said pertaining to the governance of the realm was that 'the good government of kings and magistrates' should be directed at 'righteousness of the poor and neidy and for the breaking of the oppressor', for 'all gods people might certainly expect this from Chrysts government'. In his telling, the application of the text was to tell his audience that they 'had reasone to hav god hops of our king' who seemed 'weile disposed and inclined to clemency'. He did not condone the actions of the English, who had been led by an 'ill cause'. Furthermore, he had warned his congregants that 'if the work of the reformation was abandoned', then they should not blame Charles II, but rather the 'malignant misinforming knaves that were constand enemies to it'. Though unwilling to criticise the new king in an explicit way, Adair greatly distrusted those Charles II had put into power in Scotland and elsewhere. Indeed, his preaching had cast aspersions only on those who 'continued to call the building of Jerusalem rebelling against the king'.[28] So far, the king had issued declarations that suggested that he would leave the kirk be, and his government was not (yet) targeting those still committed to the covenants. But the Ayr minister had seen enough in his career to curtail any optimism.

Adair's warnings about those around the king turned out to be prescient. In the spring of 1661, the Scottish Parliament – filled with figures sympathetic to, and appointed by, the newly restored monarch – rescinded all acts passed by the covenanter parliaments of the previous decade. In their place, a series of acts passed by Charles's government over the next two years required ministers to recognise the supremacy of the monarch in ecclesiastical matters and, for those appointed after 1649 when lay patronage had been dispensed with, to actively accept the authority of bishops.[29] By the end of 1662, the covenants themselves had essentially been deemed illegitimate. To hardliners like Adair and his brethren in the southwest, this struck at the Erastian heart of their lives' work; these new measures were, on their face, an affront to the godly project and God himself. While two-thirds of the Scottish clergy did conform to the directives, more than half in the southwest did not. Men like William Eccles lost their jobs; those who, like Adair, had been in post since before 1649 were confined to their parishes, where they became, as Robert Wodrow put it, 'eyesores' to the bishops.[30]

The sense of betrayal was acute, even if the ecclesiastical settlement was, in a way, a 'pyrrhic ideological victory' for the protestors who had always doubted the sincerity of Charles II's commitment to upholding the covenants.[31] Covenanters of many stripes would have agreed with Robert Baillie's lament that, in a letter penned in May 1662, 'we had lost so much blood at Dunbar, Worcester, and elsewhere, and at laist our libertie' in the cause of the king, only to have been betrayed.[32] Though we do not have any of Adair's own words on the return of episcopacy, it is safe to assume that he largely shared the sentiments of fellow protestors James Guthrie and Archibald Johnston of Wariston, who both gave scaffold speeches that would soon become part of covenanting martyrology. Guthrie, sentenced to die for co-authoring a seditious tract against the king, at his death deemed the covenants to be 'Sacred, Solemn, Publick Oaths of God, I believe can be loosed nor dispensed with, by no Person, or Party, or Power upon earth'; they remained 'binding upon these Kingdoms, and will be for ever hereafter'.[33] Wariston, in a similar vein two years later, reiterated his commitment not only to the National Covenant and the Solemn League and Covenant, but to the accompanying *'the Solemn Acknowledgement of our Sins, & Engagement to our duties*; to all the *grounds & Causes of Fasts* and humiliations, & of the *Lords displeasure* & contending with the Land'.[34] By this point, covenanting loyalty belonged not only to the covenants themselves, but also to the acts and disciplinary measures that embodied their aims. For the hardliners and their followers, the covenants were totalising;

no portion of their tenets nor enforcement of their mandates could be dispensed with without great affront to God. Though Adair was at times more pragmatist than high-minded idealist, he clearly concurred.

Monarchs, ministers, and magistrates

When the second session of the Scottish Parliament met in 1662, men like William Adair became targets for the new regime. According to fellow protestor James Kirkton, the members 'thought fitt to give a proof of their zeal for the new bishops' by making 'ane example of terror' to mulish presbyterians who remained unwilling to accept the episcopal settlement. 'The most considerable or most hated ministers in the west countrey' were summoned to be made an example to 'the rest of that tribe' by compelling them 'into humble submission to bishops'.[35] Kirkton may have added dramatic flair, but in any case, seven ministers, Adair among them, were summoned to be pressed in person to take the Oath of Allegiance – which recognised the king as head of the kirk – with authorities fully expecting they would refuse and might be punished accordingly. As Baillie put it, 'the guise now is, the Bishops will trouble no man, but the State will punish seditious ministers. We are in the most hard taking we have seen at any tyme'.[36] The kirk session minutes reveal a note, in Adair's hand, on the margin of the 24 April 1662 entry, that read 'Mr Wm Adair was summonded to Edinburgh and keiped till August 11', during which time little business was conducted by the session other than poor relief.[37]

While in Edinburgh, the seven ministers raised questions about the nature of the oath itself and presented to the parliament a document that acknowledged Charles II's supreme civil authority but rejected his power over the church. Kirkton noted, with frustratingly little elaboration, that Adair took a 'separate course from his honest brethren, and so saved himself, but with very great offence'.[38] He had apparently refused to sign the document until it had been first shown to the Lord Chancellor, William Cunningham, 9th Earl of Glencairn (not the same man as Ayr's sometime provost), though his fellow ministers disagreed with this course. As a result, while the others were temporarily jailed for signing, Adair was simply ordered to return home to his parish.[39] Though Adair's reasoning is unclear, this episode might best be understood as a testament to the importance of clerical connections – Adair was supported by local magistrates as well as regional nobility who either shared or were sympathetic to his cause. His half-brother, Sir Robert Adair, was an influential political figure and wealthy landowner on both sides of the Irish Sea, and he had family connections to powerful kirk figures who had been on the other side of the covenanting debate, such as Robert Douglas.

As such, he seems to have been afforded greater protection than some of his counterparts, which would allow him to hold onto his post through some of the most tumultuous decades of the seventeenth century. In return, he was at times more conciliatory than one might imagine, despite his zealous principles. Post-Restoration covenanters, though sometimes caricatured as either religious fanatics or victimised martyrs, were often neither: their connections to power remained essential, and their flexibility in certain circumstances was born of necessity and, in the case of men of Adair's generation, the experience of decades of covenanting under crisis.

For Adair, who by this point had served the parish for nearly a quarter century through war, plague, witchcraft, and occupation, the Restoration brought the greatest challenges yet. He personally knew the covenanting leaders – Guthrie, Wariston, and Argyll – executed for treason. Worse still, he lost the clerical colleague that the parish had spent over a decade trying to find. Indeed, feeling the loss of the kirk's second in command since the previous autumn, the town council sent Eccles a letter in January 1663 'desyreing him that he wold comply' with parliament's decrees and return to his charge.[40] Eccles, a man after Adair's own heart rather than those of the moderates on the council, refused and remained banned from official preaching until 1672, when he was admitted as a minister in Paisley.

For two years, Adair laboured alone. But in the winter of 1664, the Archbishop of Glasgow appointed a second minister, George White, to the parish.[41] The magistrates of Ayr, perhaps knowing their audience, still deemed it appropriate to follow the old tradition of inviting the parishioners to offer their thoughts on the new minister, even if their objections would make little difference. Of the sixty people who showed up to a meeting in the tolbooth, the majority expressed their desire to have a 'farder hearing' of White before his appointment. Others strenuously rejected his appointment, 'crying out they wold not condescend to him nor no uther because the place was sufficientlie furnished by two ministers lawfullie established', meaning Adair and Eccles.[42] These responses give us insight into the varied ways that the people of Ayr processed the disruptions wrought by the Restoration, as well as their relationship with both their ministers and the covenanting tradition. That the majority present simply wanted to hear more from White before making a judgement reminds us that those in the pews took seriously the duty of vetting the person in the pulpit, which had been a critical aspect of the minister–lay relationship since the Reformation. The faction who protested his appointment, citing that the town already had its clerical needs covered and lawfully so, critiqued what they saw as the spiritual illegality of the appointment. That most of the town could not be bothered to attend the meeting suggests an implicit rejection of White's appointment, or general dissatisfaction with the ecclesiastical establishment, or perhaps apathy driven by the sheer exhaustion of the previous years. The general sentiment towards the new minister is neatly captured by a small slip of paper – probably composed by a later minister of the parish – inserted on the final page of the volume containing the kirk session minutes between 1662 and 1666. It reads, in all caps:

THE EPISCOPAL INTRUSION.

MR. GEORGE WHITE.

1664.[43]

During the early years of White's tenure in Ayr, he faced small acts of resistance from kirk elders, some of whom openly rejected his authority by simply not showing up for meetings of the session when he was present. Indeed, Adair and White rarely attended session meetings together, neither enthusiastic about being yoked together by their charges. For years, they appear to have alternated weeks, with only a few elders joining each minister for their meetings – a marked change from the previous years, when the session had usually been staffed by at least a dozen elders at each meeting. By the second half of the decade, staffing the session became a major issue. In February 1666, the session met – with White but not Adair present – and considered 'the paucity of their number by reason there hath been no new session chosen for severall yeirs bygone and so that many of the members are dead others infirme or removed out of the town'. They put together a list of elders and deacons to be 'added to the present session to make up the number' and asked both ministers to 'speake to the severall persons listed to try their willingnesse'.[44] It is noteworthy that the following week, Adair alone was appointed to receive the new members of the session; indeed, there is every indication that the primary clerical authority remained vested in him, not only as first charge, but as someone who embodied the prevailing sentiments of the town.[45] Despite these efforts, the challenge of filling the posts of the session persisted; in 1671 the remaining members resolved 'to make a new election of deacons and elders to be added to their number' and to offer encouragement to eligible men to 'accept of the said places'.[46]

A small act of scribal resistance in a new volume of the session minutes, which began at the very end of 1666, epitomises the mood of the session during these years. All of the entries composed between the beginning of 1667 and the middle of 1669, when Adair was mostly away from the parish and fighting to hang onto his post (he was, as we will see, temporarily suspended in 1668), have been altered: 'minister' after White's name has been scratched through and replaced by 'together with', followed by the name the clerk and collector joining him.[47] At other times, 'minister' following White's name is bolded out in a deep, dark mark that nearly bleeds through the page.[48] This rhetorical stripping of White's position was likely the handiwork of a later clerk or even Adair himself, who was keeper of the physical records. If Adair did it – and the changes look to be in his distinctive scrawl – then it was an act of protest typical for a man who insisted not only on allegiance to a strict interpretation of the covenants, but also rigid adherence to procedure. White may have been an ordained minister, but in the minds of many he was not the proper minister proceeding over the session at a time when Adair was barred from preaching from his long-time pulpit.

The Restoration also roiled and divided the magistrates of the town. In the early autumn of 1661, the Oath of Allegiance and other acts passed by that year's parliament 'anent the majesties royall prerogative' were recorded in the council book, and magistrates asked to 'assure conformatie' to them. The commissioners, led by provost Cunningham, considered 'how much it may conduce to the happiness of the Royall Burrow to give obedience to the actes of Parliament now maid for establishing his majestie authority'.[49] In September 1663, as tensions flared at the national and local levels, the magistrates 'appointed a letter of thanksgiving' to be sent to the provost entreating him to 'persever in manteining of the libertie of the burghe' and offering their general encouragement for his work at the present meeting of parliament.[50] The immediate concern of the merchant-dominated council seems to have been the peace and economic prosperity of the burgh, especially given that trade had been impeded during much of the Cromwellian period.[51] In an attempt to rebuild and make up for lost revenue in the previous decade, members feared that running afoul of the king would lead to removal of the trade privileges of the burgh.

While most members of the council could support general compliance, some were unwilling to yield to the new mandates for accepting royal authority over the kirk. In late 1663, the town council declared, on order of the Scottish Parliament, that it was 'unlawfull to subjects upon pregeduce of reformatione or uther pretence whatsumever to enter into Covenants or to take up arms against the King and those commissioned by him'. The oaths 'comminlie called the nationall Covenant and the other intituled a solemne league and Covenant' were deemed to be against the 'fundamentall lawes and liberties' of the kingdom.[52] All public officials were expected to abjure the covenants, and those who refused to do so were to be barred from service on the council and in other public positions. The magistrates, clearly torn on the issue, dragged their feet. In January 1664, they received a letter from the Privy Council asking them to report 'thair diligence' in accounting for 'thos who have takin or refused to subscryve the declaration' by 18 February.[53] When the council convened in the tolbooth to do just that, all of the correspondence that Cunningham had received from the government about compliance to the various acts of parliament were publicly read by the clerk, a move that can be interpreted as both a warning to the public as well as an attempt to deflect any popular anger provoked by the forthcoming removal of the 'non-subscribers' from the council. Ten of the councillors plus the clerk resubscribed their allegiance to acts, which they had previously done in 1662, while eight of them held steadfast in their refusal to comply.[54] The motivations of those who signed remain unclear to us; some, like Cunningham, seem to have agreed to at least some extent with the royal decree, while others probably viewed it as a political necessity if further conflict was to be avoided. For those who refused, though, the reasoning was clear: they could and would not abjure the covenants which, at this point, had been central to their identities for most of their adult lives.

These divisions had major implications for the governance of the town, and in 1664, the Privy Council noted that 'a difficulty has arisen in connection with the Declaration' in Ayr. The 'difficulty' was that so many had refused to deem the covenants unlawful as per the government's orders that now Ayr struggled to staff its town council.[55] As such, it was ordained that those already sitting on the council who had complied would be allowed to continue in their posts well past the typical new election date, 'until they consider what course to take anent the said burgh'.[56] In short, this allowed the compliant members of the council to both re-elect themselves and strategically appoint like-minded magistrates, which they did in 1665. In September of 1666, the Privy Council sent a letter to the town council, reminding them that no magistrates were to be elected 'bot such as are knoune to be affected to the Kings service and present government' and that it was 'their pleasur' for William Cunningham to continue in service as provost for another year. This was, for the burgh, an unprecedented amount of governmental oversight.[57] To maintain order and compliance regarding the government's ecclesiastical policies, partnerships between local and national leaders were essential, and Ayr was by no means the only burgh to experience such interference.[58] Cunningham was the king's man on the inside (apparently an unpopular one at that), and his authority was central to keeping nonconformists there in check.[59] As a result, and in ways that bucked the civil–ecclesiastical collaboration in town over at least the last three decades, council leadership was often at odds ideologically with the kirk session. As we will see, this imperilled and altered the community's culture of covenanting in significant ways.

The nuances of the political and ecclesiastical debates in Ayr should not obscure the very challenging interpersonal dynamics at play here. The town was not small, but it was also very much a tight-knit community, one that had been bound together, even amid disagreements, by the manifold challenges of the previous years. Indeed, the magistrates who had complied with government orders noted that they were 'verie tender of the weillfair of thair nighbours', which explains in part why the provost had, for two years, put off removing noncompliers from positions of public trust.[60] Subscription to the covenants had been a fundamentally corporate act, one that helped to stitch together the social fabric of Ayr. Rejecting them or their defenders outright threatened, in no small way, to provoke its unravelling.

Rebellions, big and small

The people of Ayr, far from being disinterested bystanders, understood and at times acutely felt the changes wrought by the Restoration in ways both material and spiritual. By the autumn of 1662, emotions and anxieties were running high in the town. The community purse ran low and poor relief lists ran long, due in part to the fines levied by Charles II's government in 1662 as retribution against those who had 'associat[ed] themselffs in most treasonable declarations and protestations' or 'joyned in councill or armes with the murderers of the king', among other crimes.[61] Soon, the lists of those receiving poor relief regularly filled multiple pages in the session records. In 1662 Adair was often away in Edinburgh grappling with the aftermath of the ecclesiastical settlement, and a new and controversial provost had been elected. Two years later, discord worsened when George White was imposed upon the parish, but even before then, cracks in the communal clay had grown increasingly visible. To add insult to injury, on 28 October 1662, the burgh records report that that the magistrates had levied 1,500 pounds 'for defraying of ane pairt of the charges given out the town the tyme of the Commissioner his being in town with the nobles and his majesties lyf guard'.[62] Apparently, the Earl of Middleton, commissioner of Scotland and one of the architects of the episcopal settlement, had visited the town over the course of the previous month, accompanied by a number of Scottish nobles and the king's guards, and taken advantage of all the food and drink the town had to offer. As one local historian colourfully put it, Middleton and his men had engaged in 'daily and nightly drunkenness resembling a heathen bacchanal' and 'brought shame unspeakable upon the Christian religion'.[63] James Kirkton also notes that during this 'rant' through the West Country, 'at Air [Middleton's] company drank the devil's health at the cross at the night time'.[64] Of course, these are not the recollections of neutral observers, but obvious biases notwithstanding, it seems likely that such a visible display of the excesses and priorities of the new regime would have caused both amusement and anger among the people in the town.

Things came to a head on the final day of October 1662, when John Caldwell, the deacon convener of trades – an elected position of significant importance and influence in the community – together with the heads of other trades appeared before the town council for their offence of gathering together in a 'mutinous and seditious way'.[65] Apparently, Caldwell, accompanied by the 'whole deacons tradesmen journeymen and prenteis [apprentices]' had marched down the high street in a 'contemptuous and menassing maner' towards the mercat cross. Provost Cunningham, having gotten wind of the manoeuvrings of the 'tumultuous crew', ordered them to disperse at once. Caldwell and his associates ignored the order, and things escalated very quickly from there. Cunningham then commanded the men to go to the tolbooth so that they could meet with the minister and be questioned by the magistrates as to the cause of the chaos. To this, the rebellious group began to cry out in unison, 'no Tolbuth, no Tolbuth at all'![66] Thanks to the help of the baillies and other men of the town not involved in the rising, Caldwell and his crew, despite their 'most wicked and willfull resistance', were finally hauled away to jail.

The exact cause of the turmoil remains unknown – apparently, some of the crowd's fury was directed at George Grier, a tailor, but extant records do not say why. When pressed about his actions, Caldwell simply said that 'it wes his deutie which he had done'.[67] Regardless of the origins of the uprising, in the minds of the magistrates, the contempt for their authority could not be abided. In order to encourage the other residents to 'live peaceable and with subjection to the power and authoritie of the magistrates of this burghe', Caldwell and the other ringleaders of the rising were put in the stocks. They were then led from the tolbooth to the centre of town on the next busy market day, bare-footed with a cord around their necks, to be 'led be the hand of the hangman' to stand for an hour on the platform at the base of the mercat cross. Pasted to each of their foreheads was a piece of paper with the inscription: 'Beholders tak example feir God and obey your lawful magistrates.' They were then banished from Ayr, though Caldwell was later allowed to resume trade within the burgh.[68]

The Caldwell episode, even if not directly related to the ecclesiastical changes introduced by the Restoration, offers a useful window into the brewing crisis of leadership in the town. Cunningham was not a man who took challenges to his authority lightly – a trait he had in common with the minister he seemed to greatly dislike. The great error of Caldwell and company was gathering without having been convened by the magistrates and repeatedly ignoring the orders of the provost. The oath that burgesses took upon admission was explicit in its mandate that the directives of the magistrates be obeyed; Caldwell's uprising was in direct opposition to this promise.[69] What is more, they had demonstrated 'heigh contempt' for the acts of parliament made against 'unlawfull convocations of the people' – something that was an especially acute concern of the new government.[70]

It is clear that Cunningham was anxious to exercise unhindered his authority in town, particularly due to concerns that Ayr's radical, nonconformist reputation might invite retribution from the government and further impede the economic prosperity of the community. Additionally, the Privy Council had gotten wind of the 'great trouble raised in the toune of Air amongst the inhabitants' and asked the magistrates to lawfully proceed against them.[71] The motivations of Caldwell – or what 'duty' he thought he was performing by his conduct – remain unclear. Tantalisingly, there is a 'Caldwell' listed among the men in Ayrshire fined by the parliament in exception to the Act of Indemnity in 1662, but the first name is obscured, and it may well be another Caldwell.[72] Regardless, the fact that he and so many of the town's tradesmen felt angry and empowered enough to act testifies to the atmosphere of discontent during these years.

The Pentland Rising

Of all the rebellions that touched Ayr in the decade following the Restoration, none received more national attention than the Pentland Rising. Beginning in November 1666, the rising emerged out of a potent and muddled cocktail of political, economic, and spiritual discontent in the southwest. It was a challenging time for the region, as the second Anglo-Dutch War had disrupted trade while requiring funding from Scottish taxes. The loss of the nonconforming ministers ejected from their parishes four years prior was still fresh, and tensions were high. Though often described as a rather spontaneous insurrection by nonconformists against supporters of the government, the rising may have been in the works since the previous summer, when a cohort of nonconformist ministers held secret meetings in Edinburgh.[73] Regardless of the circumstances, the armed covenanters moved through Ayrshire and attempted to advance upon Edinburgh. On 26 November, while encamped in Lanark, they renewed the Solemn League and Covenant – a clear articulation of the principles for which these men were willing to die.[74] Two days later, they were intercepted and thoroughly routed by the royal army at Rullion Green, ten miles south of the capital.[75]

There is no direct evidence that Adair was involved in the plans for the rising, though he was also conspicuously absent from most session meetings between late May 1666 and April 1667, dates that encompass the summer when nonconformist members were meeting secretly in Edinburgh. The session records themselves are surprisingly quiet on the rising and its aftermath, but members of the wider community certainly knew people involved in the insurrection – or were involved in some way themselves. Eight of the thirty-six convicted for their involvement in the rising were sentenced to be hanged and beheaded in Ayr in December 1666. One of them, Cornelius Anderson, was a tailor from the town. The sentiments of the community were made manifest in the fact that authorities struggled to carry out the executions; the usual hangman fled the town, because, as Kirkton dramatically recounted, 'he would not murther the innocent'.[76]

The situation growing desperate, William Sutherland, the hangman of neighbouring Irvine, was sent for, but he also refused. For his disobedience, authorities put him in the tolbooth. According to his account, while there he was visited by minister George White, who told him that the convicted men had engaged in crimes deserving of death and that their rebellion was comparable in severity to 'the sin of witchcraft' – punishments for which the hangman had previously carried out.[77] According to Sutherland's testimony, White lost patience and cried out 'Away with thee! The devil is in thee, and thou hast dealing with familiar spirits'. Brought before several authorities in the town, Sutherland was asked whether he was a covenanter. This he denied, but also asked 'what Covenant will ye give us? If ye take away the Covenant of God, ye will give us the Covenant of the devil, for there is but two Covenants, a good one in a bad one'.[78] Provost Cunningham stepped in, haranguing the resistant executioner – 'What! are you afraid of the country folk?' – and offering to pay him off. But he stood fast.[79] At last Cunningham alighted on a solution, and told the local tailor, Cornelius Anderson, that if he carried out the execution, his own life would be spared. Anderson agreed, but only after seeking forgiveness from his fellow rebels. Sensing that the makeshift executioner might lose his nerve at the last minute, the provost reportedly 'took care to make him almost drunk with brandy' on the day of.[80] The execution of the rebels must have been a messy, morose scene indeed, one that left a lasting impression on the people who witnessed it. As for Anderson, we have two endings to his story, both equally sad: one says that his conscience so tormented him after the deed was done that he died of heartbreak a few days later; the other suggests that he fled to Ireland, where his house was soon after burned down, either by arsonists or in a suicide.[81]

This grim tale of the search for an executioner, even filtered through the hands of presbyterian polemicists, tells us quite a lot about the prevailing sympathies of the day. It seems clear that both the Ayr and Irvine executioners did fear the backlash that might be invited by carrying out the sentences in a community that sympathised – if not supported – the rebel cause. Sutherland's assertion that there only existed a divine covenant and a demonic one testifies to the widely held fear that by denying the truth of the covenants to which they had sworn, God himself would be denied. The culture of covenanting had bred an enduring solidarity among the inhabitants of Ayrshire and empowered them to resist the orders of authorities who acted in ways deemed contrary to both God and community.

Strange new world

Between the chaos of the Pentland Rising and the end of the decade, Adair was rarely present for meetings of the session. The elders, too, were mostly absent – generally, only White, the clerk, and the treasurer were present, while those elected in 1666 and 1667 had ceased showing up. The agenda of the formerly active session was now down to a bare minimum in dealing only with poor relief and other financial matters, such as monies given to James Tobias, a surgeon, for 'cureing Agnes Dickie her leg it was broken'.[82] There are also signs that the traditional practices of piety – at least in officially sanctioned venues – were not being kept to the usual standards. In May of 1667, for example, the barebones session paid six shillings to James Campbell 'for keeping away children from breaking the church glass windows'.[83] Late that year, a new local boy was hired 'for keeping dogs out of Church in the sabbath day'.[84] When typical disciplinary cases did occur for issues such as sex before marriage, no public repentance was required, only fines for 'pious uses'.[85] What is apparent is that in the handful of times Adair was present between 1666 and 1670, he was joined by between five and seven elders, who otherwise absented themselves when White presided. Their loyalties shone clear – their consciences would not countenance regular cooperation with a minister imposed upon them by an archbishop.

While the number of elders consistently showing up for the session meetings may have decreased, the presence of international visitors in the town rose precipitously. The community had always been a hub of trade with England and Ireland, and from the mid-1640s onward, Ayr merchants had been travelling across the Atlantic to and from destinations in the Caribbean and the British colonies in North America.[86] The following decade, the Cromwellian occupation had brought a stable presence of English soldiers, some of whom married Scottish women or were made burgesses of the town, despite the council's insistence in November 1660 on removing from the town any disbanded Englishmen who were usurping local trade.[87] These ongoing international connections, and the wealth they had previously brought to the town in the pockets of local merchants as well as international investors, were fundamentally challenged by the domestic and foreign policy decisions of Charles II's government. The Navigation Acts of 1660 and 1663 excluded Scottish ships from many trading routes, and the Second Anglo-Dutch War (1665–7) interrupted trade with one of Ayr's most important trading partners.[88] For all levels of the community, this meant hard times; to many, it seemed like adding economic insult to episcopal injury.

A town council minute from the summer of 1670 titled 'Reasons of the Decaying Trade' reflected the general sentiment of fiscal frustration and idealised nostalgia for a more prosperous past. Composed to explain why the town did not send aid to Dundee following the destruction of its harbour during a massive storm in 1668, the minute lists a litany of troubles over the previous decade: trade to Barbados, France, and Norway had been interrupted by war and exorbitant excises; commerce with Ireland had collapsed; and the town's few remaining ships were deteriorating. The very infrastructure of the town was, reportedly, crumbling under the weight of want and neglect: 'Our harbour is totallie ruined and decayed, which we are not abill in the leist to maintain. Our bridge daylie failing, by great spaits, and yce coming down in the winter tyme on it'.[89] The seriousness of the situation was epitomised by the fact that the previous year, the town council had issued an order to inhabitants to assist in the physical repairs of the harbour or else pay a fine.[90] Yet despite these economic challenges and the council's claims of poverty, the picture is muddy: the harbour, for example, was nonetheless well-maintained, with the council making substantive payments for its repair during the Restoration era.[91] Moreover, Ayr burgh accounts show profits accrued in nearly every year of the 1660s, complicating desperate depictions of 'decay'.[92] While the overall economic health of the town is not the focus here, what can be confidently asserted is that the fiscal pressures on the community were great, and they cannot be divorced from ecclesiastical and political issues of the day. Amid its 1670 inventory of economic complaints, for example, the town council noted that in 1667, 'we had 450 men on frie quarter for the space of seaven months belonging to Generall Dalzell' – meaning the much-hated 'Bluidy Tam' Dalyell, who subdued the covenanters at the Pentland Rising – 'which cost the town of Air above fourtie thousand merks Scots money'.[93] Rebellion was clearly a costly business.

Despite this challenging economic situation, the town's international connections continued to develop. In the early 1660s, some of the town's traders found creative ways to circumvent the rules of the Navigation Acts: a number of the Englishmen who were made burgesses at the start of the decade partnered with Ayr merchants to give the appearance of English owned ships that were, in actuality, staffed by Scots bound for the West Indies.[94] And even as Scottish merchants were effectively barred from important trading routes, foreign merchants and seamen increasingly arrived on Ayr's shores – often due to bad weather rather than planned visits – as did international news. We hear echoes in the archives of prayers for plagues abroad, a fast day held for 'a happy successe to the Royall Navy', and calculations for money doled out by the session to strangers who had been shipwrecked near the town.[95] 1668 was an especially interesting year for visitors, as the kirk allocated small sums of aid to 'six shipbroken Frenchmen', 'ane shipbroken gentleman in new England', and most intriguingly, 'Thomas Mitchell ane converted jew'.[96] Clearly, any financial straits were superseded by both the kirk's moral imperative to assist the poor – as well as potential for establishing positive relationships through this sort of targeted aid. More generally, being part of an increasingly interconnected world seems to have been part and parcel of the townspeople's identity, especially, of course, for those who made their livings on the sea.

The popular importance of these international connections is made manifest by the fact that even today, in the 'Sailor's Loft' in the Auld Kirk of Ayr hangs a model of a French ship called the 'Arethusa', which was driven ashore in 1662 by treacherous weather. According to local accounts, the townspeople were so kind to the shipwrecked sailors that the model of the barque was presented as a measure of thanks for both moral and material support.[97] The actual story is a bit messier and testifies to both the communal importance of international connections as well as the brewing leadership crisis sparked by debates over the Restoration settlement. The town council minutes note that in June 1662, the magistrates had found 'ane ship hung above the mariners loft by some of the seamen'.[98] Apparently, some of the sailors had claimed to have permission from the council to put it there, when in fact they did not. This angered members of the council, who, already feeling their authority challenged by divisions in the town, removed the ship. The sailors, after making sincere apology for their misdeed, 'humblie craved' that the ship be restored to its prior location. The council granted their request, but also took the opportunity to issue a warning that if any man within the burgh 'put up any monument or decorment within the kirk or any public place' without proper consent, 'they sall be severlie published as usurpers of the lawes liberties and priviledges of the burgh'.[99] This episode, like the Caldwell rebellion the following autumn, reveals the increasingly heavy hand of the council on the town, while the anxiety over monuments and decoration also suggests growing concern about dissent manifesting itself materially in the built environment of the burgh. The replica ship was deemed innocent enough, but public spaces throughout Scotland – parish kirks, mercat crosses, tolbooths, and other sites of authority – had become increasingly contested. That the sailors earnestly requested that the model French ship be restored to its place in the kirk reminds us that sacred space was as much the site of economic hopes, international connections, and communal negotiations as it was a spiritual conduit.

Throughout the 1660s, amid a crisis of leadership at the local level, order remained elusive. Adair, because he had been in his post prior to 1649 and was thus confined to his parish, provided some degree of stability for his parishioners. Still, his frequent absences from the parish due to ongoing questioning by the government as well as the imposition of George White in

1664 posed a genuine spiritual hardship for the town. After all, Adair had been their minister for three decades. In 1667, the highest officials in the Scottish government debated whether to remove him from his post, likely due to fears that he was aiding and abetting the radicals involved in the events of the Pentland Rising. For the previous year or so, the refusal of Adair and like-minded ministers, particularly in the southwest, to attend church courts in protest of episcopacy had been 'tolerated' by the Scottish archbishops, even those with reputations as dogged opponents of presbyterians.[100] Apparently, however, there were some whose patience for Adair had run out. In a letter from privy councillor Sir Robert Moray to the Earl of Lauderdale, Moray raised up the issue of whether Adair should be 'put out' – that is, deposed. Moray's position was that it would be 'of advantage to the Kings service and quyet of the parts where he resides' not to proceed against him.[101] He painted Adair as a potential moderate who the government could keep onside: 'I hear he is a sober man, & already out of the good opinion of the fanatically disposed people as being almost come over to the full length of compliance with episcopacy.'[102] Lauderdale did not heed his colleague's advice, and Adair was suspended from his post in spring 1668.

Upon hearing the news of the loss of the long-time leader of the town, deacon convener Robert Cunningham, on behalf of the 'whole trades of the burgh', petitioned the council to intercede on Adair's behalf so that he could be reinstated as minister of Ayr.[103] Adair, when consulted by newly elected provost Thomas Knight about this petition moving forward, gave his consent but also noted that the magistrates should 'engage nothing for him to the Bishop', who the minister saw as fundamentally illegitimate.[104] Adair was restored to his position in late summer 1669 due to his 'peaceable deportment during his silence' and 'his aversioun to all illegal disourders and clandestine meitings'.[105] He, like many others in the western shires, would be allowed to exercise his ministry in Ayr so long as he did not explicitly attempt to subvert the government's general episcopal policies. Some contemporaries – as well as some modern historians – have interpreted those who accepted these carve outs as caving to demands in contradiction to their presbyterian commitments. In reality, however, 'conforming' ministers in the southwest and beyond worked in parallel to or in collaboration with unindulged and nonconformist ministers in furtherance of the presbyterian church.[106] Adair, in his mid-50s by 1670, had not so much lost his zeal as gained pragmatism. He laboured to make sure his community and nation did not fall afoul of the covenants while also not attracting too much unwanted attention from the Restoration regime, a similar strategy to the one he employed during the Cromwellian occupation. Above all, he wanted to make this strange new world old again, a project which would become increasingly untenable as he moved into the final decade of his ministry.

Notes

1. On Richard Cromwell, see Jason Peacey, 'The Protector Humbled: Richard Cromwell and the Constitution', in Patrick Little (ed.), *The Cromwellian Protectorate* (Woodbridge: Boydell, 2007), pp. 32–52.
2. Sharon Adams, 'In Search of the Scottish Republic', in Sharon Adams and Julian Goodare (eds), *Scotland in the Age of Two Revolutions* (Woodbridge: Boydell, 2014), pp. 97–114.
3. Alan R. MacDonald, *The Burghs and Parliament in Scotland, c. 1550–1651* (Aldershot: Ashgate, 2007), pp. 184–5.
4. For an introduction to the Restoration in Scotland, see Clare Jackson, *Restoration Scotland, 1660–1690: Royalist Politics, Religion and Ideas* (Woodbridge: Boydell, 2003); Tim Harris, *Restoration: Charles II and His Kingdoms, 1660–1685* (London: Penguin, 2006); Alasdair Raffe, 'Presbyterian Politics and the Restoration of Scottish Episcopacy, 1660–1662', in N.H. Keeble (ed.), *'Settling the Peace of the Church': 1662 Revisited* (Oxford: Oxford University Press, 2014), pp. 144–67.
5. On this point, see, for example, Alasdair Raffe, 'Who Were the Later Covenanters?', in Chris R. Langley (ed.), *The National Covenant in Scotland, 1638–1689* (Woodbridge: Boydell, 2020), pp. 197–214, at pp. 198–202 and Jamie Murdoch McDougall, 'Covenants and Covenanters in Scotland, 1638–1679' (PhD thesis, University of Glasgow, 2017), chapter 4.
6. Alasdair Raffe, *The Culture of Controversy: Religious Arguments in Scotland, 1660–1714* (Woodbridge: Boydell, 2012), pp. 69–70.
7. For parish dynamics outside of the southwest during the Restoration, see, for example, Alison G. Muir, 'The Covenanters in Fife, c. 1610–1689: Religious Dissent in the Local Community' (PhD thesis, University of St Andrews, 2002), chapter 4.
8. Raffe, 'Who Were the Later Covenanters?', p. 197.
9. The importance of grassroots radicalism is a central argument in Neil McIntyre's 'Saints and Subverters: The Later Covenanters in Scotland, c. 1648–1682' (PhD thesis, University of Strathclyde, 2016); the nature of the post-Restoration period in Ayr supports many of McIntyre's key findings.
10. On the protestors who became separatists, see McIntyre, 'Saints and Subverters', pp. 42–3; Kyle David Holfelder, 'Factionalism in the Kirk during the Cromwellian Invasion and Occupation of Scotland, 1650–1660: The Protestor-Resolutioner Controversy' (PhD thesis, University of Edinburgh, 1998); and Adams, 'In Search of the Scottish Republic'.
11. Robert Baillie, *The Letters and Journals of Robert Baillie*, 3 vols, ed. David Laing (Edinburgh: Bannatyne Club, 1841–2), ii, p. 484.
12. Ayrshire Archives, Town Council Minutes, B6/18/2, fo. 161v. Cunningham had been elected provost the previous October; see fo. 167r.
13. B6/18/2, fo. 175r.
14. National Records of Scotland (hereafter NRS), CH2/751/3/2, fo. 552r.
15. CH2/751/3/2, fo. 552r.

16 CH2/751/3/2, fo. 552v.
17 CH2/751/3/2, fo. 552v.
18 CH2/751/4, p. 185.
19 According to the Survey of Scottish Witchcraft, only six witches within the larger county of Ayr were accused during the 1661–2 hunts, as compared to forty-seven during the 1658–9 trials. See Julian Goodare, Lauren Martin, Joyce Miller, and Louise Yeoman, 'The Survey of Scottish Witchcraft', https://witches.hca.ed.ac.uk (archived January 2003, accessed 23 September 2023).
20 CH2/751/3/2, fo. 562v.
21 CH2/751/4, p. 111. On demonic rhetoric and the language of insult, see Michelle D. Brock, *Satan and the Scots: The Devil in Post-Reformation Scotland, ca. 1560–1700* (London: Routledge, 2016), chapter 5.
22 As Margo Todd points out, 'the vast majority of witchcraft charges in the kirk session books were answered by mediation of a quarrel rather than pursuit of presumed sorcery'. Margo Todd, *Culture of Protestantism in Early Modern Scotland* (New Haven: Yale University Press, 2002), p. 248.
23 An act was passed by the town council in January 1662 'for demolishing the walls of the citadel', though ruins would long remain. B6/18/2, fo. 190v.
24 See Chapter 4, this volume. On the complicated responses to the end of the Cromwellian occupation, see Allan Kennedy, 'The Urban Community in Restoration Scotland: Government, Society and Economy in Inverness, 1660–C.1688', *Northern Scotland*, 5:1 (2014), 26–49, at 35–6.
25 Baillie, *Letters and Journals*, iii, p. 404.
26 National Library of Scotland (hereafter NLS), Wod. Fol. XXVI, 'Letter from William Adair to Robert Doulas, justifying his behavior under commonwealth, 6 Sept., 1660', fo. 120r.
27 *KJV*, Psalm 92:7.
28 NLS, Wod. Fol. XXVI, 120r–121r.
29 For an overview of these events, see Jamie McDougall, 'Covenants and Covenanters in Scotland, 1638–1679' (PhD thesis, University of Glasgow, 2017), pp. 135–8.
30 Robert Wodrow, *The History of the Sufferings of the Church of Scotland, from the Restauration to the Revolution*, 4 vols (Edinburgh: James Watson, 172), vol. 1, p. 403. In Ayrshire, confined ministers held more than one-third of the 53 parish charges. See Elizabeth H. Hyman, 'A Church Militant: Scotland, 1661–1690', *Sixteenth Century Journal*, 26 (1995), 49–74; at 55.
31 McIntyre, 'Saints and Subverters', p. 50.
32 Baillie, *Letters and Journals*, iii, p. 486.
33 As printed in James Stewart, *Naphtali, or, the Wrestling of the Church of Scotland for the Kingdom of Christ* (Edinburgh, 1667), p. 207.
34 Stewart, *Naphtali*, p. 211. Italics are Stewart's.
35 James Kirkton, *A History of the Church of Scotland 1660–1679*, ed. Ralph Stewart (Lewiston: Edwin Mellen, 1992), pp. 78–9.
36 Baillie, *Letters and Journals*, iii, p. 487.
37 CH2/751/3/2, fo. 568v.

38 Kirkton, *History*, p. 79.
39 Wodrow, *History*, vol. 1, pp. 294–6.
40 Ayrshire Archives, B6/18/3, Ayr Council Book. 1655–1663, n.p., 13 January 1663. The town council had also attempted to get him to comply the previous September, having sent him a letter asking to speak with him about the recent acts of parliament. B6/18/2, fo. 200r.
41 White first appears in the kirk session records on 26 December 1664. There was no formal admission or welcome to the parish by the session, as had previously been the tradition. CH2/751/4, p. 257.
42 B6/18/2, fos. 225v–6v.
43 CH2/751/4, p. 289.
44 CH2/751/4, pp. 277–8.
45 CH2/751/4, p. 278.
46 CH2/751/5, p. 228.
47 See, for example, CH2/751/5, pp. 5, 20, and 58.
48 See, for example, CH2/751/5, pp. 22, 54, and 60.
49 B6/18/2, fo. 186v.
50 B6/18/2, fo. 215r.
51 On the economic priorities and makeup of the town council, see Tom Barclay and Eric J. Graham, *The Early Transatlantic Trade of Ayr, 1640–1730* (Ayr: The Ayrshire Archaeological and Natural History Society, 2005).
52 As quoted in Archibald Mackenzie, *William Adair and His Kirk: The Auld Kirk of Ayr, 1639–1684* (Ayr: Ayr Advertiser, 1933), p. 66; *Records of the Parliaments of Scotland to 1707* (hereafter *RPS*) ed. Keith M. Brown et al., www.rps.ac.uk (accessed 2 January 2024), 1663/6/33.
53 B6/18/2, fo. 220v.
54 B6/18/2, fos. 220v–222.
55 *The Register of the Privy Council of Scotland* [hereafter *RPCS*], series 1–3, ed. P. Hume Brown (Edinburgh, 1881–1933), 3rd series, vol. I, p. 601.
56 *RPCS*, 3rd series, vol. I, p. 601.
57 For Privy Council oversight of the elections of the town council, see *RPCS*, series 3, vol. II, pp. 95 and 195.
58 Edinburgh and Glasgow, too, dealt with the central government's meddling in their local elections. See John Toller, '"Now of little significancy"? The Convention of the Royal Burghs of Scotland, 1651–1688' (PhD thesis, University of Dundee, 2010), pp. 104–5.
59 Cunningham's unpopularity in some quarters of the town was demonstrated by a conflict he had with John Ferguson, former ballie of the burgh, which grew large enough that it came to the attention of the Privy Council in early 1668. Cunningham claimed that Ferguson had slandered him by calling him 'a lyar and spyting him and all his kin', and for the injunction Cunningham had imprisoned Ferguson. Ferguson's testimony to the Privy Council painted Cunningham as a man who ruled the town with a tight circle of like-minded lackies and used the town council to deal with his personal business. He reported that Cunningham had for the past seven years used the levers of power to 'oppresse

him and almost all the honest men and old magistrats of that place'. What was more, 'to the better of effectuating [Cunnigham's] designes, his comon practice has always been to make every privatt quarrel a tounes action, having no body upon the councill bot some few young men of his owne inbringing who are little acquaint with the affairs of the burgh, he having keepd out always those of better experience by the suggestions and groundless informations of ther disloyalty'. Ferguson asked the Lords 'as ane act of justice and charity, that they might appoint some indifferent persons of ther owne number to take notice of the oppressions and distractions under which that poor place groans, which cryes aloud for help'. The Lords claimed that they would look into things, but Ferguson unexpectedly and inexplicably dropped his accusations that June, saying he did 'rashlie' speak against Cunningham and 'was sory for it'. The matter was declared settled. *RPCS*, 3rd series, vol. II, pp. 418 and 461.

60 B6/18/2, fo. 220v.
61 See, for example, *RPS*, 1662/5/87 and 1662/5/96.
62 B6/18/3, n.p.
63 Mackenzie, *William Adair and His Kirk*, p. 63.
64 Kirkton, *History*, p. 90.
65 B6/18/2, fo. 204v.
66 B6/18/2, fo. 205r.
67 B6/18/2, fo. 205r.
68 B6/18/2, fo. 207v.
69 An eighteenth-century copy of the oath is transcribed in Alistair Lindsay and Jean Kennedy (eds), *The Burgesses and Guild Brethren of Ayr, 1647–1846* (Ayr: Ayrshire Federation of Historical Societies, 2002), p. xv.
70 B6/18/2, fo. 205v.
71 *RPCS*, 3rd series, vol. I, pp. 275–6.
72 *RPS*, 1662/5/96.
73 McIntyre, 'Saints and Subverters', p. 62.
74 On the covenant renewal at Lanark, see James Wallace, 'Narrative of the Rising at Pentland', in Thomas M'Crie (ed.), *Memoirs of Mr. William Veitch, and George Brysson* (Edinburgh: W. Blackwood, 1825), pp. 388–432; and Alasdair Raffe, 'Confessions, Covenants and Continuous Reformation in Early Modern Scotland', *Études Épistémè*, 32 (2017), 15–19.
75 For an overview of the Pentland Rising, see Charles Sandford Terry, *The Pentland Rising and Rullion Green* (Glasgow: Maclehose & Sons, 1905) and, more recently, McIntyre, 'Saints and Subverters', pp. 61–6.
76 Kirkton, *History*, p. 146.
77 Sutherland's account is printed in Wodrow, *History*, ii, pp. 54–8, and also printed as *The Genuine Declaration of William Sutherland, Hangman at Irvine; Wherein his Knowledge of the Scriptures, His Courage, and Behaviour Towards the Persecutors, And Their Barbarous Treatment of Him at Air are Plainly Set Forth* (Edinburgh, 1821).
78 Wodrow, *History*, ii, p. 57.
79 Wodrow, *History*, ii, pp. 54–5.

80 Wodrow, *History*, ii, p. 54.
81 Woodrow, *History*, ii, p. 54.
82 CH2/751/5, p. 139. These payments are also recorded in the kirk session account books, which are extant from 1664. See, in particular, CH2/751/19 and CH2/751/20.
83 CH2/751/5, p. 32.
84 CH2/751/5, p. 56.
85 See, for example, CH2/751/5, pp. 113 and 134.
86 Tom Barclay and Eric J. Graham, *The Early Transatlantic Trade of Ayr, 1640–1730* (Ayr: The Ayrshire Archaeological and Natural History Society, 2005).
87 Barclay and Graham, *The Early Transatlantic Trade of Ayr*, p. 17.
88 Barclay and Graham, *The Early Transatlantic Trade of Ayr*, p. 17.
89 B6/18/4, fos. 22r–v.
90 Hugh McGhee, 'The Harbour', in Annie I. Dunlop (ed.), *The Royal Burgh of Ayr: Seven Hundred Fifty Years of History* (Edinburgh: Oliver and Boyd, 1953), pp. 197–211, at p. 207.
91 John Strawhorn, *The History of Ayr: Royal Burgh and County Town* (Edinburgh: John Donald Publishers, 1989), p. 69.
92 For a discussion of the challenges in assessing the fiscal health of the burghs during the Restoration, see Toller, 'Now of little significancy', pp. 113–34; figures for the Ayr accounts are graphed on p. 312.
93 B6/18/4, fo. 22v.
94 Barclay and Graham, *The Early Transatlantic Trade of Ayr*, p. 19.
95 See, for example, Ch2/751/4, pp. 77, 263, 268; CH2/751/5, p. 157.
96 CH2/751/5, pp. 87, 94, 76. Funds were given to another 'converted Jew' in August 1670 (CH2/751/5, p. 197), but this is the last we hear of either man in the records.
97 Archibald Mackenzie, *An Old Kirk and Burns Memories* (Kilmarnock: Standard Printing Works, 1943), p. 3.
98 B6/18/2, fo. 190v.
99 B6/18/2, fo. 190v.
100 On this policy of unofficial and limited toleration, see Andrew Carter, 'Episcopal Church of Scotland, 1660–1685' (PhD thesis, University of St Andrews, 2019), esp. pp. 81–4.
101 Osmund Airy (ed.), *The Lauderdale Papers*, 3 vols (London: Camden Society, 1884), vol. 1, pp. 43–4. Thank you to Alasdair Raffe for pointing me towards this reference.
102 Airy, *Lauderdale Papers*, pp. 43–4.
103 B6/18/2, fo. 295v. This episode is also recounted in John H. Pagan, *Annals of Ayr in the Olden Time, 1560–1692* (Ayr: Alex Fergusson, 1897), p. 34.
104 B6/18/2, fo. 295v.
105 B6/18/2, fos. 298v–9r.
106 On this point, see Hyman, 'A Church Militant'.

6

The old protestor

Ten years after the end of the Cromwellian occupation, and more than three decades after the swearing of the National Covenant, the people of Ayr seemed to want a return to something, though to what or when they did not necessarily agree. On 25 January 1670, the town council heard a petition from 'verie manie of the comunitie' requesting that the former practice of hearing weekday sermons, which had been suspended with the Restoration, be reinstated on Tuesdays and Thursdays. Some complained 'heavilie' of their want of more regular preaching. Others registered their dissatisfaction with the way that 'Mr. William Adair and Mr. George White have divydit the town betwixt them', Adair apparently overseeing the south side and White the north end. This had impeded the ability of townsfolk to get their children baptised by the minister of their choice, who, understandably, seems to have been the man who had served their parish for a generation.[1] Such a request was an auger of things to come. Over the next decade, the ordinary men and women of the burgh would continue to push back, often with greater force than their leadership, on the ecclesiastical policies of local and national authorities.

For now, though, the issue was how the town council might handle this collective complaint about the deal struck by its ministers. When the two men appeared before the council to discuss the issue, Adair rejected the idea that he should perform clerical duties on the north side of town, which had been assigned to White. To do so, he said, would 'discurrage and disgrace Mr. George in his ministrie'. Moreover, he had promised White to uphold this division of labour, and his word 'he would not break'. Remarkably, given the early antagonism between the two men, Adair in this instance defended White, calling him 'ane godly, pious and discreet man' who was perfectly suitable to administer the sacrament of baptism; indeed, Adair noted that he had 'baptized his oun child with him'. Ever the proponent of the autonomy of the kirk from secular authority, Adair 'marvelled much' that the magistrates would dare to 'meddle' in the affairs of 'church and churchmen'.[2] The town council, which appears to have been caught off guard by this reaction, decided to table the matter until a time when the community could 'be callit together' to offer their thoughts on the best course of action.

It is hard to know precisely what had transpired to make Adair so willing to compromise with and even defend a man with whom he had once deigned to share a seat on the kirk session. It may well be that after years of working together, the two ministers had come not only to a logistical arrangement for performing their duties, but even mutual respect. At first glance one wonders if White was quite moderate in his views, conforming only superficially to the episcopal settlement, but his later writings and actions suggest otherwise.[3] Perhaps Adair's recent experience of suspension had dampened his combative ardour, or at least made him more cautious in his willingness to anger his ecclesiastical higher-ups. Indeed, this was a moment, as we shall see, when indulged clergy were under a tremendous amount of scrutiny, particularly with regard to whether they were encouraging mistreatment of 'loyall', conforming clergy as well as fomenting more general dissent.[4] What is clear, however, is the level of consistency in the old protestor's insistence that secular authorities stay out of spiritual affairs: they should not meddle, in Adair's words, with things that 'did not concerne them'.[5]

Robert Wodrow, in his role as presbyterian hagiographer as much as a historian, wrote the following assessment of Ayr's long-time minister in his *Analecta:* 'Mr Adair, as I hear, was a zealous Protester in his youth against the Publick Resolutions; but in his latter dayes he seemed to decline somwhat from his former zeal and forwardness; so that his first wayes did far excell his last wayes.'[6] In the last full decade of his career, Adair's ability to preach in the parish kirk – which had been built under his watchful eye – hung in the balance. He had been briefly suspended in the late 1660s for his ongoing refusal to comply with episcopacy, and this would not be the last time he faced such censure. As the government increasingly began to pursue policies meant to quiet dissent and keep nonconforming ministers in check, men like Adair faced difficult, intensely personal decisions about the extent to which holding onto their posts was worth countenancing certain policies of the Restoration state. Wodrow's diagnosis elides the fact that over time, Adair increasingly worked to balance pragmatism with principle. At times he prioritised the former more than the latter, placing him at odds with some of the flock he had shepherded through the development of a staunch covenanted identity, but he never abandoned the commitments that had guided his adult life. Historians have increasingly acknowledged the complexities of resistance and compliance following the Restoration, fruitfully complicating our understandings of religious identities in this era.[7] What the final decade of Adair's career reveals is the personal toll that local divisions, competing priorities, and changing national stakes could take on both ministers and the communities they served.

Navigating nonconformity

Just as the sentiments and actions of the people of Ayr were not a monolith, neither were the policies of the government, which in the 1670s continued to be a muddle of accommodations, frustrations, and eventually, intense repression. For the people of the town, it was a confusing and at times dangerous mess. By the end of the 1660s, Charles II's government had been pursuing a tactic of 'limited rapprochement'; the indulgences many ministers in the southwest accepted in 1669 was one key part of this approach.[8] In 1670 Robert Leighton, at the time archbishop of Glasgow, set about attempting to unite episcopalian and presbyterian factions through shared governance of the kirk.[9] This aspirational compromise – 'the Accommodation' – was first outlined in Edinburgh in August and then in Paisley in January 1671. Adair attended this latter meeting and, according to Wodrow's account, grew worried that his engagement with the deal might eventually be used as 'a handle against the whole of Presbyterian ministers'.[10] He asked, along with the like-minded minister James Naismith, that they be able to consider the proposals in writing before signing on. Though the Accommodation itself was never implemented, Adair's presence at the meeting and reactions to the proposal are telling. We often have a black-and-white image of ministers in this period as either for the religious settlement, or wholly, dogmatically against it. And yet even a man like Adair was open to compromise born not of ideology, but a combination of necessity and strategy. Indeed, the southwestern part of Scotland was home to a power base of indulged presbyterian ministers who took a similar approach. Far from having capitulated to the government and abandoned their former covenanting zeal, men like Adair viewed staying in their posts – which did not preclude them from collaborating with those who practised their ministry illicitly – as most advantageous for both their flocks and the movement.[11]

In April 1671, a year after both the failed Accommodation and the petition from the townspeople to reinstate weekday preaching, the Ayr kirk session held an election for elders and deacons, observing the 'fewnes of ther number by reason of the death and absence of many of ther old members'.[12] The newly constituted session quickly moved to unanimously nominate Adair to be their 'constant moderator'. Ever a stickler for proper process, Adair responded that his being moderator was by right of his office and not by vote.[13] The issue was taken up again in May when both ministers were present, and Adair further clarified that any working with the session while White was also sitting was not to be interpreted as 'homologating of any errour in the constitution of the said judicatory or in approbation of anie corruptione in any constituent member thereof'. According to his principles alone did he join in the 'incontraverted acts of discipline with the said judicatory and their determinations by the major pairt of them for incoragement of piety in censuring of sin scandal and vice'.[14] He would go along to get along for the sole aim of promoting godliness among his flock. Not to be ignored, White too spoke up: his 'not interrupting' Adair's role in moderating should 'not be interpreted as a passing from his oun right and priviledge to moderat per vices in the kirk session', and he might once again take up the rule of moderator when 'he finds it convenient'.[15] In response, the elders and deacons unanimously insisted that they be allowed to 'adheir to their former resolution and act accordingly' – meaning maintain Adair as constant moderator – and that 'ther sitting in the session with Mr George Whyte may not be interpret any concurrence with any error that may be in the judicatory'.[16] Whatever elements of conformity existed within the session, undercurrents of protest at the ongoing 'episcopal incursion' subtly but regularly surfaced. Still, their shared goal of implementing discipline and community stability was enough to maintain some cohesion, albeit imperfectly and temporarily.

Things were even less agreeable on the town council than on the session, and the thorny issues of recent years remained sharp, made worse by persistent poverty – described by the Convention of the Burghs in 1671 as so severe as to risk 'the outter rowin of that ancient burgh' – and the rising enthusiasm among local residents for illicit preaching.[17] As it had done a decade prior, in 1675 the Privy Council ordered all public office holders in the burgh to, upon their election, subscribe a declaration affirming the unlawfulness of both covenants and nonconformist meetings (conventicles, as we will see, were on the rise). A number of influential men, including former provost John Moor and current treasurer John Ferguson, refused.[18] On 1 March 1676, the Privy Council learned that several members of the Ayr town council had still declined to sign the declaration. In response, they asked those members who had complied with the government's mandate to 'meit, elect and choyse uther persons in place of those who have refused to subscrybe the same, who will sign the Declaration', which they did.[19] The continuity of the problem and ensuing divisions is illustrated by a copy of the declaration inserted into the minute books, which listed all thirty-three men who had subscribed the document between 1664 and 1676, implicitly calling out those who had refused.[20]

In the last decade of Adair's career, the burgh's schools also became an ideological battleground.[21] Schoolmasters in seventeenth-century Scotland stood with one foot in the clerical world – they had sometimes been trained as ministers, were involved in the religious education of local children, and were typically vetted by kirk sessions and presbyteries – but they also ultimately served at the pleasure of local magistrates. Like the rest of the men in positions of influence in the town, schoolmasters were not shy about expressing their views on the decisions and impositions of the government, and in return, their actions were increasingly regulated by the town council. In May 1675, master of the Scots school William Wallace demitted his position, due to a combination of age, infirmity, and an aversion to signing the declaration. Soon after, the council began their search for a new schoolmaster. David Skeoch, invited to take up the post, responded that he was 'clear and reddie' to do so, meaning not otherwise employed, but he 'refuised to be tyed to cum to the paroch church at all times'. His meaning is opaque here – did he not want to hear from either White or Adair, or did he have another reason for his resistance to mandate church attendance? – but the impact of ecclesiastical controversy on the education of Ayr's young people is clear. After some wrangling Skeoch was hired, and the inhabitants were told not to put their children in any other grammar school but the one kept by Skeoch or 'anie Scots School except it be to learne the Catachis and pslam buik' as authorised by the council.[22] The suspension of James Anderson, doctor of the grammar school, also attests to how the ongoing ideological power struggle affected local education. In June 1676, Anderson had refused to sing the doxology – like many covenanting hardliners, he found the structured ritual of praise a touch too popish – and accordingly lost his post, though he soon relented and was reinstated a month later.[23] His tenure was not to last, and in 1677 he resigned from his positions as both reader of the church and doctor of the grammar school.[24]

Discipline and worship

The unprecedented crisis of authority of these years translated, at times, into an equally disruptive crisis of discipline. In September 1674, for example, the kirk session ordered Jean Peattie to be whipped and banished from town for her frequent breaking of the sabbath day by 'drinking and whoredome within the burgh the many yeirs bygain'; the addition of the timeframe highlights not only the severity of her crime, but the fact that her misconduct had been allowed to persist for so long.[25] Many of the disciplinary issues of these years involved secular crimes handled by the local magistrates. In a time of economic hardship, crimes of desperation, particularly theft, crept steadily upward, resulting in a rash of banishments of both men and women, some of whom were 'scurged [whipped] through the toun' in the 1670s.[26] There was also a subtle but noteworthy shift in the attitudes of both the session and town council about how to deal with deviance. While kirk discipline had always foregrounded the desire to bring the ungodly back into the fold, during the 1670s fines and private forgiveness became the primary course of action, at times supplanting the previously requisite public repentance. The reasons for this were probably practical rather than ideological; Adair was at times away from the community, White seems to have been mistrusted by much of the congregation, and the unevenness of discipline due to ecclesiastical tumults required an 'as and when' approach.

In February 1670, for example, we find Hew Mcquhirtor, former messenger of the town, in 'the blak hous of the tolbuth of Air for his repairing and coming back to this Burgh'. Two years prior, he had been forcibly removed for living a 'base sinfull and drunken lyf', which had culminated in Mcquhirtor making a dramatic final appearance at the place of public repentance while inebriated and picking a fight with both a kirk officer and the minister. Now he was back in town and in jail, being fed only 'with bread and water' according to the punishment prescribed by the act that had formerly banished him. Despite his past history of 'sin upon sin', the magistrates, in collaboration with Adair, choose mercy: 'being desirous to reclaim him by love rather then force', they declared that 'if anie tyme heirafter it sall please God to reclaim him And he to behaiv himself as ane good Christian and give obedience to the Church', they would make the previous act of banishment void and restore him to his former liberties.[27] Given the general chaos and controversy of the decade, it is notable that in such and other cases, the town council and session continued to cooperate in pursuit of quotidian aims.[28]

Still, all was not well in this aspirational covenanted city upon a hill. Politics and kirk discipline had always mixed, but in the 1670s, the former impeded upon the latter more than ever. On 24 April 1671, the session met, with both Adair and White present, to consider 'the great desuetude [disuse] of discipline in this congregatione' and 'ther oun deuties as Christians' and to pass an act for its remedy.[29] As they had done all those years ago when facing the plague of 1647, the elders began with their own shortcomings. They reaffirmed their own duties to promote the 'trew reformed Christian religion within the burgh and paroch both in public and privat', a long-standing commitment which took on a renewed urgency in the context of present ecclesiastical struggles.[30] Among the list of virtues they sought to recommit themselves to were unity, the 'harmonius and peaceable exercise of discipline', and the careful prevention and suppression of 'all such evill motions as are apt to breid invy, stryfe, division, or skisme, either in the session or congregation'.[31] Apparent in these vows was the divisiveness of recent years in a community used to being on the same religious page. The Restoration had destabilised this, as residents took different approaches to conformity and compliance, dissent and disobedience. The ministers and elders also stressed the need to visit the families of the parish and to take stock 'of every persones condition and cariage'.[32] The goal was both a public relations campaign during a period when the legitimacy of institutions like the session faced new challenges and an opportunity to anticipate and prevent future issues. The factions within the session itself were also laid bare by the commitment of the elders and ministers that the body as a whole would 'harmoniously submit unto' the disciplinary judgements made by the 'free vote of the major pairt' about how to deal with 'scandalous persones'.[33] Clearly, the divisiveness of its members had impeded the ability of the session to agree on the best courses of action in matters of discipline; this is doubtlessly one of the reasons the kirk session minutes are comparatively sparse in the post-Restoration period when compared to previous decades.

This April 1671 call to action included a list of 'scandals' that reveals several concerns that we have not seen before, or to the same extent, in Ayr. It specified that the session should collaborate closely with the civil magistrates in the censure of ten distinct but at times overlapping groups, including those who 'manifestly by word or wryte to deny the trew God or his sone Jesus Christ' by speaking in ways either blasphemous, 'atheisticall', or supportive of 'pagans, Turks, or Jews', and those who 'worship false Gods, such as the elements, starrs, spirits'.[34] It is unclear precisely who the session had in mind here, but the Restoration era had coincided with both a declining sense of control and a rise of international incomers to the town, as well as a flourishing of debates about spirits and the nature of the cosmos that, while concentrated in England, surely made their way north of the border in the early years of what would become the Scottish Enlightenment.[35] The need to control the religious narrative was more imperative – and more impossible – than ever for those on the session who, varying levels of conformity aside, appear to have remained committed presbyterians.

The other concerns listed here are more quotidian: unchristian speeches and 'neidless swearing', theft and lying, people given to 'charms, sinfull lusts, and superstitious practices', those neglecting the sabbath and family worship, 'promiscuous dancing' of men and women anyone engaging with 'filthy unclean and scurrilous discourses, lascivious songs, books, pictures, stage playes', and so on.[36] Especially revealing is the concern for the neglect of the 'honour and duety' that God's word demands be given to 'superiors' such as magistrates, ministers, and elders – the civil and spiritual 'parents' of the town. The act suggests a real vulnerability in its citing not only of general disobedience, but also the 'slanderous and backbiting speiches' about things like the infirmities of local leaders; the elders were 'grieved for such words and actions as naturally lend to weaken ther authority and esteem among the people'.[37] As had been done according to a November 1648 act, the session carved the town into divisions to be overseen by appointed elders and deacons. This throwback to a measure enacted at the zenith of radical covenanter power suggests a desire to return to a period of greater presbyterian hegemony and oversight – it was earlier that month that the newly elected session had unanimously appointed Adair 'constant moderator' over his episcopal counterpart – while also avoiding disorder that might attract unwanted attention from the government. This was easier endeavoured than done, and as in recent years, the continued absences of both ministers meant that with some regularity 'ther was no sessione not discipline because ther can be no rightly constitut sessione without a minister to moderat therin'.[38] On these days, the clerk was often present with one of the deacons to hand out poor relief, but little else could be accomplished.

Still, as the decade neared its midpoint, and despite hurdles imposed by divisions and absences, the Ayr session grappled with some of the usual fare in ways that reflect consistency in disciplinary priorities: Agnes Rowan complained that Janet Muir had slandered her good name by publicly calling her 'ane common notorious whoore'; James Dunbar and Thomas Donaldson were sentenced to public repentance for drinking when they should have been in kirk on the sabbath; a local miller accused the spouse of a tailor for calling him a thief and hoping 'to see him hang'; and William Kelso admitted that by the 'suggestions of Satan and his own corrupt nature' he had fallen in fornication with Agnes McGrath.[39] Fornication cases involving soldiers stationed in or near the town continued to be an issue for the session. The southwestern port was a useful rendezvous point, and the presence of soldiers spiked during events like the lead up to the Anglo-Dutch War in 1672 and, as we shall see, the arrival of the government's large 'peace-keeping' forces later in the decade.[40] Ayr's seaside location also meant that the session continued to offer regular relief to international visitors – people like 'six sea broken French men' in 1671, 'Mr. Nicolas a Gretian' for the relief of his son and brother who had been taken into 'captivity under the turks' in 1679, and 'a broken west India planter and his comrade' in 1680.[41] In 1676, the session received a sizeable donation from John McColm, one of the owners of a ship called the *James*, recently returned from the Caribbean carrying sugar and tobacco.[42] The money was for 'the use of the poor', a charitable gesture that would assure the owners remained on good terms with both the session and with God.

A sense of providential anxiety is also apparent in the pages of the session records during these years, when periods of dearth and lurid tales of suffering compounded the ongoing political turmoil. A fast held in autumn 1673 due to the unseasonable weather and poor harvest was followed by another the next March, and the session clerk noted how God had manifested his displeasure through 'frost and storm that hes lyen on now so long this tyme of the year to the hinderance of the laboureing of the ground, the generall death and mortality of cattell for want of food, and by extream cold'.[43] The problems continued, and in May 1675 the session called for a day of prayer and supplication to God for the relief of 'the great drought wherewith the land is afflicted, together with the dearth and povertie and death that has followed thereupon' over the past two years.[44] This prefigured an act from the Privy Council later that summer calling for a fast in response to the 'sad and pinching dearth, that hes reduced many to a starving conditione'; the session, though 'they have allready aggried upon and also publickly keept a day of solemn humiliatione, for the same causes', complied.[45] By the late 1670s, stories of local men who had been made 'galley slaves with the Turks at Algiers' and tormented until they 'forsake the Christian religion' circulated in the town. In 1681, the session took up a collection to fund the ransom so that the captives might be freed.[46] For those in Ayr who believed fervently in the covenanted cause, these latest rounds of hardship only strengthened their resolve to worship in the ways that they believed to be divinely sanctioned.

Conventicles

The story that reveals most about parish religion and its challenges in the 1670s is not found in the scattered cases of parishioners acting in ways unbefitting a covenanted community, but rather in the townsfolk's emphatic disobediences in defence of the covenants, actions that formed part of a larger pattern of nonconformist resistance in the region. These disobediences took different forms, but most visibly, some residents regularly defied orders by attending outlawed conventicles – passionate worship services, at times in homes and others in large field gatherings, in which the presbyterian ordinances were followed in full, much to the chagrin of the government. Ongoing conversations in the session about crowded seating in the parish kirk suggests that the prominence of conventicles in the region was not attended by substantive withdrawal from regular worship in the kirk, as was the case in other regions.[47] This may seem surprising at first glance, but hearing sermons by Adair – who appears to have been in regular conversation and collaboration with nonconformists in the region – likely would not have been a contradiction in the minds of most parishioners.

Ayr was part of a visible centre of nonconformity in the southwest, and while the largest conventicles took place in the eastern lowlands during the 1670s, the region witnessed its fair share of these illicit meetings. And though the western parishes were filled with indulged and confined ministers like Adair who the government hoped would, in Robert Leighton's words, 'burn away', the region remained a major threat, as 'something like a schismatic church seemed to have arisen' there.[48] So much of our evidence for the precise happenings at conventicles, be they in private homes or in the local hills, is imprecise, shrouded as these events were in secrecy and polemic. But it is clear that these meetings were taking place around and within Ayr, attended by people from across the social spectrum, and condoned and even outright supported by local leaders.[49]

Accordingly, throughout the 1670s, the Scottish Privy Council exerted considerable energy trying to bring Ayrshire and adjacent areas to heel. On 11 June 1669, a committee appointed by the Privy Council to 'consider the fittest course to be taken for the suppression of conventicles in the west' ordered that a letter be sent William Cunningham, currently Ayr's provost, 'to repair to this towne and to take all the information hee can have anent any conventicles that are keiped in that countrey, and what are the designes and practices of the disaffected partie there'.[50] The government's aim was initially to understand the scope of the problem in the southwest and beyond; it was, as the Privy Council soon learned, significant and deeply concerning. An act of 7 April 1670 complained that 'sundry disloyall and seditious persons, especially in the shyres of Lanerk, Air, Renfrew' had gone beyond mere absences from parish kirks; some residents had engaged in the 'disorderly maryeing and baptizing their children, making attempts upon and offering serverall affront and injuryes to loyeall and peaceable ministers, dealing with and minacing them to live their churches'.[51] In response to these flagrant violations of the law, the Privy Council set up commissions to go to the shires and get a handle on the misbehaviour, by force if necessary – a pattern that would continue throughout the decade.[52] Government measures for the suppression of dissent during the 1670s were, by comparison to earlier policies centred on conciliation, severe.

At the centre of these policies was a tremendous amount of scrutiny of the behaviour of indulged and confined ministers in the southwest. In April 1670, the commissioners to the western shires were asked to 'call before yow the ministers allowed to preach by the Councill' and to 'take tryall of their carriages and behavior since they were allowed to preach'.[53] In October 1673, a report from the synod of Glasgow and Ayr detailed how despite efforts to the contrary, 'conventicles still abound more publicly and avowedly ... and these are kept by both men that are indulged and others who are not'.[54] Apparently the indulged ministers in the area, though not leading the conventicles, attended them, and they also stepped on the toes of the conforming clergy by baptising, catechising, marrying, and otherwise ministering to their parishioners. In June 1675, the Privy Council received a letter from His Majesty's Government lamenting the recent uptick in the holding of conventicles and other nonconformist activity throughout the country after a period of relative quiet; as the letter put it, the king had learned that 'more effects of that seditious spirit doe break out afresh'. Among the litany of offences, it had come to the attention of the government that in Ayrshire, 'ther hath latly bein a meiting of indulged and outed ministers who have issued orders forsooth for keiping of fastes, and other illegal injunctions, as if they had bein a judicatory'.[55] The degree to which Adair participated in these activities is hard to gauge with any precision. On the one hand, he clearly endeavoured not to encroach on the ministerial purview his episcopal colleague White, much to the chagrin of some of the local residents. On the other, however, he was deeply connected to local networks of nonconforming ministers, and later events demonstrate that in these years he condoned, and at times directly continued to engage in, such activities in defiance of episcopacy.

Regardless of Adair's precise involvement in local disorder, the government's frustration with the region continued to grow as the decade progressed. Things went from bad to worse, for both sides, in the final years of the decade. In 1677, the Privy Council sent a missive to the major peers from the southwestern shires – the Earls of Glencairn and Dundonald and Lord Ross – noting that they had learned of the 'extraordinary insolencies' committed in their respective region. The issue was not only the harassment of orthodox clergy and the holding of conventicles but also reports of behaviour that threatened 'his Majesties authority and government and to the peace of the kingdome in generall'.[56] The Privy Council expressed great resentment 'in his Majesties name' at 'the forsaids outrages and affronts done to the government in these shires of Air and Renfrew'. From the government's perspective, these 'most considerable seminaries of rebellion in this kingdome', despite their manifold disobedience, had 'eminently tasted of his Majesties clemency' through both formal indulgences for their ministers and more informal head-turning at their abuses. But enough, it seemed, was enough. The Council called upon the commissioners of the militia and justices of the peace from Ayrshire and Renfrewshire to help impose order on their regions. They then ordered that the heritors – essentially, the Scottish gentry – from those shires should be collectively summoned about what to do about this disobedience. If those local elites should fail to help suppress these rebellions, the councillors reported that they were 'fully resolved to repress by force ... all such rebellious and factious courses without respect to the disadvantage of the heretours, whom his Majestie will then looke upon as involved in such a degree of guilt as may allow the greatest severity that can be used against that countrey'.[57] Essentially, if the most privileged men in Ayrshire could not bring their social inferiors into line, then they too would be held to account.

A letter sent to the Privy Council from Glencairn, Dundonald, and Ross the next month reveals the scope of the dilemma: neither the local commissioners nor heritors believed they had the power to 'quyet these disorders'.[58] In December 1677, taking into account 'the great and unsufferable insolencies latly committed by the fanaticks', especially in the shires of Ayr,

Renfrew, and 'other adjacent places', the king pointedly informed the councillors that the crown's forces had been readied at the English border and in Belfast and gathered in the Highlands with plans to shortly assemble in Stirling. He asked that the Privy Council be ready to assist in marshalling forces to go to those places 'so infested with such rebellious practices' and to do what was necessary – from fines to imprisonment to banishment – to compel all inhabitants to take the Oath of Allegiance.[59] What was necessary, it turned out, was the creation of a committee in early 1678 to 'sit in the West for the suppression of disorder'. This committee was at least in part the brainchild of the increasingly frustrated Scottish bishops, and it was to be backed by a substantial military force that came to be derisively known as the 'Highland Host'.[60] For four months, between late January and late April, eleven men were appointed commissioners to administer justice in the southwest, usually from their base in Ayr.[61]

The Committee and the Host

The dramatic events of recent years and the mid-seventeenth century more generally loomed large in what came next, informing both the indignant stamina of the dissenters and the growing ire felt by the government. The authorisation for 'Committee in the West' and the attending forces, written on behalf of Charles II, explained that 'forasmuch as wee cannot bot too weell remember that, whilst wee were engadged in a warr abroad in the year 1666, many in the westerne shyres were so unduetifull as to ryse in rebellion against us and our authority'.[62] The disloyalty that had fuelled the Pentland Rising had continued, despite the indulgences given to ministers in the region during the previous decade, which the government thought ought to have inspired gratitude and a sense of duty. What is more, the Privy Council had, in its view, shown leniency by inviting the leading figures of these shires 'to redresse these wronges and to secure our government against the same for the future'.[63] These local leaders had been told that if they failed, the government would have no choice but to act because of the risks of the disobedience snowballing and spreading. 'Least any of our other good subjects in any of our three kingdomes might againe be involved in thee fatal miseries' – a reference to the lead up to the British civil wars – the government had ordered a combined army of standing forces, militia men, and Highlanders 'to march into these shyres'.[64]

This allusion to the years between 1637 and 1649 – to the first decade of Adair's career – was again echoed in a March 1678 letter from the Privy Council to the king. In offering an update on the prosecution of religious dissent in the western shires, it noted its ongoing consideration of 'what fatall steps our country was formerly led into that execrable rebellion' and its regret to 'see that some courses latly taken in severall disaffected shyres did resemble to much the beginnings of those unhapy tymes'.[65] No doubt statements born of both genuine sentiment and a desire to maintain an effective working relationship with their monarch, the councillors understood their audience. It is often remarked that the guiding force in Charles II's kingship was an overriding desire not 'to go on his travels again', an adage that, through perhaps a touch trite, animated his government's policies towards his northern as well as southern kingdom.[66]

Ayr was not alone in its reputation as a hotbed of presbyterian rebellion, but central and southern Ayrshire were areas of particular concern, and the burgh itself was noted by authorities as 'the centre of a great circle of the disaffected'.[67] Indeed, the suppression of dissent in Ayr was considered a precondition of progress elsewhere. The letter forming the 'Committee in the West' was followed by a series of remarkably detailed directives that framed Ayrshire as both a test case for the government's increasingly vigorous strategy and as an evident incubator of national dissent. These centred on two main objectives: the total disarming of the shire and the 'rigorous' prosecution of all those who attended, hosted, or in any way condoned the holding of local conventicles.[68] The Committee was also to gather all the names of the 'heretours, lyfrenters and landlords' so that they might be called and compelled to give formal agreement to live in a way that was 'orderly and obedient to the laws'.[69] Yet the goal was not just to ensure that local elites would help maintain order; the Privy Council also established that the Committee would summon 'the haill tenents and masters of families' to agree, on behalf of themselves and their dependents, to good behaviour. The Committee was told that after enacting this plan in Ayr and reducing the 'same to order', by force if necessary, they were to then move to the other unruly shires and do the same there.

Hearing what was afoot in Edinburgh, on 28 January 1678 the Ayr town council sent a letter to the Privy Council in response to the band of obedience sought by the Committee in the West. They reported that, theoretically, members of the council and trades were 'reddie and willing to subscribe the band for keiping of the kirk and abstaining from conventicles', but that 'the Counsell and certain tradesmen of the town cannot subscrybe the band' until they saw 'what is thairin contained'.[70] Basically, the Privy Council had made some vague asks, and the local men wanted concrete terms before signing on – a practice fully in line with how presbyterians had long approached determining the extent to which they could comply with government decrees that might contravene their sincerely held beliefs. The magistrates did not, however, want to further contribute to the burgh's trouble-making reputation. 'We doe assure you', they told the members of the Privy Council, 'that we will gie as much obedience to His Majesty's lawes as any burgh in Scotland'.[71] The following month, however, the Committee reported back to the Privy Council that the jurisdictions within the shire of Ayr were 'in a condition farr different' from the others under their scrutiny, because even the local 'commissioners of excise and militia thereof' had ignored directives for 'securing the peace and freing the country of disorders'. The commissioners moved, with the king's approval, to draw up a formal band of obedience for all Ayrshire office holders to subscribe.[72] The Committee was then given the green light to sit at Ayr throughout the winter and early spring of 1678 to administer justice and enforce obedience.

The ensuing 'Band of Relief at Air' was remarkably broad in its remit: it bound not only the magistrates and councillors of the burgh to in 'no wayes be present at any conventicles and disorderly meetings in tyme coming' and to live 'orderly in obedience to the law conform to the acts of parliament made there anent', but also their wives, children, servants, and successors.[73] It also specified that the magistrates were responsible for ensuring that all inhabitants adhered to the letter of the law. The band is revealing of the government's specific anxieties about illicit activities in the town and surrounding areas. It mandated that adherents not 'reset supplie nor commune with' treasonous persons or prohibited preachers and instead compelled magistrates to apprehend such men and turn them over to the authorities. In an echo of the combination of individual and corporate language that had long characterised the covenanting culture of the town, by subscribing the band, the magistrates promised that 'we and ilk one of us for our own parts' would endeavour to control not only their own behaviour but also to ensure the obedience of their fellow magistrates and their successors.[74] Their motivations for complying were complex: there is, for example, evidence of council members upholding the band in order to receive 'licence to wear their armes' or to avoid the economic and physical threat of having troops forcibly quartered upon them.[75] In the end, facing an array of consequences ranging from the loss of offices to the ever-present threat of military retaliation, many in Ayr complied with the band, but we should not assume this was a decision based on affirmative sentiment rather than necessity and expediency.[76]

Were the Committee's efforts to prevent Ayrshire residents from attending conventicles and supporting the presence of condemned preachers in their communities successful? The persistence of illicit activity well after 1678 suggest that the answer is an emphatic no. One of the things revealed by the findings of the Committee in the West was the breadth of the demographic makeup of those who steadfastly and at times flagrantly defied governmental orders. Those at the very top of the burgh hierarchy continued to attend conventicles and, perhaps worse, support and shelter fugitive preachers who had shown a willingness to speak not only against episcopacy, but even the actions of the king himself. The case of John Moor, former provost of Ayr and former kirk session elder, is both a dramatic example and emblematic of the level of resistance by certain burgh leadership. In February 1678, he was called before the Lords of the Committee for a litany of offences, dating back to his refusal to subscribe the so-called declaration earlier in the decade. More recently, he had, in 1677 and into the current year, attended conventicles with his family, including four held at his own home.[77] The Committee claimed that he had invited several notorious nonconformist preachers to these meetings, such as John Welsh and Donald Cargill, who 'did vent and express seditious and schismatically doctrin, and uttered many scandalous, calumnious and reproachfull speeches against his Majesties'.[78] One such meeting was reportedly held 'within the citedale of Air', a once-sacred space that, as the former parish kirk and the site of the swearing of the National Covenant and Solemn League and Covenant, must have created an especially evocative atmosphere. In the end, after having been repeatedly called to appear before the Privy Council to answer for his crimes and failing to do so, the erstwhile provost was denounced as 'his Majesties rebell'. Moor was then 'put the horn' – publicly proclaimed, to three blasts of the horn, to be an outlaw – and accordingly, all his worldly possessions were to be given to the crown's use as payment for Moor's 'contempt and disobedience'.[79]

Moor's case is especially interesting in what it reveals about not only his own part in the burgh's well-known defiance of the government, but also the sentiments and actions from other corners of the community. Up until this point, it appears that Adair had been playing nice with the government for much of the 1670s, having escaped suspension in 1669 due his good behaviour and 'aversioun to all illegal disorders and clandestine meitings'.[80] And he had, in 1670, defended the honour of his episcopal counterpart, George White. But amid the accusations against Moor was the allegation that Adair had composed a letter to 'severall indulged ministers who had mett at Machline' – referring, perhaps, to his former protestor compatriots, or to a more recent gathering. This letter, delivered by Moor, asked for their assistance in planting a minister in the parish in order to oust the 'present regular minister ther'. The group in on the plot – a mix of like-minded local ministers and magistrates – met at Adair's house where the old minister reportedly 'satt as in presbyterie and session with them' as they debated ways to exclude White from his position. In the end, the group decided to not go forward with any such plans due to reports of the establishment of the Committee in the West.[81] This does not seem to have been the first time Adair presided over deliberations that replicated an official ecclesiastical meeting. In October 1676, at a time when the official session records are unusually bare, Adair reported to the session the expenses of 'conveining of the people to a meeting of the session and court at the cunningpark'; these were lands owned, at this time, by the session, but a meeting beyond the walls of the parish would have almost certainly been unsanctioned. Unfortunately, the identities of 'the people' in attendance, the specific proceedings, and frequency of such meetings went – one imagines purposefully – unremarked.[82]

The findings from the Committee in the West also reveal, albeit in more indirect ways, the involvement of ordinary residents of the burgh in the illicit activities. Along his litany of offences, Moor had apparently been collecting 'considerable soumes of money' for the outlawed preachers from the inhabitants of Ayr, which suggests popular support in the parish for funding the activities of such men at a time when cash was tight. We do not have names of many specific residents involved in these activities, but in early 1678, two female residents of the town, Helen Leslie and Helen Purveyance, were both cited for their involvement in keeping of conventicles. Leslie, likely the wife of a heritor, had been hosting local gatherings, while Purveyance, a winemaker in the burgh, was accused of 'being present at diverse conventicles' and providing goods at the illegal communion held by John Welsh south of the town.[83] Emblematic of the centrality of women to the strength of nonconforming movement throughout Scotland, Purveyance also corresponded with Welsh and spoke herself at the communion, for which she was imprisoned in Ayr until she paid a very stiff fine of 300 merks.[84]

In February 1678, the Privy Council ordered James Kennedy, 7th Earl of Cassillis, to raze two illicit meeting houses in Carrick, the seat of the Kennedy lands in southern Ayrshire, which he did. Not content to merely see the houses demolished, the Council requested that he bring back the timber from the buildings, cut it into pieces, and 'burne the same to ashes' in the places they used to stand. The meeting houses in Carrick – long a favourite haunt of the covenanters – were very likely attended by residents from the burgh who were only a short horseback journey away, including the presently imprisoned Purveyance. The order that the timber from the illegal gathering places be burned on the spot reveals a desire on the part of the government not just to suppress dissent, but to destroy it literally and symbolically as a warning to others.[85] But it was not only at conventicles that the words of dissenting preachers shaped the religious experiences of the people of Ayr. On 11 March 1678, the Committee in the West reported learning that 'some irregular ministers have bein permitted to preach in the kirk of Air by the allowance or connivance of some of the magistratts or ministers thereof'; Adair was clearly willing to share his pulpit with likeminded presbyterians, and the magistrates too had looked the other way. One wonders what minister White made of all of this, but he surely felt unnerved, for the following year he was transported – at his request, it seems – to the kirk of Maryculter in Aberdeenshire.[86]

The Committee in the West was ultimately short-lived. Over the course of spring 1678, a debate over the legality of the Privy Council's plans to bring nonconforming western landowners to heel ensued as a group of local nobles led by the Earl of Cassillis appealed directly to the king. This appeal eventually led to a cessation of the activities of the Committee, which seemed to be doing more harm than good.[87] The commissioners had come to Ayr equipped with a sense of urgency and thorough directives, but these were easier ordered than executed. As Ronald Lee has pointed out, 'the whole policy' of subduing the west was 'the result of weakness rather than strength'.[88] The town magistrates, even those who seem to have shared the aims of the government, resented the top-down imposition of oversight which ultimately made their jobs harder; some local heritors clearly felt assailed by the demand that they personally compel their tenants to subscribe the band against conventicles; and everyone felt the presence of the quartering of the so-called Highland Host. Kirk discipline ground to a halt, and no session was held for much of February and at all between 3 March and 8 April, because both ministers were absent.[89] All told, the Committee in the West sat at Ayr for four months, between late January and late April 1678, and it seems to have only added fuel to the fire of rebellion there.

This failed experiment in containment had several discernible impacts on the lived experiences of the townspeople. Most obviously, the increased military presence wrought economic, social, and psychological consequences for Ayr's residents. To enforce the band against conventicles and their other directives, the Committee had brought with them 'a regiment of rid coats, four bress gunes, twelve wagons' and 'a squad of the kings hose guard consisting of fourtie'.[90] This smaller force represented only a fraction of the military presence felt acutely by the community; according to town council minutes, 'six or seven thousand northland men and highland men quartered in this schyre round about the Burgh'. Regardless of whether this was a numerical exaggeration, the economic strain would have been profound: once again, as a product of its religious and political positions, the town faced unwanted occupation and the associated costs of maintaining government forces. The council clerk reported bitterly that those compelled to host them were given little to no payment for their quarters, and with typical lowlander prejudice, complained that 'those of the north highlands' were 'much given for stelth'. What was more, he added, 'it is to be remembered that the clerk nor his men got no drink money, but great paines, trouble, and vexation'.[91] Some of the soldiers in Ayr took quarter at Cunningpark, land belonging at the time to the session, and one of the residents later sought payment from the elders 'for quartering of 60 men and boys and 6 horse for the space of

24 hours when the host was here'.[92] To reduce further disorder, and perhaps to provide additional security for the residents of the burgh, the magistrates by late autumn 1678 had arranged for a guard 'be keiped nightlie within the town, consisting of sixteen in number, to convein at ten o'clock in night, and to dissolve in the morning at day light' until January of the following year – yet another expense the town could scarcely afford.[93] But clearly, the issues remained unresolved, for in March 1679, the government sent two companies of foot soldiers and one on horseback to the town to keep the peace.[94]

We cannot know precisely what most men and women in the community made of these dramatic events, but certainly the augmented military presence was felt by all residents. As it had been in the past, the effects were gendered. The session – when it had a minister present and could administer discipline – grappled with a now-familiar spike in fornication cases between local women and the soldiers stationed there.[95] In early 1681, for example, Agnes Wood was convicted of carnal dealings with a soldier named John Mussman. Witnesses nearby the home where it took place knew the act had been committed due to their hearing 'all the breathings', and Wood was deemed an 'unfit person to come to public repentance' and fled town.[96] The experience for women was, at times, brutal. In January 1679, for example, Barbara Law was called before the session for the sin of uncleanness with an unnamed 'Highland Man'; during her questioning, she denied having had intercourse, but explained that she had been in his company and that he 'threw hir over in a saller [cellar]' in an attempt to have sex with her. To the session, that this seems to have been an appalling case of attempted rape was beside the point: witnesses confirmed seeing the man 'betwixt hir leggs in such a posture as men use to be when they commit filthyness with women'. One of them went so far as to deem Law, soon to be sentenced to public repentance, 'a vile woman ... and an abomination in the side of God Almighty!'.[97] This was, sadly, typical; in early modern Scotland, what mattered was that both parties had engaged in a sinful act, not intent or consent.[98] Accordingly, the session sentenced Law to public repentance. Just as they had during previous periods of martial occupation, women bore the brunt of the presence of strange men quartered in their community.

From the records of the Privy Council, the town council, and the kirk session, we can discern with confidence the general sympathies of the town. The people of Ayr were at the very least receptive and in many cases outright desirous of presbyterian worship; illicit preachers spoke numerous times in the parish kirk, including John Brown, who had apparently been allowed by the magistrates to preach 'to a large multitude'.[99] Ousted ministers like John Welsh, Gabriel Semple, George Barclay, and 'other rebels' had, according to allegations from the Privy Council, 'feasted' in the houses of the former provost, the sheriff clerk, and the former treasurer and were 'entertained by others within the burgh'.[100] Though these cases centre on the actions of local elites, it is apparent that nonconforming ministers and other covenanting rebels were welcomed and supported by many in the community. Laura Stewart and Neil McIntyre have suggested that involvement in organising and sustaining conventicles – which included not only elite men, but women, servants, labourers, and others without obvious access to power – should be viewed as part of a long and complex legacy of the covenanting revolution, which had offered all Scots a clear stake in the political debates and moral reform of their community.[101] Ayr, a still-covenanted community during the Restoration, attests to this legacy.

The final test

Adair's final few years as minister were far from harmonious, though perhaps this was fitting for a man who first took up his first and only post in a time of crisis. On 3 May 1679, the much-maligned James Sharpe was brutally murdered by a group of covenanter extremists. After about a month of planning, a party of nine men overtook the archbishop's coach and, while Sharp was on his knees begging for mercy, stabbed him to death in front of his daughter.[102] While the assassination, which was both planned and executed in Fife, went unremarked in the minute books of the Ayr kirk session or town council, it was followed by violent events much closer to home. In the following weeks, Sharp's assassins journeyed west to hold a large conventicle at Loudon Hill – on the border of Ayrshire and Lanarkshire – with like-minded nonconformists in the region. The gathering never fully materialised, due to reports of the approaching government forces commanded by John Graham of Claverhouse come to suppress the rebels. The Battle of Drumclog that ensued on 1 June about twenty-five miles northeast of Ayr was a massive victory for the covenanters, whose knowledge of the boggy local terrain had given them the upper hand. A victorious group then travelled to the burgh and took down 'the heads of severall rebells' that had previously been 'affixt on the publick places there', giving them proper internment.[103] The provost at the time, William Cunningham the younger, would later be accused of and imprisoned for allowing them to publish, with accompaniment by the town drummer, 'their traiterous declaration at the mercat croce' – almost certainly a reference to the Rutherglen Declaration composed at Glasgow in late May, which condemned all the acts committed by the government against the covenanters.[104]

This display, following so closely on the heels of Sharp's murder, must have caused a major spectacle in the town, eliciting loud cheers as well as a few jeers. Any jubilation was short-lived; the armed rebellion met its end at Bothwell Bridge on 22 June 1679. The only indication of how this event impacted Ayr, beyond the presence of several men from the parish and many more from the broader shire at the battle, is a terse entry in the town council minutes from 9 July 1679, which reads: 'The which day John Graham of Clavers, captain to ane of his Majesties troop of horse, Francis Stewart, captain to ane of his Majesties dragoons, and Charles Baird, cornet, were maid burgesses and gild brethren of the burgh.'[105] For some on the council, these privileges were surely begrudgingly bestowed, if not outright compelled.

Sometime later that year, in the early autumn, George White left the parish to take up a new post in Aberdeenshire, where he likely found a more receptive audience for his views.[106] He had been absent from the session for much of the year before his formal departure, and there was a notable uptick in the regularity of discipline and attendance by the elders now that the 'episcopal intrusion' had gone. Perhaps the most amusing example of this renewed discipline comes from the case of James Tannehill, who in early 1681 claimed that Adam English had told him that members of the kirk session said Tannehill could name his dog 'unitie and trinitie'. They had, I think we can be certain, not said this, and when English also denied the allegation, the author of the blasphemous pet name had to make public repentance.[107]

On 8 September 1679, the session voted to ask the Privy Council, with support from the burgh magistrate, to allow Adair's former colleague William Eccles 'to return to his own place and stipend again'.[108] When approached later that month, Eccles expressed his strong desire to return to his old parish, but unsurprisingly, given that he had been regularly fined for not observing the anniversary of the Restoration, no approval came. Adair continued as the kirk's sole minister until August 1682, when William Waterson, formerly minister of Dunbar, was installed.[109] The call to Eccles was part of a larger pattern of the session trying to regain what had been lost over the previous decades, and another sign that the efforts of the government to the contrary had not changed hearts and minds. On 19 April 1680, the session considered that 'in times past several differences' had emerged between the preferences of the minister and session on one hand, and the magistrates and town council on the other. 'Severall incroachments', the clerk noted, had been made upon the role and rights of kirk leaders in the appointment and dismissal of 'schoolmasters, doctors, precenters, readers and clerk to the session'.[110] Referring back to privileges granted by a 1648 decree, they hoped, with 'God's assistance', to reclaim their former oversight.[111]

These divisions would soon be overshadowed by the shared rejection of the Test Act. Passed in July 1681 by the Scottish Parliament, this religious test was to 'to be taken by all persons in public trust' – including all ministers as well as magistrates. This unhelpfully complex oath required that its adherents acknowledge, among other things, that they had 'no obligation' from either the National Covenant or Solemn League and Covenant.[112] This time, the majority of the council refused to take the Test, and in early October 1681 they also refused to hold elections so that more compliant councillors could their positions.[113] According to allegations by his Majesty's Advocate, the rebellious magistrates 'did most presumptuously, in face of the people, at the foot of the tolbooth stair call for the toune officers and dismisse them, telling them there was to be no more government in that place'.[114] This must have provoked a tremendous amount of uncertainty and confusion in the burgh, not least because no town council met between October 1681 and January 1682. The Privy Council responded by deeming the burgh incapable of holding its own elections and appointed magistrates who could take the Test 'without any equivocation mentall reservation or any maner of evasion whatsoever'.[115] Still, six of the newly nominated group refused, and there were ongoing challenges in ensuring that voting tradesmen in the town complied (or else lose 'their liberties and priviledges').[116] Two schoolmasters also resigned when faced with the Test, though one would eventually capitulate in order to get his job back.[117] When the Privy Council met on the eve of the next town council election cycle in September 1682, it noted that 'there are some differences and tumult like to fall out at the election of magistrats and councill of the burgh'; hoping to prevent 'farder disturbance', it sent a party of royal forces to quarter in Ayr until it was clear that the process had been peaceably completed.[118]

By far, though, the biggest impact of the Test was felt by the kirk. As Andrew Carter has explained, the Test Act of 1681 'provoked resistance and chaos in the church', and for men like Adair, this was finally a bridge too far.[119] On 26 December 1681, the minutes note that 'no session nor sermon last Sabbath in regard that Mr. William Adair was suspended for not taking the test'.[120] No session met for nearly three months in his absence, and upon his return in mid-March of the following year he told the reconvened group that 'now the third time he had in god's providence escaped from the restraints were put upon him in the exercise of his ministrie'.[121] He had been granted connivance – meaning, essentially, that the authorities had decided to look the other way and allow him to continue in his ministry, so long as he did not misbehave further.[122]

This respite was short-lived. On 26 August, Adair followed a familiar course and gave a 'protestation' before the session, noting that:

> in respect there are several alterations and changes of the members of the session as I have formerly so I do now for tyme to come declare for a salve to my judgment that I do sit and moderate in the session as formerly and according to my known principles and do concur with this judicatory in the uncontroverted

duties of charitie and discipline and do also declair that this concurrence in the qualitie forsd art not to be interpreted to impart any allowance of or compliance with any corruption or error of this judicatorie either in the constitution or constituent members there of or in any other acts or proceedings there of.[123]

What is most notable here is the minister's elaboration that this declaration was a 'salve' to his judgement. He needed present company as well as posterity to recognise him as man of 'known principles' – pragmatic, yes, but at his core always a presbyterian who cared about process.

Perhaps he knew that this latest 'protestation' would be his last. By the end of August, William Waltersone was now a second minister in the parish; licensed by the bishop of Edinburgh, he was surely one of the 'alterations' to which Adair referred. Finally, on 11 December 1682, after being asked once more to subscribe the Test, Adair received his final sentence of deposition because 'he would not conform'. The old protestor's zeal, in his waning years, was quieter but still present after all. Added in a different hand in the minutes is a line that reads: 'he was ordained minister here in September 1639'.[124] The sense of loss was palpable; so too was the weight of history and all that had come before. Adair died two years later, at age 70, just one year before James VII and II ascended the throne, eventually sparking yet another protestant revolution that would see the minister's beloved presbyterian kirk, though altered, restored.

Notes

1 Ayrshire Archives, town council book, B6/18/4, fo. 9r.
2 B6/18/4, fo. 9v.
3 Hew Scott (ed.), *Fasti Ecclesiae Scoticanae*, vol. VI: Synod of Aberdeen and Moray, new edn (Edinburgh: Oliver and Boyd, 1926), p. 61.
4 *The Register of the Privy Council of Scotland* (hereafter *RPCS* series 1–3, ed. P. Hume Brown (Edinburgh, 1881–1933), series 3, vol. 3, p. 157.
5 B6/18/4, fo. 9v.
6 Robert Wodrow, *Analecta; or, Materials for a History of Remarkable Providences* (Edinburgh: Maitland Club, 1842), vol. 3, p. 74.
7 For two relatively recent discussions of Restoration identities, see Alasdair Raffe, 'Who Were the Later Covenanters?', in Chris R. Langley (ed.), *The National Covenant in Scotland, 1638–1689* (Woodbridge: Boydell, 2020); and Jamie Murdoch McDougall, 'Covenants and Covenanters in Scotland, 1638–1679' (PhD thesis, University of Glasgow, 2017), chapter 4.
8 This term is Neil McIntyre's in 'Saints and Subverters: The Later Covenanters in Scotland, c. 1648–1682' (PhD thesis, University of Strathclyde, 2016), p. 117.
9 Andrew Carter, 'Episcopal Church of Scotland, 1660–1685' (PhD thesis, University of St Andrews, 2019), pp. 136–42.

10 Robert Wodrow, *The History of the Sufferings of the Church of Scotland, from the Restauration to the Revolution*, 4 vols (Edinburgh: James Watson, 1722), ii, pp. 180–1.
11 On this point, see Elizabeth H. Hyman, 'A Church Militant: Scotland, 1661–1690', *Sixteenth Century Journal*, 26 (1995), 49–74.
12 NRS, Ayr kirk session minutes, CH2/751/5, p. 228.
13 CH2/751/5, p. 244.
14 CH2/751/5, p. 244.
15 CH2/751/5, p. 244.
16 CH2/751/5, p. 244.
17 James D. Marwick (ed.), *Extracts from the Records of the Convention of Royal Burghs, 1615–1676*, vol. III (Edinburgh, 1866), p. 626. Ayr was not alone in its suffering; the southwestern burghs of Irvine and Dumfries were noted by the Convention as in similarly dire straits in the early 1670s.
18 B6/18/4, fos. 106r–v. Moor's last name is also spelled, variously, 'Mure' and 'Muir'.
19 *RPCS*, 3rd series, vol. 4, p. 551. This also happened in Kirkcudbright, though there only two had refused to sign.
20 B6/18/4, fo. 107r.
21 Burgh schools were generally grammar schools, meaning the main subject taught was Latin grammar and literature; in Ayr, there was both a school master who focused on Latin grammar, and a 'doctor of the grammar school' who taught general reading and writing. In the late sixteenth century Ayr also established a 'sang school', or Scots School, which focused on teaching younger pupils, including girls, to sing, read, and write in English. It is noteworthy that Ayr was, as James Grant put it in his *History of the Burgh Schools of Scotland*, 'conspicuous for the careful regulations made in it from a comparatively early period for supplying the scholars with an English education' – that is, the language of the kirk. See James Grant, *History of the Burgh Schools of Scotland* (Edinburgh: William Collins, 1876), p. 91. Even before 1600, pupils could study English in the grammar or Scots school. For more on schooling in Ayr, see John Strawhorn, *750 Years of a Scottish School: Ayr Academy, 1233–1983* (Ayr: Alloway Publishing, 1983).
22 B6/18/4, fos 92r–3.
23 B6/18/4, fo. 110r.
24 B6/18/4, fos. 124r and 126v; CH2/751/6, 374.
25 B6/18/4, fo. 77r.
26 See, for example, B6/18/4, fos. 87v–88r, 91r, 92r, 98v, 104v, 158r–v, 173r.
27 B6/18/4, fos. 11r–v.
28 In March 1671, for example, the town council considered how to deal with the familiar problem of 'manie young lous women that takes up hous', raising suspicions that they lived 'ane sinfull and vicious life' – a reference to potential sex work. A list was to be made of 'single women that keeps house', and three councillors were then to speak with Adair 'anent the course that sallbe taken with such persons'. B6/18/4, fo. 32v.

29 CH2/751/5, p. 234.
30 CH2/751/5, p. 234.
31 CH2/751/5, p. 234.
32 CH2/751/5, p. 235.
33 CH2/751/5, pp. 235–6.
34 CH2/751/5, pp. 236–7.
35 For an overview of the core ideas of the Scottish Enlightenment, see Alexander Broadie (ed.), *The Cambridge Companion to the Scottish Enlightenment* (Cambridge: Cambridge University Press, 2003).
36 CH2/751/5, pp. 237–9.
37 CH2/751/5, p. 237.
38 CH2/751/6, p. 23; see also, for example, in 1674: no session held due to absence of the minister on 13 April, 27 July, 24 August, and in 1675, the session could not meet between late June and late July, or between late August and late September.
39 CH2/751/5, pp. 246, 258, 306, and 310; CH2/751/6, p. 370.
40 See, for example, CH2/751/5, pp. 257, 276, 289, 294, 300, 316, and 328. On Scotland and the Anglo-Dutch Wars, see Steve Murdoch, *The Terror of the Seas? Scottish Maritime Warfare, 1513–1713* (Leiden: Brill, 2010), chapter 6.
41 CH2/751/5, p. 227 and CH2/751/6, pp. 452 and 494.
42 CH2/751/6, p. 289. On the James, which travelled from Ayr not only to the West Indies, but also to continental Europe and the Carolinas, see Tom Barclay and Eric J. Graham, *The Early Transatlantic Trade of Ayr, 1640–1730* (Ayr: The Ayrshire Archaeological and Natural History Society, 2005), pp. 26–38.
43 CH2/751/6, pp. 65 and 101.
44 CH2/751/6, p. 197.
45 CH2/751/6, p. 211.
46 CH2/751/6, pp. 535–6. For references for Scots captured by Barbary corsairs, see also CH2/751/6, pp. 69, 88, 426, 461, 507, and 553.
47 On discussions about seating, which revolved around the prohibition of long stools or benches that overly crowded the kirk as well as the need for the infirm to sit closer to the pulpit, see CH2/751/6, pp. 142–5.
48 Hyman, 'A Church Militant', 50–9.
49 For more on the involvement of lay people in organising and attending conventicles, see Neil McIntyre, 'Conventicles: Organising Dissent in Restoration Scotland', *Scottish Historical Review*, 99 (2020), 429–53.
50 *RPCS*, series 3, vol. 3, p. 624.
51 *RPCS*, series 3, vol. 3, p. 157.
52 For more examples of the government's attempt to suppress conventicles in Ayrshire and the broader southwest during the 1670s, see, for example, *RPCS*, series 4, vol. 4, pp. 425, 578, 581; vol. 5, pp. 279–80.
53 *RPCS*, series 3, vol. 3, pp. 159–60.
54 Wodrow, *History*, vol. ii, p. 263.
55 *RPCS*, series 3, vol. 4, p. 413.
56 *RPCS*, series 3, vol. 5, p. 270.
57 *RPCS*, series 3, vol. 5, pp. 270–1.

58 *RPCS*, series 3, vol. 5, pp. 279–80.
59 *RPCS*, series 3, vol. 5, p. 298.
60 See 'suggestions by the Bishops of Scotland for the Suppression of Conventicles in the West' printed in *The Lauderdale Papers*, ed. Osmund Airy, 3 vols (London: Camden Society, 1884), iii, pp. 95–8.
61 The members appointed to the Committee in the West were: the Earls of Linilithgow, Strathmore, Airlie, Glencairn, Caithness, Moray, Perth, Mar, and Wigton, the Lord Rosse, and the Marquis of Athol. *RPCS*, series 3, vol. 5, p. xvi.
62 *RPCS*, series 3, vol. 5, p. 319.
63 *RPCS*, series 3, vol. 5, p. 319.
64 *RPCS*, series 3, vol. 5, pp. 319–20.
65 *RPCS*, series 3, vol. 5, p. 395.
66 On Charles II, see Ronald Hutton, *Charles the Second, King of England, Scotland, and Ireland* (Oxford: Oxford University Press, 1989) and Tim Harris, *Charles II and His Kingdoms, 1660–1685* (London: Penguin, 2006).
67 *Lauderdale Papers*, vol. 3, p. 95.
68 *RPCS*, series 3, vol. 5, pp. 321–2.
69 *RPCS*, series 3, vol. 5, p. 322.
70 B6/18/4, fo. 134r.
71 B6/18/4, fo. 134r.
72 *RPCS*, series 3, vol. 5, p. 338.
73 National Library of Scotland (hereafter NLS), Wod. Qu. XXXVI, 'Band of relief at Air', February 1678, p. 33.
74 Wod. Qu. XXXVI, 'Band of relief at Air', February 1678, p. 33. Later that month, a 'Band of relief signed be the inhabitants of the borrowfield of Air and Barronie of Alloway' was issued and subscribed along the same lines. See Ayrshire Archives, B6/39/12.
75 *RPCS*, series 3, vol. 5, pp. 529, 550, and 554.
76 For the receipt of the band and the orders to meet at the kirk and subscribe the band, under warning of the 'highest pain that efter may follow', see B6/18/4, fo. 134v.
77 *RPCS*, series 3, vol. 5, p. 543.
78 *RPCS*, series 3, vol. 5, p. 544.
79 *RPCS*, series 3, vol. 5, p. 545.
80 B6/18/2, fos. 298v–9r.
81 *RPCS*, series 3, vol. 5, p. 544.
82 CH2/751/6, p. 321.
83 *RPCS*, series 3, vol. 5, pp. 543 and 550.
84 *RPCS*, series 3, vol. 5, p, 553. On women and Scottish nonconformity, see Alasdair Raffe, 'Female Authority and Lay Activism in Scottish Presbyterianism, 1660–1740', in Sarah Petrei and Hannah Smith (eds), *Religion and Women in Britain, c. 1660–1760* (Farnham: Ashgate, 2014), pp. 59–74; Alan James McSeveney, 'Non-Conforming Presbyterian Women in Restoration Scotland: 1660–1679' (PhD thesis, University of Strathclyde, 2005).
85 *RPCS*, series 3, vol. 5, pp. 420–1.

86 *Fasti*, vol. vii, p. 61.
87 Ronald Arthur Lee, 'Government and Politics in Scotland, 1661–1681' (PhD thesis, University of Glasgow, 1995), pp. 266–8.
88 Lee, 'Government and Politics in Scotland, 1661–1681', p. 265.
89 CH2/751/6, pp. 407–11.
90 B6/18/4, fo. 136v.
91 B6/18/4, fo. 136v.
92 CH2/751/6, p. 448.
93 As quoted in Archibald Mackenzie, *William Adair and His Kirk: The Auld Kirk of Ayr, 1639–1684* (Ayr: Ayr Advertiser, 1933), p. 83.
94 B6/18/4, fo. 148r.
95 CH2/751/6, pp. 415, 436–7, 443.
96 CH2/751/6, pp. 527 and 530.
97 CH2/751/6, p. 443.
98 Gordon DesBrisay, 'Twisted By Definition: Women Under Godly Discipline in Seventeenth-Century Scottish Towns', in Yvonne Galloway Brown and Rona Ferguson (eds), *Twisted Sisters: Women, Crime and Deviance in Scotland Since 1400* (East Linton: Tuckwell, 2002), p. 146
99 *RPCS*, series 3, vol. 6, p. 164.
100 *RPCS*, series 3, vol. 6, p. 164; B6/18/4, fos. 148v–9r.
101 See McIntyre, 'Saints and Subverters', and Laura A.M. Stewart, *Rethinking the Scottish Revolution* (Oxford: Oxford University Press, 2016).
102 For an account of the murder, see James Russell, 'Account of the Murder of Archbishop Sharp', in James Kirkton, *A History of the Church of Scotland 1660–1679*, ed. Ralph Stewart (Lewiston: Edwin Mellen, 1992), pp. 397–431. The planning and significance of the murder are discussed in McIntyre, 'Saints and Subverters', pp. 203–6.
103 It is unclear precisely who the former owners of these heads were, or when the heads had been displayed, or how many were taken down, but some were likely from the Pentland Rising of 1666. See Chapter 5, this volume.
104 *RPCS*, series 3, vol. 7, p. 256; B6/18/4, fo. 183r.
105 According to Mark Jardine's count, eight of the men declared fugitives in 1684 for having been present at the battle were from Ayr; many more – 446 – were from Ayrshire more broadly. See Mark Jardine, 'The United Societies: Militancy, Martyrdom and the Presbyterian Movement in Late-Restoration Scotland, 1679 to 1688' (PhD thesis, University of Edinburgh, 2009), p. 204. For the entry from the town council minutes, see B6/18/4, fo. 151v.
106 *Fasti*, vol. vi, p. 61.
107 CH2/751/6, pp. 526–8.
108 CH2/751/6, p. 473.
109 CH2/751/6, p. 591.
110 CH2/751/6, p. 496.
111 CH2/751/6, p. 496.
112 *Records of the Parliaments of Scotland to 1707* (hereafter RPS), ed. Keith M. Brown et al. (St Andrews, 2007–11), 1681/7/29.

113 B6/18/4, fo. 182r.
114 *RPCS*, series 3, vol. 7, p. 255.
115 B6/18/4, fos. 182v–4r. As Alasdair Raffe has noted, Ayr was not the only burgh to require such intervention, but it was the 'most prominent case' of this sort of resistance and governmental response. Alasdair Raffe, *Scotland in Revolution* (Edinburgh: Edinburgh University Press, 2019), p. 85.
116 B6/18/4, fos. 184v and 186r.
117 James McClelland, 'Schools', in A.I. Dunlop (ed.), *The Royal Burgh of Ayr: Seven Hundred Fifty Years of History* (Edinburgh: Oliver and Boyd, 1953), p. 215.
118 *RPCS*, series 3 vol. 7, p. 548.
119 Carter, 'Episcopal Church of Scotland', p. 119.
120 CH2/751/6, p. 566.
121 CH2/751/6, p. 571.
122 On the informal policy of 'connivance', see Carter, 'Episcopal Church of Scotland', pp. 81–3.
123 CH2/751/6, p. 590.
124 CH2/751/6, p. 605.

Epilogue: afterlives

Auld Ayr, wham ne'er a town surpasses,
For honest men and bonnie lasses.

Robert Burns, 'Tam O'Shanter'[1]

In reading through the kirk session and town council records of seventeenth-century Ayr, one might be struck by the general lack of fanfare at the passing of the burgh's longest serving and arguably most influential minister. Just over a year after his final stand against the Test Act and ensuing deposition, he lay in his deathbed. A new minister, Alexander Gregorie, had taken his clerical place after having been transferred from St Quivox in 1683.[2] On 11 February 1684, second minister William Waterson reported to the elders that he had received from Adair 'four books of register' which were given to the session clerk, along with a box containing the rights to the land of Cunningpark and other papers.[3] The next day, the man who had occupied the pulpit of the parish kirk for four and a half decades, guiding multiple generations of Ayr families through personal and communal 'plagues of the heart', drew his final breath.[4]

The following summer, Adair's son and namesake approached the town council to ask for permission to build a monument 'above his umquhill [deceased] fathers burial place'. The magistrates granted this request, with the stipulation that the younger Adair ensure that the monument did not block the light of any kirk windows.[5] And so this testament in stone stands today, facing the River Ayr (see Figures 1 and 2). The inscription above it, translated from Latin, reads 'Mr. William Adair, from the most ancient family of KINHILT, legitimate Pastor of the church of Ayr for 44 years, who died and was buried here 12 Feb 1684, aged 70'.[6] The inscription was most likely written by Adair the younger, and it is telling that he selected 'legitimus' – translating to lawful or legitimate – to describe his father's life's work and position. This graveside monument is the only extant image we have of the man at the centre of this book, and it is fitting that it depicts him kneeling in prayer, an act for which he was reported to have 'an eminent gift'.[7] It is also rarefied – I have not come across any similarly ornate monuments to

Figure 1 Photo of Adair monument at the Auld Kirk of Ayr taken by the author.

Figure 2 Etching of Adair's monument by Robert Bryden from *Ayrshire Monuments* (1915), Wikimedia Commons.

specific covenanting clergy, which no doubt testifies to the relative wealth of Adair's family as much as the importance of his ministry.[8]

By the close of the seventeenth century, Ayr's longest serving minister was gone, and so too, in many ways, was Scotland's covenanting movement. But the individuals and ideologies of Ayr had important afterlives, looming large in popular memory and carving legacies into ongoing practices. The town's culture of covenanting, forged during seventeenth-century crises but born of far older ideas, proved durable and influential because it was purposefully fashioned not only for the present, but for posterity.

Ayr after Adair

The difficulties and dramas of the years following the deposition of Adair reveal the persistence of the crisis of authority that had ensued since the Restoration. At times tensions flared between some of the residents and the government, but as often, between residents themselves in ways that reveal how the previous decades had left an indelible mark on the community. In late 1682, infighting broke out on Ayr's town council between Robert Hunter, William Brisbane, and William Cunningham the younger, and the complicated conflict reached its apex in 1684. Involving libels and counter libels that go on for many pages in the town council book and Privy Council minutes alike, the whole affair can be summed up as each man reporting to the Privy Council that the others and their associates had acted in extraordinary ways against the wishes of the government.[9] Willian Brisbane, former provost (he served in 1683), was accused by Robert Hunter of 'great & manifest contempt of his Majesties authoritie' by the 'the incouradgment of fanaticall interest in the toun of Air', where 'the growth of fanaticism is much to be feared'.[10] According to the judgement of the Privy Council, it would have 'bein the utter ruine of the church in that place' if Brisbane had continued unabated, as the townspeople were 'more inclined to follow disaffected & presbyterian min[iste]rs than to wait upon the ordinances under the orthodox ministry'.[11] Most sensationally, Brisbane was accused of manoeuvring for the election to the town council of 'severall Inglish fanaticks' who, as the Privy Council put it, had 'served during the rebellion under the usurper in that place', showing their 'villainous rebellious principles' by deserting General Monck during the Restoration.[12] Here again, we see just how large Oliver Cromwell and his men loomed in the imaginations of the public and Restoration government alike, both of whom at times conflated the realities of the past with the perceived threats of the present.

In this convoluted case, Brisbane was not the only party in trouble. Indeed, the Privy Council also judged former provost William Cunningham the younger (he served in 1678–81) and former baillie Robert Hunter to be guilty of crimes 'contrair to the standing lawes of the Kingdom'. Cunningham, Brisbane alleged, committed manifold crimes early in the decade: among them, encouraging the rebels present at Bothwell Bridge and compelling the town clerk to provide some of them quarter; 'gratifying the fanatics' by inviting unlicensed minister James Brown to preach in the pulpit over the course of several sabbath days; and convincing members of the trades of the town to ignore orders from the government to appear and subscribe the Test in 1683.[13] Hunter had, apparently, 'intertained and supplied' James Paterson – another rebel at Bothwell Bridge – at his home, and collaborated with Cunningham to bar compliant magistrates from council meetings and to encourage others through both bribery and force to 'desert his Majesties service'. Ultimately, the Privy Council judged the allegations against Brisbane to be 'not sufficiently proven' and delayed the proceedings against Hunter indefinitely. They deemed Cunningham, who drew the short end of the disciplinary stick, 'incapable of all public office' and fined him 500 pounds; he was to be imprisoned until the money was paid in full.[14]

This ongoing drama with the council in the year of Adair's death reveals several things. First, ideological differences did little to fuel this conflict; indeed, all parties accused the others of being willing to countenance and even support the harbouring of rebels and illicit preachers in the burgh during the early years of the 1680s. Second, this general sympathy for the presbyterian cause was not limited to the elites of the community; ordinary men and women had filled the parish kirk to hear the sermons of unlicensed minister James Brown, attended conventicles, and, following the deposition of Adair, been easily persuaded to abandon orthodox ministers to 'follow disaffected & presbyterian' pastors. Third, the seriousness with which the Privy Council took this situation confirms the lasting impact of the disorders of the previous years. They decided, given the 'animosities and divisions amongst the Inhabitants', to forgo typical elections and use the now well-worn tool of choosing compliant men to serve as magistrates and town council members for the following year.[15] The previous month, a commission had also been set up at Ayr to deal with these disorders, and it required all the heritors of the shire to gather in Ayr's kirk or tolbooth until they took the Test and were cleared from suspicion of sheltering rebels.[16] According to Robert Wodrow – who heard about these events from a narrative sent to him by 'a gentleman of honour then present' – the commissioners erected a gibbet at Ayr's market cross and, pointing to it, reminded all in earshot that 'yonder tree will make you take Test'.[17] While these sorts of reports in Wodrow's *History* ought to be taken with a hefty grain of salt, there is little doubting the gravity with which the government approached the ongoing resistance and noncompliance of Ayr and its surrounding regions, and the degree to which the latest crackdown must have shaken local inhabitants.

With the deposition of Adair, the community had not only lost its popular pastor, but also a critical source of stability during uncertain times. The session minutes during the ministry of Alexander Gregorie testify to this loss. Shortly after he made his first appearance in the minutes in June 1683, witnesses reported to the session that 'ane stranger in the habit of a minister' had married residents William Mitchell and Anna Kennedy. The session deemed Mitchell 'guilty of schism by his disorderly marriage without proclamatione or ane order from the Bishop'.[18] Though the strange man in clerical garb is not again mentioned in the records, we have to wonder whether he was one of the fugitive preachers sheltering in the town or an ousted minister from a nearby parish.

The following month, Gregorie presided over a series of consequential meetings that reflected a level of general discomfort with the new leadership as well as challenges in ensuring attendance both on the session and at the sabbath. On 2 July 1685 the session, which had for a long time met on Mondays at nine in the morning, determined that this was an hour in which many of the members were 'most busie' and thus unable to attend; the meeting time was moved to 2pm in the afternoon. The seven men present alongside ministers Gregorie and Waterstone also considered the regular absences from the session and asked that all elders and deacons appear at the next meeting to 'declare whither they will continue and officiat or not'.[19] On 9 July, of those who answered the session's call to appear, six said they would serve until Martinmas, another for another year, and three men for six months. At the next meeting, four additional members agreed to officiate 'for a tyme' but would not commit further.[20] This rescheduling of the session for convenience and the inconsistency of the terms of service suggests that membership on the kirk's governing body no longer held the cache it once did, nor was it a top priority for its members. Still, the vast majority of the men who agreed to continue their service on the session for various lengths of time – and no doubt with varied enthusiasm – had also served with Adair during his final months as minister. Though some of them would abandon this role within the year, their loyalty, dampened as it may have been, seems to have been to the institution as much as the minister who ran it.

Such was not the case for many of the townspeople, and during Gregorie's ministry, large numbers of them withdrew from the parish kirk. On 3 August 1683, the minutes note that 'the sabbath is ill observed', with many parishioners engaging in drinking and other recreations rather than attend sermons.[21] The minister issued an intimation seeking to curb the problem the following Sunday, but unsurprisingly, given how few people seem to have been present to hear said warning about poor attendance, 'the great abuse that is comitted on the Lords day' persisted.[22] The following autumn, the session, at the desire of the provost, appointed elders to search sections of the town to find out 'what children were keept unbaptised'.[23] In February 1684, the session lamented the 'idle and profane persons' who traipsed up and down the streets and gathered in 'considerable numbers' rather than attending services as they should. Exasperated by those who did 'flight and condemn' the authority of the session by not appearing when called, the elders and deacons agreed with the town officers that they should be empowered to commit such persons to prison 'unless their excuse to be such shall be found relevant to the elders and deacons'.[24] In April, noting the 'disorders of that place' due to declining church attendance, the session determined that 'the people be solemnly warned and Christianly advertised to keep better order for the future on their peril'.[25]

Of course, even at the height of the covenanter's disciplinary regime, things like sabbath-breaking were problems, but generally, infractions involved individual delinquents, and there is no evidence of any comparable withdrawal during Adair's long and difficult ministry. These actions suggest a lack of enthusiasm for the new clerical regime – indeed, it is a testament to Adair's sway over the community that this had not happened earlier, given his confined, conforming status and the local keenness for conventicles. At the same time, it is almost certainly the case that in these years many took advantage of the enfeebled disciplinary capacity of the session – itself a reflection of the general lack of communal buy-in – to sleep in on Sundays, go drinking with their friends, raucously celebrate marriages, and enjoy previously barred pastimes. There was at once an acute longing for the past and an embrace of the opportunities posed by the present.

The road to revolution, again

Things would continue to be chaotic in the town through the years leading to the Revolution of 1688–9. In the winter of 1685, during the deadliest year of the so-called 'Killing Time', six companies of footmen were sent to the burgh to bring any rebels to heel. This dramatic period of government crackdown, which has had an outsized role in shaping popular memory of this period, continued a policy of military repression in the southwest that had done little to quiet presbyterian dissent.[26] The infighting on the town council persisted, coming to name-calling and fisticuffs on the High Street.[27] Alasdair Raffe, assessing the drama on the Ayr council during the latter half of the 1680s, has rightly described the town's local politics as 'characterised by a factionalism of bewildering complexity'.[28]

Things were not any calmer within the kirk session, and the new ministers faced marked resistance from within and beyond the community. In

1687, motivated by a desire to extend toleration for his fellow Catholics, James VII and II issued an Act of Indulgence, giving nonconformists in Scotland (save the most extreme among them) freedom to hold their own meetings and religious services.[29] Within a matter of weeks, John Moor – covenanting stalwart and former provost (he served from 1673 to 1675) – and a few like-minded men had purchased the old church of St John the Baptist, then in private hands, and converted it into a meeting house to host a presbyterian session. For over a year and a half, Ayr had two rival sessions, and minister William Eccles, having previously been denied the opportunity to return to the parish, presided over the dissenting one. The first presbyterian meeting was on 6 September 1687, staffed by Adair's old allies, though the 'official' – that is, episcopal – minute books note that additional poor relief was being collected in the old church from 18 July of that year, only 13 days after James VII's indulgence had been proclaimed.[30] The Ayr presbytery was also reconvened that August, meeting too in St John the Baptist.[31] What ordinary parishioners made of having, perhaps for the first time in their lives, a free choice in where to worship we cannot be sure. The steps toward greater pluralism are often confused and messy. But the reports of established churches in the southwest being deserted after 1687 coming from both sides of the confessional divide suggests an enthusiasm, at least in places like Ayr, for the revival of permitted presbyterian worship.[32] For some of the older members of the community, a return to the kirk of St John's and to the services of their youth must have felt like coming home.

Whatever spiritual unity Adair had cultivated in his decades-long ministry, imperfect as it was, only partially survived him. What remained of the covenanting movement was subsumed within the growing extremism – in tactic as much as ideology – of a small subset of presbyterians known as the Cameronians. This group of militants originated in the late 1670s and rejected any and all compromise with the government, and they were well represented in southwestern Scotland, though there is little evidence of many of these so-called 'Hillmen' coming from the burgh itself.[33] Perhaps this is because the town's spiritual leadership was for so long embodied by a man who, while zealous in his commitments to the covenants, at times recognised the necessity of side-lining purity in favour of stability. Regardless, the Cameronians, now organised into the United Societies, made their presence known in Ayr in early 1689, when the official session minutes note that for the first four months of the year no meeting was held, 'nor sermon nor collection Last Sabbath, both the ministers being discharged to preach by ane armed partie of hillmen upon their perill'.[34] According to reports, on 11 January Alexander Gregorie had received a paper 'commanding him and all his Brethren to leave their Ministers against the fifteenth under the pain of death'. Because he initially disregarded this directive, eleven armed men showed up at his house a few days later and commanded him 'Preach no more in the Church of Air'.[35]

Such intimidation tactics in the midst of revolution worked. While there is little evidence of Ayr residents directly involved in this rabbling, there is also no evidence of anyone stepping in to aid Gregorie and Waterson. By May 1689, after the Revolution of the previous year returned the kirk to presbyterian hands, Eccles resumed his role as head minister at Ayr, presiding over the parish where he had taken up his first post in 1656 and where he would serve until his death in 1694.[36] Eccles's installation as official first minister took place the same month that William III and Mary II of England accepted the Scottish throne. According to a report by Thomas Morer, an English minister travelling in Scotland in the early eighteenth century, it was in Ayr that the new monarchs 'were first proclaimed, and own'd for their sovereign'.[37] While this may have been slight exaggeration, the Ayr town council did appoint that William's Scottish *Declaration of Reasons* for his invasion be read aloud at the market cross on 29 December 1688.[38] John Moor was re-elected provost at the Revolution, after a brief interlude when the position was held by William Wallace, a Catholic landowner who had been appointed by James VII and II in November 1687.[39] There was no episcopal service for nearly a half century until a congregation was formed in 1743.[40]

The events of the years after Adair's deposition and subsequent death, much like the years of his life, reflect the degree to which national politics and high-level decisions shaped and were shaped by lived communal experiences. Directives from the top exacerbated pre-existing rivalries, provided new fodder for defamation, sparked renewed spiritual anxieties, and impeded the management of local affairs at multiple levels. In turn, national authorities made decisions in direct response to disruptions in places like Ayr, though not always fully understanding the complex dynamics (and difficult personalities) of local communities.[41] And despite heated disagreement with certain decisions made by the government, members of Ayr's town council – even those of the presbyterian persuasion – sought assistance from the Privy Council in adjudicating internal divisions. The events of these years offer no clear-cut narrative of town versus king or one confessional commitment versus another, though both of these dynamics were present. Instead, the period between Adair's deposition and the Revolution witnessed a messy struggle for control, influence, and stability, one informed by the spiritual anxieties and practical concerns of the period and intensified by the absence of the town's long-time minister.

Covenanted memory

Memory looms large in the course and afterlife of the covenanting movement.[42] Adair and his ilk made decisions informed by the tumultuous events of the recent decades and an ardent desire to return to an imagined period of past godliness, be that the early days of the Scottish Reformation or the apex of their own political and religious influence. When the reconvened presbytery and session of Ayr chose to meet in the newly purchased St John the Baptist, this was not simply a matter of convenience, but an intentional homecoming in the place where both covenants had been sworn. At the same time, the choices of the covenanters were profoundly forward-looking, shaped by a conscientiousness about how their words and actions would become the subject of memory; this is apparent in the composition of kirk session records (the reoccurring 'it is to be remembered' was both a practical and aspirational phrase), sermons, wartime polemics, the diaries kept in the post-Restoration era, and more. At the Revolution of 1688–9, memories of the civil wars and the later struggle for presbyterian worship informed both willingness to support the new monarchs and the pronounced anti-Jacobite sympathies of the southwest and beyond.[43]

The years of Adair's ministry have held an important place in both the academic study of Scotland and the popular imagination of many Scots, though Adair himself has been little more than a footnote in the former, and the years of his ministry have often been transformed into hagiography in the latter. The covenanters have been memorialised in a wide and often contradictory range of ways: as principled Scottish patriots and unyielding religious extremists, as heroes and as villains. Even in academic studies, they have been subjects of, as Ian Cowan aptly put it, 'excessive adulation' and 'denigration' alike, though more recent histories have generally offered a useful and nuanced corrective.[44]

The adulation of popular memory is neatly illustrated by a stone laid in 1814 by the incorporated trades of Ayr in memory of those executed in the town after the Pentland Rising of 1666. Like Adair's memorial, it looks towards the River Ayr. On the front, seven names are listed as those who died 'for their adherence to the Word of GOD and Scotlands Covenanted work of Reformation'. On the back, it reads:

> Here lie seven Martyrs to our Covenants,
> A sacred number of triumphant Saints.
> Pontus M'Adam the unjust sentence was passed,
> What is his oun the world will know at last:
> And Herod Drummond caused their heads affix,
> Heaven keeps a record of the sixty-six,
> Boots, thumbkins, gibbets, were in fashion then,
> LORD, let us never see such days again.[45]

That the stone was erected by the incorporated trades of the town is fitting and revealing. These were the heirs of those who shaped the covenanting movement in Ayr and endeavoured to uphold it, at times by means more radical than those of their minister. In the mid-seventeenth century, the men of the professions had sworn the covenants alongside their wives and children, confessed to their violations when the plague came in 1647, attended conventicles, and in many cases rejected government directives to abjure the lodestones of their religious and political identities. Nearly two centuries after the swearing of the National Covenant, at a time when Scottish history was being increasingly romanticised, their lives had become local and national legend, the stuff of myth as much as history.

Ayr's location on the sea was central to both its comparative radicalism and its influence on the impact and memory of the covenanting movement beyond Scottish shores. The region's location meant that at times of turmoil, covenanting ministers from the southwest could seek refuge in Ireland while maintaining contact with their networks back home.[46] As a port city, Ayr essentially had a religious safety valve in times of persecution, and Adair's more radical counterparts could thus flee while continuing to support and collaborate with like-minded minsters who had held onto their posts. The proximity to the sea also meant that, when boarding ships to sail to places like Barbados and Virginia, the merchants of Ayr – many of whom also held prominent positions as local elders and magistrates – took the culture of covenanting with them. When they traversed the Atlantic and eventually began to settle in the British colonies in substantial numbers in the later seventeenth and early eighteenth centuries, sometimes directly from Ayr and other times via Ireland, they established religious and commercial networks that profoundly influenced the evolution of British North America. As Craig Gallagher has persuasively demonstrated, the militant protestantism inspired by generations of Scottish covenanters from places like Ayr was at the heart of what would become the American revolutionary vision.[47]

More generally, the culture of covenanting in Ayr and throughout Scotland cannot be divorced from its European and transatlantic contexts. As the story of Ayr reveals, covenanting was in many respects a communal practice, born of local histories, concerns, and personalities. But at the same time, it was part of an international theological movement that inspired regionally specific spiritual praxes. John Coffey has persuasively suggested that ministers like Adair 'should be considered as part of the Puritan tendency within English speaking Reformed Protestantism'. He notes that 'to describe them simply as Presbyterians or Covenanters focuses attention on their particular ecclesiological or political positions, whilst obscuring the ethos and spirituality that they shared with zealous Protestants beyond Scotland'.[48] This is a crucial point. Here, I have tried to consider the 'culture of covenanting' as a Reformed palimpsest: European in its theological origins, transatlantic in its influence, national in its political dimensions, but fundamentally shaped by the communities in which it was practised. These communities, like the

Epilogue: afterlives 185

individuals who made them, can rarely be neatly categorised over long periods of time. The 'radicals' and 'conservatives' of the past are not always those of the future, and from the outset, the covenants were imbued with calculated ambiguity and implicit flexibility. Ayr's culture of covenanting demonstrates that Reformed protestant piety, despite outdated assumptions about individualism or rigidity, was fundamentally a communal project negotiated over decades of lived experience and born of moments of crisis.

****

Today, the National Library of Scotland in Edinburgh is home to one of the most remarkable extant copies of the National Covenant. Signed by hundreds of men from Ayr in the spring of 1638, it is a large and delicate piece of parchment, protected in plastic, extending nearly three feet long and over two feet wide. The signature of 'Mr. William Adair', then newly come to the parish, is near the top of the list of local signatories in a distinctive scrawl. It would surely be ill-advised to judge historical figures by their handwriting, but Adair's seems emblematic of the man: unobtrusive, formal, not especially neat but exceptionally clear. This copy, often called the 'Ayr Covenant', was donated to the then Advocates Library in 1875 by John Cowan, the grandson of Mary Adair, who was the granddaughter of William Adair.[49] For five generations and nearly two centuries, it had been kept in the Adair family, passed on from the man to whom it meant so much to his children and their children. I think our minister would have liked the document's final resting place, available for viewing by scholars from Scotland and far beyond, preserved, as he hoped its ideals would be, 'for all tyme coming'.

Notes

1 Robert Burns, 'Tam O'Shanter', first published in Francis Grose (ed.), *The Antiquities of Scotland*, 2 vols (London: S. Hooper, 1789–91), II, pp. 199–201.
2 Hew Scott (ed.), *Fasti Ecclesiae Scoticanae*, vol. III: Synod of Glasgow and Ayr, new edn (Edinburgh: Oliver and Boyd, 1920), p. 9.
3 National Records of Scotland (hereafter NRS), CH2/751/6, p. 657.
4 This phrase comes from a sermon of Thanksgiving delivered by Adair after the plague of 1647. See Chapter 2, this volume, and NRS, CH2/751/3, fo. 60r.
5 Ayrshire Archives, Town Council Book, B6/18/4, fo. 247r
6 Thank you to Dr Richard Raiswell and Dr Sarah Bond for help translating the inscription.
7 Robert Wodrow, *Analecta; or, Materials for a History of Remarkable Providences* (Edinburgh: Maitland Club, 1842), vol. 3, p. 73.
8 Thank you to Dr Mark Jardine, who also confirmed the uniqueness of this sort of effigy among the many covenanter memorials.

9 This whole convoluted affair is recorded in *The Register of the Privy Council of Scotland* (hereafter *RPCS*), series 1–3, ed. P. Hume Brown (Edinburgh, 1881–1933), series 3, vol. 8, pp. 438–448, and B6/18/4, fos. 239v–244v.
10 B6/18/4, fo. 239r. The dates of all former provosts in Ayr are listed in John Strawhorn, *The History of Ayr: Royal Burgh and County Town* (Edinburgh: John Donald Publishers, 1989), pp. 283–5.
11 B6/18/4, fo. 239v.
12 B6/18/4, fo. 240r.
13 B6/18/4, fo. 242r.
14 B6/18/4, fo. 244v. The sentence barring Cunningham from public office was lifted in September 1685, and he served as provost again in 1686. The sitting magistrates were unhappy with this decision, and they soon accused Cunningham of 'using fraudulent and sinistruous designes to get himself elected proveist for the ensuing year', an allegation which required the Privy Council to again intervene in local elections. See *RPCS*, series 3, vol. 11, pp. 179 and 194.
15 B6/18/4, fo. 244v.
16 Strawhorn, *The History of Ayr*, p. 66.
17 Robert Wodrow, *The History of the Sufferings of the Church of Scotland, from the Restauration to the Revolution*, 4 vols (Edinburgh: James Watson, 1722), iv, p. 128.
18 CH2/751/6, p. 624. On 'disorderly' marriage, see Katie Barclay, 'Marriage, Sex, and the Church of Scotland: Exploring Non-Conformity Amongst the Lower Orders', *Journal of Religious History*, 43:2 (2019), 163–79.
19 CH2/751/6, pp. 626–7.
20 CH2/751/6, p. 628.
21 CH2/751/6, p. 631.
22 CH2/751/6, p. 635.
23 CH2/751/6, p. 640.
24 CH2/751/6, p. 658.
25 CH2/751/6, p. 668.
26 *RPCS*, series 3, vol. 11, p. 256; Allan Kennedy, 'The Legacy of the Covenants and the Making of the Restoration State', in Chris R. Langley (ed.), *The National Covenant in Scotland, 1638–1689* (Woodbridge: Boydell, 2020), pp. 179–96, at pp. 190–1.
27 See, for example, testimony in January 1684 about the behavior of William Cunningham, who was trying to be elected provost, and a town baillie. *RPCS*, series 3, vol. 11, p. 472.
28 Alasdair Raffe, *Scotland in Revolution* (Edinburgh: Edinburgh University Press, 2019), p. 99.
29 On the 1687 Act of Indulgence and its general effects, see Raffe, *Scotland in Revolution*, chapter 2.
30 The members present at the first gathering in the 'meeting house' on 6 September 1687 were John Muir, Alexander Campbell, John Ferguson, John McColme, Thomas Millikin, Henry Smith, Robert Colville, William Muir, Robert Paton, and Robert Strauton. In February 1689, John Crawford, Hugh Crawford, John

Osburn, Robert Muir, Willian Tough, and Robert Paterson were added to the session. Nearly all of these men had served on the session at some point with William Adair. See CH2/751/7, fos. 45r and 23r. The activities of the presbyterian session are also recorded in the session account book from these years. See CH2/751/24.
31 CH2/532/2, p. 1.
32 See Raffe, *Scotland in Revolution*, pp. 52–3.
33 On the Cameronians – or more accurately, the United Societies – and their geographical representation, see Mark Jardine, 'The United Societies: Militancy, Martyrdom and the Presbyterian Movement in Late-Restoration Scotland, 1679 to 1688' (PhD thesis, University of Edinburgh, 2009).
34 CH2/751/7, fo. 43r.
35 John Sage, *Case of the Present Afflicted Clergy* (London, 1690), pp. 2–3.
36 CH2/751/7, fo. 54r. Eccles was not, according to Scott's *Fasti*, formally admitted into this role until 1692, but he served as moderator of the session from May 1689 until his death.
37 Thomas Morer, 'A Short Account of Scotland', in Peter H. Brown (ed.), *Early Travellers in Scotland* (Edinburgh: David Douglas, 1891), pp. 266–90, p. 290.
38 According to Alasdair Raffe, the first public reading of the Declaration was in Glasgow around 25 December, but this was not officially approved by the town council and was instead spearheaded by local presbyterian leaders. See Raffe, *Scotland in Revolution*, pp. 122–3.
39 B6/18/4, fo. 306r. Wallace seems to have had little involvement in the day-to-day affairs of the burgh, which is perhaps why there was not as much outcry in the records about his appointment as one might expect; his removal in 1689 in favour of John Moor, however, was 'in regaird he is a Papist'. B6/18/4, fo. 335r, and John H. Pagan, *Annals of Ayr in the Olden Time, 1560–1692* (Ayr: Alex Fergusson, 1897), p. 47.
40 Strawhorn, *The History of Ayr*, p. 124.
41 On this point, see Raffe, *Scotland in Revolution*.
42 Until recently, this topic has been little explored by Scottish historians. For a welcome intervention, see Neil McIntyre, 'Remembering the Revolution: Identity and Ideology in Restoration Scotland', in Chris Langley (ed.), *The National Covenant* (Woodbridge: Boydell, 2020), pp. 163–79.
43 For a helpful overview of anti-Jacobite ideology in Scotland and its connection to Covenanting histories, including areas beyond the southwest, see Chris Whatley, 'Reformed Religion, Regime Change, Scottish Whigs and the Struggle for the "Soul" of Scotland, c.1688–c.1788', *Scottish Historical Review* (April 2013), 66–99.
44 Ian Cowan, 'The Covenanters: A Revision Article', *Scottish Historical Review*, 47:143 (April 1968), 35–52, at 37.
45 John H. Henderson, *The Martyr Graves of Scotland* (Edinburgh: Oliphant, Anderson & Ferrier, 1903), pp. 310–11.
46 Sharon Adams, 'A Regional Road to Revolution: Religion, Politics and Society in South-West Scotland, 1600–50' (PhD thesis, University of Edinburgh, 2002), pp. 12–13.

47 On the influence of Scottish presbyterians in the British colonies that became the United States, see Craig Gallagher, ' "Them that are dispersed abroad": The Covenanters and their Legacy in North America, 1650–1776', *The Scottish Historical Review*, 99 (December 2020), 454–72.
48 John Coffey, *Politics, Religion and the British Revolutions: The Mind of Samuel Rutherford* (Cambridge: Cambridge University Press, 1997), pp. 17–18. On terminology and the question of Scottish 'puritans', see also Margo Todd, 'The Problem of Scotland's Puritans', in John Coffey and Paul C.H. Lim (eds), *The Cambridge Companion to Puritanism* (Cambridge: Cambridge University Press, 2008), pp. 174–88.
49 National Library of Scotland, Adv. MS. 20.6.17, 'Ayr Covenant'.

Select bibliography

Manuscript sources

Ayrshire Archives, Ayr

Acc. 483, Papers of William Adair, c. 1633–1656, vols I and II.
ATO/42/1/34, 'Contract of Marriage Adair and Kennedy'.
B6/12/9, Burgh court book, 12 February 1640 to 2 July 1668.
B6/18/2, Ayr council book, 29 September 1647 to 24 August 1669.
B6/18/3, Ayr council book, 9 July 1655 to 24 November 1663.
B6/18/4, Ayr council book, 21 September 1669 to 31 January 1694.
B6/18/5, Ayr council book, 21 February 1678 to 29 January 1690.
B6/24/1, Minute book of the Wrights and Squaremen of the Burgh of Air, 1556–1724.
B6/24/2, Minute book of the Walkers of the Burgh of Air.
B6/24/3, Dean of Guild court book.
B6/30/81, 'Extract decreet of Reduction of the instance of Mr William Adair, 24 Feb. 1648'.
B6/30/82, 'Tack by Mr. William Adair, 26 Feb. 1648'.
B6/36/1, Council and police papers, 1609–1706.
B6/39/8, 'Contract between the magistrates and Council of the burgh of Ayr'.
B6/39/9, 'Account of what moneyes has been payit to ministers in the tyme of the vaccancie of ane collige, 27 January 1657'.
B6/39/12, 'Band of relief signed be the inhabitants of the borrowfield of Air and Barronie of Alloway'.
B6/39/13, 'Copy discharge and assignation by Arthur, Archbishop of Glasgow, in favour of William Cunyngham, provost of Air'.
B6/39/16, 'Receipt by the sherrifs of Ayr to the Baillie of Air'.
Hendry, Alastair. 'Witch-Hunting in Ayrshire: A Calendar of Documents, etc'. Unpublished, May 1998.

National Library of Scotland, Edinburgh

Adv. MS. 20.6.17, 'Ayr Covenant'.
Adv. MS. 34.7.9, 'List of ministers who refused to submit to "prelacy"'.
MS. 941, 'Extracts from the minute book of the mariners of Ayr'.
MS. 3430, 'Petition to the General Assembly for planting another minister at Ayr'.
MS. 5770, 'Notebook of seventeenth-century sermons'.
MS. 7173, 'Sermon notes of William Eccles'.

MS. 10335, 'Extracts from the minutes of the Ayr town council, copied ca. 1820'.
Wod. Fol. XXV, Letters to and papers of Robert Douglas, c. 1631–51.
Wod. Fol. XXVI, Church and state papers, c. 1654–1709.
Wod. Qu. XXXVI, Miscellaneous religious manuscripts, c. 1660–1714.
Wod. Qu. LXXXIII, Miscellaneous religious manuscripts, c. 1660–1714.

National Records of Scotland, Edinburgh

CH2/532/1, Ayr presbytery minutes, 1642–51.
CH2/751/2, Ayr kirk session minutes, 1621–46.
CH2/751/3/1, Ayr kirk session minutes, 1646–53.
CH2/751/3/2, Ayr kirk session minutes, 1653–62.
CH2/751/4, Ayr kirk session minutes, 1662–6.
CH2/751/5, Ayr kirk session minutes, 1666–72.
CH2/751/6, Ayr kirk session minutes, 1672–86.
CH2/751/7, Ayr kirk session minutes, 1686–93.
CH2/751/19, Ayr kirk session accounts, 1664–7.
CH2/751/20, Ayr kirk session accounts, 1667–71.
CH2/751/21, Ayr kirk session accounts, 1670–6.
CH2/751/22, Ayr kirk session accounts, 1676–81.
CH2/751/23, Ayr kirk session accounts, 1682–6.
CH2/751/24, Ayr kirk session accounts, 1687–96.
GD25/6/151A, 'Letters of renunciation by William Adair'.
JC 26/25, High Court of Justiciary, process notes, 1658.
JC 26/26, High Court of Justiciary, process notes, 1659.

Printed primary sources

Acts and Proceedings of the General Assembly of the Church of Scotland (Edinburgh: Edinburgh Printing and Publishing Co, 1843).
Ayr Burgh Accounts, 1534–1624, ed. and trans. George S. Pryde (Edinburgh: Scottish History Society, 1937).
Baillie, Robert, *The Letters and Journals of Robert Baillie*, 3 vols, ed. David Laing (Edinburgh: Bannatyne Club, 1841–2).
Burns, Robert, 'Tam O'Shanter', in *The Antiquities of Scotland*, 2 vols, ed. Francis Grose (London: S. Hooper, 1789–91).
The Constitutional Documents of the Puritan Revolution, 1625–1660, 2nd edn, ed. Samuel R. Gardiner (Oxford: Oxford University Press, 1899).
Douglas, Robert, *The Forme and Order of the Coronation of Charles the Second, King of Scotland, England, France, and Ireland* (Aberdeen, 1651).
Early Travellers in Scotland, ed. Peter H. Brown (Edinburgh: David Douglas, 1891).
The Egerton Papers, ed. John P. Collier (London: J.B. Nichols and Sons, 1840).
Extracts from the Records of the Convention of Royal Burghs, 1615–1676, ed. James D. Marwick (Edinburgh: William Paterson, 1866).
The Genuine Declaration of William Sutherland, Hangman at Irvine; Wherein his Knowledge of the Scriptures, His Courage, and Behaviour Towards the Persecutors, And Their Barbarous Treatment of Him at Air are Plainly Set Forth (Edinburgh: D. Webster and Sons, 1821).

Kirkton, James, *A History of the Church of Scotland 1660–1679*, ed. Ralph Stewart (Lewiston: Edwin Mellen, 1992).
Kirkton, James, *The Secret and True History of the Church of Scotland from the Restoration to the year 1678* (Edinburgh: James Bannatyne and Co., 1817).
The Lauderdale Papers, 3 vols, ed. Osmund Airy (London: Camden Society, 1884).
Memoirs of Mr. William Veitch, and George Brysson, ed. Thomas M'Crie (Edinburgh: W. Blackwood, 1825).
Miscellany of the Scottish History Society, vol. 3 (Edinburgh: Scottish History Society, 1919).
New Statistical Account of Scotland (Edinburgh: W. Blackwood and Sons, 1834–45).
The Records of the Commissions of the General Assemblies of the Church of Scotland holden in Edinburgh in the years 1648 and 1649, ed. Alexander F. Mitchell and James Christie (Edinburgh: Scottish History Society, 1896).
Records of the Kirk of Scotland Containing the Acts and Proceedings of the General Assemblies, ed. Alexander Peterkin (Edinburgh, 1843).
The Register of the Privy Council of Scotland, series 1–3, ed. John Hill Burton, David Masson, P. Hume Brown, Henry Paton, and Robert Kerr Hannay (Edinburgh: General Register House, 1881–1933).
Row, William, *The Life of Mr Robert Blair*, ed. Thomas M'Crie (Edinburgh: Wodrow Society, 1848).
Rutherford, Samuel, *The Trial and Triumph of Faith* (Edinburgh, 1645).
Sage, John, *Case of the Present Afflicted Clergy* (London, 1690).
Scotland and the Commonwealth: Letters and Papers relating to the Military Government of Scotland from August 1651 to December 1653, ed. C.H. Firth (Edinburgh, 1895).
Stewart, James, *Naphtali, or, the Wrestling of the Church of Scotland for the Kingdom of Christ* (Edinburgh, 1667).
Wodrow, Robert, *Analecta; or, Materials for a History of Remarkable Providences*, 4 vols (Glasgow: Maitland Club, 1842–3).
Wodrow, Robert, *Collections Upon the Lives of the Reformers and Most Eminent Ministers of the Church of Scotland* (Glasgow: Maitland Club, 1845).
Wodrow, Robert, *The History of the Sufferings of the Church of Scotland, from the Restauration to the Revolution*, 4 vols (Edinburgh: James Watson, 1722).

Secondary sources

Adams, Sharon, 'The Making of the Radical South-West: Charles I and His Scottish Kingdom, 1625– 1649', in John R. Young (ed.), *Celtic Dimensions of the British Civil Wars* (Edinburgh: John Donald Publishers, 1997), pp. 53–74.
Adams, Sharon, 'In Search of the Scottish Republic', in Sharon Adams and Julian Goodare (eds), *Scotland in the Age of Two Revolutions* (Woodbridge: Boydell, 2014), pp. 97–114.
Adams, Sharon and Julian Goodare (eds), *Scotland in the Age of Two Revolutions* (Woodbridge: Boydell, 2014).
Agnew, Andrew, *The Hereditary Sheriffs of Galloway* (Edinburgh: David Douglas, 1893).
Armstrong, Robert, Andrew R. Holmes, R. Scott Spurlock, and Patrick Walsh (eds), *Presbyterian History in Ireland: Two Seventeenth-Century Narratives* (Belfast: Ulster Historical Foundation, 2016).

Barclay, Katie, 'Marriage, Sex, and the Church of Scotland: Exploring Non-Conformity Amongst the Lower Orders', *Journal of Religious History*, 43:2 (2019), 163–79.

Barclay, Tom and Eric J. Graham, *The Early Transatlantic Trade of Ayr 1640–1730* (Ayr: Ayrshire Archaeological and Natural History Society, 2005).

Barrett, John and Alastair Mitchell, *Elgin's Love-Gift: Civil War in Scotland and the Depositions of 1646* (Chichester: Phillimore, 2007).

Bold, Alan, *A Burns Companion* (Basingstoke: Palgrave Macmillan, 1991).

Bowie, Karin, *Public Opinion in Early Modern Scotland, 1560–1707* (Cambridge: Cambridge University Press, 2020).

Broadie, Alexander (ed.), *The Cambridge Companion to the Scottish Enlightenment* (Cambridge: Cambridge University Press, 2003).

Brock, Michelle D., 'Enemies of God? Slander, Gender, and Witchcraft in the Scottish Parish', in Martha McGill and Alasdair Raffe (eds), *The Scottish State and the Experience of Government, 1560–1707* (Edinburgh: Edinburgh University Press, forthcoming).

Brock, Michelle D., 'Exhortations and Expectations: Preaching about the Ideal Minister in Post-Reformation Scotland', in Chris R. Langley, Catherine E. McMillan, and Russell Newton (eds), *The Clergy in Early Modern Scotland* (Woodbridge: Boydell, 2021), pp. 15–31.

Brock, Michelle D., ' "The Man Will Shame Me": Women, Sex and Kirk Discipline in Cromwellian Scotland', *Scottish Church History*, 51:2 (2022), 133–56.

Brock, Michelle D., 'Plague, Covenants, and Confession: The Strange Case of Ayr, 1647–8', *Scottish Historical Review*, 97:2 (2018), 129–52.

Brock, Michelle D., ' "She-Zealots and Satanesses": Women, Patriarchy, and the Covenanting Movement', in Mairi Cowan, Janay Nugent, and Cathryn Spence (eds), *Gender and Identity in Scotland, 1200–1800: Power, Politics, and Faith* (Edinburgh: Edinburgh University Press, 2024).

Carballo, Scott, 'Piracy, the State, and the Burghs of Southwest Scotland, 1560–1603', in Allan Kennedy (ed.), *Deviance and Marginality in Early Modern Scotland* (Woodbridge: Boydell, forthcoming).

Cipriano, Salvatore, 'The Engagement, the Universities and the Fracturing of the Covenanter Movement, 1647–51', in Chris Langley (ed.), *The National Covenant in Scotland, 1638–1689* (Woodbridge: Boydell, 2020), pp. 145–60.

Coffey, John, *Politics, Religion and the British Revolutions: The Mind of Samuel Rutherford* (Cambridge: Cambridge University Press, 1997).

Coffey, John, 'Religious Thought', in Michael J. Braddick (ed.), *The Oxford Handbook of the English Revolution* (Oxford: Oxford University Press, 2015), pp. 447–65.

Collinson, Patrick, 'Elizabethan and Jacobean Puritanism as Forms of Popular Religious Culture', in Christopher Durston and Jacqueline Eales (eds), *The Culture of English Puritanism, 1560–1700* (London: Red Globe Press, 1996), pp. 32–57.

Collinson, Patrick, *The Elizabethan Puritan Movement* (Berkeley: The University of California Press, 1967).

Cowan, Edward J., 'The Making of a National Covenant', in John Morrill (ed.), *The Scottish National Covenant in its British Context* (Edinburgh: Edinburgh University Press, 1990), pp. 68–89.

Cowan, Ian B., 'The Covenanters: A Revision Article', *Scottish Historical Review*, 47 (April 1968), 35–52.

Select bibliography

Cowan, Ian B., *The Scottish Covenanters 1660–1688* (London: Victor Gollancz, 1976).
Darcy, Eamon, *The Irish Rebellion of 1641 and the Wars of the Three Kingdoms* (Woodbridge: Boydell, 2013).
Dawson, Jane, 'Covenanting in Sixteenth-Century Scotland', *Scottish Historical Review*, 99 (December 2020), 336–48.
Dennison, E. Patricia, Gordon DesBrisay, and Lesley Diack, 'Health in the Two Towns', in E. Patricia Dennison, David Dicthburn, and Michael Lynch (eds), *Aberdeen before 1800: A New History* (East Linton: Tuckwell Press, 2002), pp. 70–108.
DesBrisay, Gordon, ' "The Civill Wars Did Overrun All": Aberdeen, 1630–1690', in Patricia Dennison, David Ditchburn, and Michael Lynch (eds), *Aberdeen before 1800: A New History* (East Linton: Tuckwell Press, 2002), pp. 238–66.
DesBrisay, Gordon, 'Twisted By Definition: Women Under Godly Discipline in Seventeenth-Century Scottish Towns', in Yvonne Galloway Brown and Rona Ferguson (eds), *Twisted Sisters: Women, Crime and Deviance in Scotland Since 1400* (East Linton: Tuckwell, 2002), pp. 137–55.
Doak, Laura, 'Militant Women and "National" Community: The Execution of Isabel Alison and Marion Harvie, 1681', *Journal of the Northern Renaissance*, 12 (2021), n.p.
Dobson, David, *Scottish Emigration to Colonial America, 1607–1785* (Athens, GA: University of Georgia Press, 2004).
Dow, Frances, *Cromwellian Scotland, 1651–1660* (Edinburgh: John Donald Publishers, 1979).
Dunlop, Annie I. (ed.), *The Royal Burgh of Ayr: Seven Hundred Fifty Years of History* (Edinburgh: Oliver and Boyd, 1953).
Dye, Sierra, 'To Converse with the Devil? Speech, Sexuality, and Witchcraft in Early Modern Scotland', *International Review of Scottish Studies*, 37 (2012), 9–40.
Edwards, Pete, 'Arming and Equipping the Covenanting Armies 1638–1651', in Steve Murdoch and Andrew Mackillop (eds), *Fighting for Identity: Scottish Military Experience c. 1550–1900* (Leiden: Brill, 2002), pp. 239–64.
Ewan, Elizabeth, 'Gendering the Reformation', in Ian P. Hazlett (ed.), *A Companion to the Scottish Reformation* (Leiden: Brill, 2021), pp. 519–21.
Falconer, Robert, *Crime and Community in Reformation Scotland: Negotiating Power in a Burgh Society* (London: Routledge, 2012).
Fissel, Mark, *The Bishops' Wars: Charles I's Campaigns against Scotland, 1638–1640* (Cambridge: Cambridge University Press, 1994).
Flinn, Michael (ed.), *Scottish Population History* (Cambridge: Cambridge University Press, 1977).
Gallagher, Craig, ' "Them that are dispersed abroad": The Covenanters and their Legacy in North America, 1650–1776', *The Scottish Historical Review*, 99 (December 2020), 454–72.
Gaskill, Malcolm, *Witchfinders: A Seventeenth-Century English Tragedy* (Cambridge: Cambridge University Press, 2007).
Gentles, Ian, *The New Model Army in England, Ireland and Scotland, 1645–1653* (Oxford: Oxford University Press, 1992).
Goodare, Julian (ed.), *The Scottish Witch-Hunt in Context* (Manchester: Manchester University Press, 2002).
Goodare, Julian, 'Women and the Witch-Hunt in Scotland', *Social History*, 23:3 (October 1998), 288–308.

Goodare, Julian, Lauren Martin, Joyce Miller, and Louise Yeoman, 'The Survey of Scottish Witchcraft', https://witches.hca.ed.ac.uk.
Graham, Michael F., *The Uses of Reform: Godly Discipline and Popular Behavior in Scotland and Beyond, 1560–1610* (Leiden: Brill, 1996).
Grainger, John D., *Cromwell against the Scots: The Last Anglo-Scottish War, 1650–1652* (East Linton: Tuckwell Press, 1997).
Grant, James, *History of the Burgh Schools of Scotland* (Edinburgh: William Collins, 1876).
Greenburg, Stephen, 'Plague, the Printing Press, and Public Health in Seventeenth-Century London', *Huntington Library Quarterly*, 67:4 (December 2004), 508–27.
Gribben, Crawford, 'Polemic and Apocalyptic in the Cromwellian Invasion of Scotland', *Literature and History*, 23:1 (2014), 1–18.
Hall, David D., *The Puritans: A Transatlantic History* (Princeton: Princeton University Press, 2019).
Harris, Tim, *Restoration: Charles II and His Kingdoms, 1660–1685* (London: Penguin, 2006).
Harris, Tim, 'Revisiting the Causes of the English Civil War', *Huntington Library Quarterly*, 78:4 (Winter 2015), 615–35.
Henderson, John H., *The Martyr Graves of Scotland* (Edinburgh: Oliphant, Anderson and Ferrier, 1903).
Hood, Nathan, 'Corporate Conversion Ceremonies: The Presentation and Reception of the National Covenant', in Chris R. Langley (ed.), *The National Covenant in Scotland, 1638–1689* (Woodbridge: Boydell, 2020), pp 21–38.
Hughes, Ann, *Gender and the English Revolution* (London: Routledge, 2012).
Hughes, Paula, 'Witch-Hunting in Scotland, 1649–1650', in Julian Goodare (ed.), *Scottish Witches and Witch-Hunters* (London: Palgrave, 2013), pp. 85–102.
Hunter, Michael and David Wooton (eds), *Atheism from the Reformation to the Enlightenment* (Oxford: Oxford University Press, 1992).
Hutton, Ronald, *Charles the Second, King of England, Scotland, and Ireland* (Oxford: Oxford University Press, 1989).
Hyman, Elizabeth H., 'A Church Militant: Scotland, 1661–1690', *Sixteenth Century Journal*, 26 (1995), 49–74.
Jackson, Clare, *Devil-Land: England Under Siege, 1588–1688* (London: Penguin, 2021).
Jackson, Clare, *Restoration Scotland, 1660–1690: Royalist Politics, Religion and Ideas* (Woodbridge: Boydell, 2003).
Jillings, Karen, *An Urban History of the Plague: Socio-Economic, Political and Medical Impacts in a Scottish Community, 1500–1650* (London: Routledge, 2018).
Johnson, Alfred, 'Scandalous Ayr: Parish-Level Continuities in 1650s Scotland', in Fiona McCall (ed.), *Church and the People in Interregnum Britain* (London: University of London Press, 2021), pp. 171–92.
Kennedy, Allan, 'Military Rule, Protectoral Government and the Scottish Highlands, c.1654–60', *Scottish Archives*, 23 (2017), 80–102.
Kennedy, Allan, 'The Urban Community in Restoration Scotland: Government, Society and Economy in Inverness, 1660–C.1688', *Northern Scotland*, 5:1 (2014), 26–49.
Kishlansky, Mark A., *A Monarchy Transformed: Britain, 1603–1714* (London: Penguin, 1997).
Langley, Chris R. (ed.), *The National Covenant in Scotland, 1638–1689* (Woodbridge: Boydell, 2020).

Langley, Chris R., 'Parish Politics and Godly Agitation in Late Interregnum Scotland', *Church History*, 90 (2021), 557–8.
Langley, Chris R., 'Sheltering under the Covenant: The National Covenant, Orthodoxy and the Irish Rebellion, 1638–1644', *The Scottish Historical Review*, 96:2 (October 2017), 137–60.
Langley, Chris R., *Worship, Civil War and Community, 1638–1660* (London: Routledge, 2015).
Langley, Chris R., Catherine E. McMillan, and Russell Newton (eds), *The Clergy in Early Modern Scotland* (Woodbridge: Boydell, 2021).
Larner, Christina, *Witchcraft and Religion: The Politics of Popular Belief* (Oxford: Oxford University Press, 1984).
Levack, Brian P., 'The Great Scottish Witch Hunt of 1661–1662', *Journal of British Studies*, 20:1 (1980), 90–108.
Levack, Brian P., *The Oxford Handbook of Witchcraft in Early Modern Europe and Colonial America* (Oxford: Oxford University Press, 2013).
Levack, Brian P., 'The Prosecution of Sexual Crimes in Early Eighteenth-Century Scotland', *The Scottish Historical Review*, 89 (October 2010), 172–93.
Levack, Brian P., *Witch-Hunting in Scotland: Law, Politics and Religion* (London: Routledge, 2008).
Lindley, K.J., 'The Impact of the 1641 Irish Rebellion upon England and Wales, 1641–5', *Irish Historical Studies*, 18 (1972), 143–76.
Lindsay, Alistair and Jean Kennedy (eds), *The Burgesses and Guild Brethren of Ayr, 1647–1846* (Ayr: Ayrshire Federation of Historical Societies, 2002).
Little, Patrick and David L. Smith, *Parliament and Politics during the Cromwellian Protectorate* (Cambridge: Cambridge University Press, 2007).
Lynch, Michael, *The Early Modern Town in Scotland* (London: Routledge, 1987).
Lynch, Michael, *Edinburgh and the Reformation* (Edinburgh: Edinburgh University Press, 1981).
MacDonald, Alan R., *The Burghs and Parliament in Scotland, c. 1550–1651* (Aldershot: Ashgate, 2007).
MacDonald, Alan R., 'Urban Archives: Endless Possibilities', *Journal of Irish and Scottish Studies*, 9:2 (2019), 29–49.
Macinnes, Allan I., *The British Revolution, 1629–1660* (Basingstoke: Palgrave, 2005).
Macinnes, Allan I., *Charles I and the Making of the Covenanting Movement* (Edinburgh: John Donald, 1991).
Macinnes, Allan I., 'Covenanting Ideology in Seventeenth-Century Scotland', in Jane H. Ohlmeyer (ed.), *Political Thought in Seventeenth-Century Ireland: Kingdom or Colony* (Cambridge: Cambridge University Press, 2000), pp. 191–220.
Mackenzie, Archibald, *An Old Kirk and Burns Memories* (Kilmarnock: Standard Printing Works, 1943).
Mackenzie, Archibald, *William Adair and his Kirk: The Auld Kirk of Ayr, 1639–1684* (Ayr: Ayr Advertiser, 1933).
MacKenzie, Kirsteen M., *The Solemn League and Covenant and the Cromwellian Union 1643–1663* (London: Routledge, 2017).
Makey, Walter, *The Church of the Covenant 1637–1651: Revolution and Social Change in Scotland* (Edinburgh: John Donald, 1979).
Mann, Alastair J., *The Scottish Book Trade, 1500–1720: Print Commerce and Print Control in Early Modern Scotland* (East Linton: Tuckwell Press, 2000).
McCallum, John, 'Charity and Conflict: Poor Relief in Mid-Seventeenth-Century Dundee', *The Scottish Historical Review*, 95:240 (April 2016), 30–56.

McCallum, John, *Poor Relief and the Church in Scotland, 1560–1650* (Edinburgh: Edinburgh University Press, 2018).
McCallum, John, *Reforming the Scottish Parish: The Reformation in Fife, 1560–1640* (Aldershot: Ashgate, 2010).
McCallum, John (ed.), *Scotland's Long Reformation: New Perspectives on Scottish Religion, c. 1500–c. 1660* (Leiden: Brill, 2016).
McIntyre, Neil, 'Conventicles: Organising Dissent in Restoration Scotland', *Scottish Historical Review*, 99 (2020), 429–53.
McIntyre, Neil, 'Remembering the Revolution: Identity and Ideology in Restoration Scotland', in Chris Langley (ed.), *The National Covenant* (Woodbridge: Boydell, 2020), pp. 163–79.
McIntyre, Neil and Jamie McDougall, 'Reframing the Covenant: *A Solemn Acknowledgment* (1648) and the Resubscription of the Solemn League and Covenant', *Seventeenth Century*, 37:5 (2022), 733–56.
Mearns, Natalie and Alec Ryrie, *Worship and the Parish Church in Early Modern Britain* (Farnham: Ashgate, 2013).
Mills, Jane A. (ed.), *Cromwell's Legacy* (Manchester: Manchester University Press, 2012).
Morris, James, *The Auld Toon o' Ayr* (Ayr: Stephen and Pollock, 1928).
Mullan, David G., 'Women in Scottish Divinity, c. 1590–1640', in Elizabeth Ewan and Maureen M. Meikle (eds), *Women in Scotland, c. 1100–c. 1750* (East Linton: Tuckwell Press, 1999), pp. 29–41.
Mullet, Charles F., 'Plague Policy in Scotland, 16th – 17th Centuries', *Osiris*, 9 (1950), 435–56.
Muravyena, Mariana, 'Do not Rape and Pillage without Command: Sex Offenses and Early Modern European Armies', *Clio: Women, Gender, History*, 39 (2014), 53–77.
Murdoch, Steve (ed.), *Scotland and the Thirty Years' War* (Leiden: Brill, 2001).
Murdoch, Steve, *The Terror of the Seas? Scottish Maritime Warfare, 1513–1713* (Leiden: Brill, 2010).
Murdoch, Steve and Alexia Grosjean, *Alexander Leslie and the Scottish Generals of the Thirty Years' War, 1618–1648* (London: Routledge, 2014).
Normand, Lawrence and Gareth Roberts, *Witchcraft in Early Modern Scotland: James VI's Demonology and the North Berwick Witches* (Exeter: University of Exeter Press, 2000).
Nugent, Janay, 'Reformed Masculinity: Ministers, Fathers and Male Heads of Households, 1560– 1660', in Lynn Abrams and Elizabeth Ewan (eds), *Nine Centuries of Man: Manhood and Masculinities in Scottish History* (Edinburgh: Edinburgh University Press, 2017), pp. 39–57.
Ó Ciardha, Éamonn, 'Tories and Moss-Troopers in Scotland and Ireland in the Interregnum: A Political Dimension', in John R. Young (ed.), *Celtic Dimensions of the British Civil Wars* (Edinburgh: John Donald Publishers, 1997), pp. 141–57.
Ohlemeyer, Jane (ed.), *The Civil Wars: A Military History of England, Scotland and Ireland, 1638–1660* (Oxford: Oxford University Press, 1998).
Oram, Robert, '"It Cannot He Decernit Quha Are Clean and Quha Are Foulle": Responses to Epidemic Disease in Sixteenth- and Seventeenth-Century Scotland', *Renaissance and Reformation/Renaissance Et Réforme*, 30:4 (2007), 13–39.
Pagan, John H, *Annals of Ayr in the Olden Time, 1560–1692* (Ayr: Alex Fergusson, 1897).

Select bibliography

Parker, Geoffrey, 'Crisis and Catastrophe: The Global Crisis of the Seventeenth Century Reconsidered', *American Historical Review*, 113:4 (2008), 1053–79.
Parker, Geoffrey, *Global Crisis: War, Climate Change and Catastrophe in the Seventeenth Century* (New Haven: Yale University Press, 2013).
Peacey, Jason, 'The Protector Humbled: Richard Cromwell and the Constitution', in Patrick Little (ed.), *The Cromwellian Protectorate* (Woodbridge: Boydell, 2007), pp. 32–52.
Purkiss, Dianne, *Literature, Gender and Politics during the English Civil War* (Cambridge: Cambridge University Press, 2005).
Raffe, Alasdair, 'Confessions, Covenants and Continuous Reformation in Early Modern Scotland', *Études Épistémè*, 32 (2017), n.p.
Raffe, Alasdair, *The Culture of Controversy: Religious Arguments in Scotland, 1660–1714* (Woodbridge: Boydell, 2012).
Raffe, Alasdair, 'Female Authority and Lay Activism in Scottish Presbyterianism, 1660–1740', in Sarah Petrei and Hannah Smith (eds), *Religion and Women in Britain, c. 1660–1760* (Farnham: Ashgate, 2014), pp. 59–74.
Raffe, Alasdair, 'Presbyterian Politics and the Restoration of Scottish Episcopacy, 1660–1662', in N.H. Keeble (ed.), *'Settling the Peace of the Church': 1662 Revisited* (Oxford: Oxford University Press, 2014), pp. 144–67.
Raffe, Alasdair, *Scotland in Revolution* (Edinburgh: Edinburgh University Press, 2019).
Raffe, Alasdair, 'Who Were the Later Covenanters?', in Chris R. Langley (ed.), *The National Covenant in Scotland, 1638–1689* (Woodbridge: Boydell, 2020), pp. 197–214.
Robertson, John, *Dundee and the Civil Wars, 1639–1660* (Dundee: Friends of Dundee City Archives, 2007).
Ryrie, Alec, *Being Protestant in Reformation Britain* (Oxford: Oxford University Press, 2013).
Ryrie, Alec, *Unbelievers: An Emotional History of Doubt* (London: William Collins, 2019).
Sanderson, Margaret H.B., *Ayrshire and the Reformation: People and Change, 1490–1600* (East Linton: Tuckwell, 1997).
Schmidt, Leigh Eric, *Holy Fairs: Scotland and the Making of American Revivalism* (Princeton: Princeton University Press, 1989).
Scott, Hew (ed.), *Fasti ecclesiae Scoticanae: The Succession of Ministers in the Church of Scotland from the Reformation*, 7 vols (Edinburgh: Oliver and Boyd, 1915–28).
Shannon, Timothy J., 'A "Wicked Commerce": Consent, Coercion, and Kidnapping in Aberdeen's Servant Trade', *The William and Mary Quarterly*, 74:3 (2017), 437–66.
Shrewsbury, John F.D., *A History of Bubonic Plague in the British Isles* (Cambridge: Cambridge University Press, 1970).
Smith, Lesley M., 'Sackcloth for the Sinner or Punishment for the Crime: Church and Secular Courts in Cromwellian Scotland', in John Dwyer, Roger Mason, and Alexander Murdoch (eds), *New Perspectives on the Politics and Culture of Early Modern Scotland* (Edinburgh: John Donald Publishers, 1982), pp. 116–32.
Smout, T.C., 'The Overseas Trade of Ayrshire, 1660–1707', *Ayrshire Archaeological and Natural History Collections*, 2nd series, vol. 6 (1961), 56–80.
Spurlock, R. Scott, *Cromwell and Scotland: Conquest and Religion, 1650–60* (Edinburgh: John Donald Publishers, 2007).

Spurlock, R. Scott, 'Problems with Religion as Identity: The Case of Mid-Stuart Ireland and Scotland', *Journal of Irish and Scottish Studies*, 6 (2013), 1–29.
Spurlock, R. Scott, 'The Solemn League and Covenant and the Making of a People in Ulster', *Scottish Historical Review*, 99 (2020), 368–91.
Stevenson, David, 'The Burghs and the Scottish Revolution', in Michael Lynch (ed.), *The Early Modern Town in Scotland* (London: Routledge, 1987), pp. 167–91.
Stevenson, David, 'The Covenanters and the Western Association, 1648–1650', *Ayrshire Archaeological and Natural History Collections*, xiii (Ayr, 1982), 147–87.
Stevenson, David, 'Deposition of Ministers in the Church of Scotland under the Covenanters, 1639–1651', *Church History*, 44:3 (1975), 321–35.
Stevenson, David, 'The Financing of the Cause of the Covenants 1638–51', *Scottish Historical Review*, 51 (1972), 89–123.
Stevenson, David, 'The Radical Party in the Kirk', *The Journal of Ecclesiastical History*, 25:2 (1974), 135–65.
Stevenson, David, *Revolution and Counter-Revolution in Scotland, 1644–1651* (London: Royal Historical Society, 1977).
Stevenson, David, *The Scottish Revolution, 1637–44* (Newton Abbot: Davis and Charles, 1973).
Stewart, Laura A.M., 'Authority, Agency and the Reception of the Scottish National Covenant', in Robert Armstrong and Tadhg O' hAnnrachain (eds), *Insular Christianity: Alternative Models of the Church in Britain and Ireland, c. 1570–1700* (Manchester: Manchester University Press, 2013), pp. 89–107.
Stewart, Laura A.M., ' "Brothers in Treuth": Propaganda, Public Opinion and the Perth Articles Debate in Scotland', in Ralph Houlbrooke (ed.), *James VI and I: Ideas, Authority, and Government* (Aldershot: Ashgate, 2006), pp. 151–68.
Stewart, Laura A.M., 'Fiscal Revolution and State Formation in Mid Seventeenth-Century Scotland', *Historical Research*, 84 (2011), 443–69.
Stewart, Laura A.M., 'Military Power and the Scottish Burghs, 1625–1651', *Journal of Early Modern History* (2011), 59–82.
Stewart, Laura A.M., *Rethinking the Scottish Revolution: Covenanted Scotland, 1637–1651* (Oxford: Oxford University Press, 2016).
Stewart, Laura A.M., *Urban Politics and British Civil Wars: Edinburgh, 1617–1653* (Leiden: Brill, 2006).
Strawhorn, John, *750 Years of a Scottish School: Ayr Academy, 1233–1983* (Ayr: Alloway Publishing, 1983).
Strawhorn, John, *The History of Ayr: Royal Burgh and County Town* (Edinburgh: John Donald Publishers, 1989).
Terry, Charles Sandford, *The Pentland Rising and Rullion Green* (Glasgow: Maclehose and Sons, 1905).
Tindol, Robert, 'Getting the Pox off All Their Houses: Cotton Mather and the Rhetoric of Puritan Science', *Early American Literature*, 46:1 (2011), 1–23.
Todd, Margo, *The Culture of Protestantism in Early Modern Scotland* (New Haven: Yale University Press, 2002).
Todd, Margo, 'The Problem of Scotland's Puritans', in John Coffey and Paul C.H. Lim (eds), *The Cambridge Companion to Puritanism* (Cambridge: Cambridge University Press, 2008), pp. 174–88.
Yeoman, Louise, 'A Godly Possession? Margaret Mitchelson and the Performance of Covenanted Identity', in Chris R. Langley (ed.), *The National Covenant in Scotland, 1638–1689* (Woodbridge: Boydell, 2020), pp. 105–25.

Young, John R., 'Escaping Massacre: Refugees in Scotland in the Aftermath of the 1641 Ulster Rebellion', in David Edwards, Pádraig Lenihan, and Clodagh Tait (eds), *Age of Atrocity: Violence and Political Conflict in Early Modern Ireland* (Dublin: Four Courts Press, 2007), pp. 219–41.
Young, John R., 'Scotland and Ulster Connections in the Seventeenth Century: Sir Robert Adair of Kinhilt and the Scottish Parliament under the Covenanters', *Journal of Scotch-Irish Studies*, 3 (2013), 16–76.
Young, John R., 'Scotland and Ulster in the Seventeenth Century: The Movement of Peoples over the North Channel', in John R. Young and William Kelly (eds), *Ulster and Scotland, 1600–2000: History, Language and Identity* (Dublin: Four Courts Press, 2004), pp. 11–32.
Young, John R., 'Scottish Covenanting Radicalism, the Commission of the Kirk and the Establishment of the Parliamentary Radical Regime of 1648–1649', *Records of the Scottish Church History Society*, 25 (1993), 342–75.
Young, John R., 'The Scottish Parliament and the Covenanting Revolution: The Emergence of a Scottish Commons', in John R. Young (ed.), *Celtic Dimensions of the British Civil Wars* (Edinburgh: John Donald Publishers, 1997), pp. 164–84.
Young, John R., 'The Scottish Parliament and Witch-Hunting in Scotland under the Covenanters', *Parliaments, Estates & Representation*, 26:1 (2006), 53–65.
Waite, Gary K., *Anti-Anabaptist Polemics: Dutch Anabaptism and the Devil in England, 1531–1660* (Thunder Bay: Pandora Press, 2023).
Whatley, Chris, 'Reformed Religion, Regime Change, Scottish Whigs and the Struggle for the "Soul" of Scotland, c.1688–c.1788', *Scottish Historical Review* (April 2013), 66–99.
White, Jason, 'Women, Gender, and the Kirk before the Covenant', *International Review of Scottish Studies*, 45 (2020), 27–53.
Whycock, Jack C., 'Ministerial Education in the Scottish Reformation', in Ian P. Hazlett (ed.), *A Companion to the Scottish Reformation* (Leiden: Brill, 2021), pp. 367–94.

Unpublished theses

Adams, Sharon, 'A Regional Road to Revolution: Religion, Politics and Society in South-West Scotland, 1600–50' (PhD thesis, University of Edinburgh, 2002).
Carter, Andrew, 'Episcopal Church of Scotland, 1660–1685' (PhD thesis, University of St Andrews, 2019).
DesBrisay, Gordon, 'Authority and Discipline in Aberdeen, 1650–1700' (PhD thesis, University of St Andrews, 1989).
Gillanders, Susan, 'The Scottish Burghs during the Cromwellian Occupation 1651–1660' (PhD thesis, University of Edinburgh, 1999).
Holfelder, Kyle D., 'Factionalism in the Kirk during the Cromwellian Invasion and Occupation of Scotland, 1650 to 1660: The Protester-Resolutioner Controversy' (PhD thesis, University of Edinburgh, 1998).
Lee, Ronald Arthur, 'Government and Politics in Scotland, 1661–1681' (PhD thesis, University of Glasgow, 1995).
McDougall, Jamie Murdoch, 'Covenants and Covenanters in Scotland, 1638–1679' (PhD thesis, University of Glasgow, 2017).
McIntyre, Neil, 'Saints and Subverters: The Later Covenanters in Scotland, c. 1648–1682' (PhD thesis, University of Strathclyde, 2016).

McMillan, Catherine E., 'Keeping the Kirk: The Practice and Experience of Faith in North East Scotland, 1560–1610' (PhD thesis, University of Edinburgh, 2016).

McNulty, Claire, 'The Experience of Discipline in Parish Communities in Edinburgh, Scotland, 1638–1651' (PhD thesis, Queen's University Belfast, 2021).

McSeveney, Alan James, 'Non-Conforming Presbyterian Women in Restoration Scotland: 1660–1679' (PhD thesis, University of Strathclyde, 2005).

Muir, Alison, 'The Covenanters in Fife, c 1610–1689: Religious Dissent in the Local Community' (PhD thesis, University of St Andrews, 2002).

Toller, John, "'Now of little significancy"? The Convention of the Royal Burghs of Scotland, 1651–1688' (PhD thesis, University of Dundee, 2010).

Yeoman, Louise, 'Heart-Work: Emotion, Empowerment and Authority in Covenanting Times' (PhD thesis, University of St Andrews, 1991).

Index

Notes: 'n.' after a page reference indicates a note number on that page; literary works can be found under authors' names.

Act of Indemnity (1662) 136
Act of Indulgence (1687) 180–1
Adair, Patrick 23
Adair, Robert 23, 129
Adair, William 2, 21, 69–74, 95, 123–7,
    131–2, 136, 147–51, 161,
    165–7, 179–80, 183, 185
  behaviour and 30–3, 36, 80,
    103–7, 109
  beliefs 4–7, 24–5, 130–2,
    138, 155–7
  Commonwealth and 108, 112–14
  contemporaries' views of 10–11, 24,
    109, 141, 148
  death 168, 174
  early life and education 23–5
  marriages 24, 77
  monument 4–5, 174–7
  preaching 10, 47–8, 51, 53–61,
    74–77, 82–3, 103–7, 113–14,
    127–9, 155
  suspension 140–1, 167–8
  travels 27, 35, 53, 81–3, 97,
    134, 152
  witchcraft and 83–7, 112
anabaptism 75, 126
Anglo-Dutch Wars 136, 138, 154
Annand, William 20–2
Army of the Covenant 26–7, 68n.102,
    69, 71, 76–7, 82, 88n.4
atheism 18, 50, 55, 153
Ayr, Scotland 26–7
  Auld Kirk 4–5, 140, 174–7

burgh court 7, 10, 84
  early history 2–3
  English occupation of 2, 4, 7–9,
    84–5, 88, 94–114, 125–7, 132
  National Covenant, swearing of 4–5,
    20–2, 36–7, 54
  plague and 44–62, 69, 71, 79, 82,
    86, 94, 139, 152, 184
  as port 3, 8, 28, 35, 44, 46–51, 87,
    94, 138–40
  professions in 3, 7, 34, 46–51, 54–5,
    57–62, 66n.67, 132, 134–7,
    159, 162, 178, 189
  refugees in 8, 25–9, 34, 37,
    139–40, 154
  religious pluralism in 96, 103–6,
    108–10, 181–2
  quartering of Highland Host
    in 163–4
  sailors in 4, 44, 47–51, 59,
    66n.67, 140
  St John the Baptist (church) 2–3, 20,
    94, 181–3
  town council 10, 44, 48, 73, 77, 82,
    94–5, 130–5, 138–41, 147,
    151–3, 159, 163–7, 169n.28,
    177, 182
  see also courts, ecclesiastical, session

Ballie, Robert 10–11, 111
baptism 108–9, 114, 121n.111, 126,
    147, 156, 180
baptists 96, 108–9, 121n.111

Barbary corsairs 36, 46–7, 79, 153–5
Battle of Bothwell Bridge (1679) 165–6, 178
Battle of Drumclog (1679) 165
Battle of Dunbar (1650) 76–7, 82, 94, 97, 123, 128
Battle of Worcester (1651) 94, 97, 128
behaviour 7–8, 21, 152
   blasphemy 35, 49, 52, 69, 78–80, 84, 109
   English occupation and 97–105, 117n.43
   sexual sins 1, 35, 47, 52–5, 79–81, 84, 87, 125–6, 151–4, 164, 169n.28
   see also drink and drunkenness; gender, behaviour and; sabbath-breaking; witchcraft and witch hunting
Bishops' Wars 19, 24, 26–7
Black Oath (1638) 25, 28–9
Blair, Robert 20–1, 27, 39n.18
Book of Common Prayer 2, 18
Boyd, Janet 24, 77
Burns, Robert 4, 174

Cameronians 181–2
Catholicism and anti-Catholicism see popery and anti-popery
Caribbean see West Indies
Charles I 2, 18–19, 26–7, 34, 69–71, 79–80, 124
   execution 75–6, 96
Charles II 4, 76–7, 123–9, 134, 138, 149, 158–9
children 24, 51, 86–7, 138, 147–8, 150–1, 160, 184
   English occupation and 100–1, 126–7
   family worship and 31–3, 54, 80, 105
   indentured servants 46–7, 50
   refugees 26–7
   see also schools and schoolmasters
colonies see New England; West Indies
Committee in the West 158–63
Commonwealth see Cromwell, Oliver; New Model Army
communion 25, 30–1, 33, 56, 71–2, 162
   expulsion from 36, 72–3, 79, 106–7
   kneeling at 5–6, 20–1, 23
   rejection of 36
confessions of faith 18, 30
courts, ecclesiastical
   General Assembly 8, 20–1, 80, 82, 121n.108
   covenants and 27, 35–6, 39n.27, 71–4
   witchcraft and 85
   presbytery 8, 10, 27, 29–30, 39n.27, 52, 60, 76, 125, 181, 183
   clergy and 21, 23, 35–6, 39n.18, 71–2, 74, 76, 82, 95
   witchcraft and 85, 111
   session 8, 148, 16n.43, 16n.46, 34, 138, 149–50, 166–8, 179–81
   behaviour and 31–3, 69, 78–83, 97–110, 125–7, 151–5, 163–5
   English occupation and 94–110, 113–14, 118n.49, 121n.108
   plague and 35–6, 60–1
   records 6–7, 10–11, 60–1, 131–2
   town council and 72–4, 77–8
   witchcraft and 83–88, 110–13
   see also Synod of Glasgow and Ayr
Cromwell, Oliver 2, 72, 76, 87, 94, 100, 177
   death 123
Cromwell, Richard 123
Cunningham, William 95, 125, 127, 132–7, 144–5n.59, 156
Cunningham, William (the younger) 165, 177–8, 186n.14

Douglas, Robert 77, 85, 118n.58, 127–9
drink and drunkenness 31, 49, 52, 55, 59, 66n.67, 69, 79–81, 107, 112, 117n.43, 126, 134, 137, 151–4
   English occupation and 97–103
Dundee, Scotland 96, 100, 101, 139

Eccles, William 82, 95, 107, 115–16n.11, 130, 166, 181–2
Edinburgh, Scotland 4, 16n.46, 19, 27, 42–3n.92, 136, 159–60
   Adair in 23–4, 129, 134
   covenants and 4, 42–3n.92

St Giles Cathedral 18–19
  witchcraft and 84
  see also Scottish Parliament
Engagement (1647) 70–7, 79–81, 85
  see also Whiggamore Raid (1648)
England 1–3, 5, 49, 58, 74, 79, 127, 138–9, 153, 182, 184
  army see New Model Army
  Parliament 19, 26–7, 70, 75, 123
  puritanism in 1, 8, 19, 70
  see also Ayr, Scotland, English occupation of; Charles I; Charles II; Cromwell, Oliver; James VI and I; James VII and II; William III and Mary II
episcopacy 20–5
  Accommodation (1671) 149
  protests against 18–19, 34, 39n.27, 131, 141, 150, 157, 160–1, 166, 182
  Restoration and 123–9, 134, 148
executions 3
  for treason 123, 130, 136–7, 183
  for witchcraft 83–5, 111–12
  see also martyrs; Pentland Rising; witchcraft and witch-hunting

family worship 49, 54–5, 59, 62, 80, 107, 153
  see also children
fasting 22, 27, 30, 71–2, 139, 154–5, 157
  plague and 44–5, 56
Fergushill, John 21–3, 25, 28, 30–1, 33–5, 57–8
Five Articles of Perth 23, 24–5
France 22–3, 112, 139
  refugees from 8, 139–40, 154

gender
  behaviour and 78–9, 107–14
  covenants and 11, 22, 32, 54
  witchcraft and 78
  see also New Model Army, women and
Glasgow, Scotland 20, 23, 95, 144n.58, 165, 187n.38
Gregorie, Alexander 174, 179, 181–2

Highland Host 158, 163–4

Ireland 5, 34–5, 47, 49, 94, 137–9, 184
  refugees from 8, 25–9, 34, 37
  see also Black Oath

James VI and I 23
James VII and II 168, 181–2

Kennedy, Janet 24
'Killing Time' 5, 180
Kirkton, James
  A History of the Church of Scotland 129, 134, 137
Knox, John 3, 45

Laud, William 18–19
Leighton, Robert, Archbishop of Glasgow 149, 155
Lord's Supper see communion

magic see witchcraft and witch-hunting
maritime trade 35, 49, 66n.61, 94, 97, 116n.17, 132, 138–9
  see also Ayr, Scotland, as port
marriage 24, 77, 83, 118n.49, 156, 179, 180
  between English soldiers and Scottish women 100–1, 114, 126, 138
  see also New Model Army, women and
martyrs 3
  covenanters 128, 130, 183–4
Mather, Cotton 61
Mauchline Muir, Scotland 6, 71
merchants 1, 3, 10, 121n.111, 184
  confession and 48–50, 66n.67
  Restoration and 132, 138–41

National Covenant (1638) 1–2, 4–11, 18–26, 28–34, 36–7, 39n.27, 58, 128, 161, 167, 184–5
  gender and 22, 32, 54
  refugees and 25–6, 28–9, 34, 37
Navigation Acts (1660, 1663) 138–9
New England 4, 8, 138–40, 184
  puritanism in 1, 8, 19, 61

New Model Army 27, 34, 58, 72, 121–2n.120
   invasion of Scotland 75–6
   occupation of Ayr 2, 4, 8–9, 84–5, 88, 94–114, 125, 132
   withdrawal from Ayr 126–7
   women and 96–102, 104, 113, 138
   see also Cromwell, Oliver

Oath of Allegiance (1661) 123, 129, 132, 158

Pentland Rising (1666) 136–7, 139, 141, 158, 183
plague 1–2, 7, 10
   arrival in Ayr 45–7
   as divine punishment 44–6, 53–4, 61–2, 86
   preventative measures 46–7, 53, 65n.61
   see also repentance, plague and
poor and poor relief 16n.44, 30, 46–8, 52, 83, 115n.9, 127, 129, 134, 138–40, 150, 154–5, 181
   religious knowledge and 105, 120n.89, 120n.91
popery and anti-popery 2, 18–21, 25–7, 34–5, 80, 151
   travel abroad and 50, 59
Presbyterianism 28–9, 56, 70–1, 108–9, 123, 141, 148–9, 153–5, 162, 164, 168
   resistance and 33, 94–5, 129, 159–60, 177–84
   witchcraft and 84–5
print 19, 44
Privy Council of Scotland 10, 18–19, 85, 132–3, 136, 141, 144n.59, 150, 155–68, 177–8, 182, 186n.14
   see also Committee in the West
puritanism 5, 8, 109, 184
   in England 1, 8, 19, 70
   in New England 1, 8, 19, 61

refugees
   from France 8, 139–40, 154
   from Ireland 8, 25–9, 34, 37
repentance
   gender and 78–9, 97–100, 103, 164

   plague and 44–62, 86
   public 26–30, 33–4, 69, 72, 82, 102–6, 108–9, 125–6, 138, 151–4, 166
Restoration 2, 4, 9–10, 123–36, 140–1, 147–8, 152–3, 165–6, 177
   see also Charles II
Revolution of 1688–9 1, 124, 180–3
Rutherglen Declaration (1679) 165

sabbath-breaking 1, 30–2, 46, 57, 78, 82, 97–8, 100–3, 107, 110, 151, 153–4, 179–90
sailors 3–4, 44, 47–51, 59, 140
   confession and 49–51, 59, 66n.67
   see also maritime trade
schools and schoolmasters 94–5, 150–1, 166–7, 169n.21
Scottish Parliament 3, 7, 10, 123, 128–9, 132–3, 166–7
   behaviour and 80, 160
   Committee of Estates 76–7, 85
   England and 70–1, 74–5
   witchcraft and 80, 84–5, 88
   see also Test Act
servants 28, 30, 52, 66n.67, 100–1, 120n.91, 160, 165
   family worship and 31–3, 54, 80
Sharp, James, Archbishop of St Andrews 165
Smith, William 21–2, 39n.24, 87
soldiers *see* New Model Army
Solemn League and Covenant (1643) 1–2, 5, 7, 34–7, 57–8, 70–2, 118n.58, 161, 167
   behaviour and 32, 36, 47–8, 125–6
   gender and 32
   renewal of 72, 74, 78, 86, 107, 125–6, 128–9, 136
Synod of Glasgow and Ayr 20, 52–3, 156

Test Act (1681) 166–8, 174
Thirty Years War 19, 23, 70
Treaty of Breda 75
Turks *see* Barbary corsairs

Wars of Independence 2–3
Wars of the Three Kingdoms 1, 26–7, 30, 102

see also Battle of Dunbar; Battle
    of Worcester; Bishops' Wars;
    Treaty of Breda
Welsh, John 45, 56, 161–2, 164–5
Western Association 71
West Indies 4, 49–50, 138–9, 154
    Barbados 8, 35, 87, 103, 139, 184
Whiggamore Raid 71
White, George 130–2, 134, 137–8,
    140–1, 144n.41, 147–52, 157,
    161–3, 166
William III and Mary II 182

witchcraft and witch-hunting 1–2, 9,
    30, 69, 76, 81, 83–8, 126–7,
    143n.19, 143n.22
    English occupation and 110–14
    gender and 78
    'Great Scottish Witch Hunt'
        (1661–2) 126–7
Wodrow, Robert 11
    Analecta 24, 148
    *History of the Sufferings of
        the Church of Scotland*
        178–9

Printed in the USA
CPSIA information can be obtained
at www.ICGtesting.com
JSHW051924200924
70253JS00003B/15